The Making of Curriculum

Studies in Curriculum History

Editor: Ivor F. Goodson University of Western Ontario, Canada

Related titles

Studies in Curriculum History

The Making of Curriculum
Collected Essays

Ivor F. Goodson

 The Falmer Press

(A member of the Taylor & Francis Group)
London · New York · Philadelphia

UK The Falmer Press, Falmer House, Barcombe, Lewes, East Sussex, BN8 5DL

USA The Falmer Press, Taylor & Francis Inc., 242 Cherry Street, Philadelphia, PA 19106–1906

First published 1988

Library of Congress Cataloging in Publication Data available on request

ISBN 1 85000 184 7
ISBN 1 85000 185 5

Jacket design by Caroline Archer

Typeset in 11/13 Bembo by Imago Publishing Ltd, Thame, Oxon.

Printed and bound in Great Britain by Redwood Burn Limited, Trowbridge, Wiltshire

Contents

Acknowledgements

To Stephen Ball, Gary McCulloch, Peter Medway, Bill Reid, and Dennis Thiessen for their help in commenting on previous drafts. Also to my publisher, Malcolm Clarkson, for his patience and continuing support. To the Faculty of Education at The University of Western Ontario for their help in providing computing and secretarial facilities and research monies from the University Excellence Fund. To my secretary Hazel Sue-Tang for her considerable skill and patience in re-typing drafts.

'History of education in Britain: Conflicting paradigms' and 'Etymologies, epistemologies and the emergence of curriculum' were first written for a triennial symposium at the University of British Columbia, Summer 1985.

'Teachers' life histories and the studies of curriculum and schooling' is a modified version of an article in HAMMERSLEY M. (Ed) *The Ethnography of Schooling*, Nafferton, 1983; the article was first published in *Interchange*, Summer 1981.

'History, context and qualitative method' is a modified version of an article which appeared in BURGESS R.G. (Ed) *Strategies of Educational Research: Qualitative Methods*, Falmer, 1985. It was written for a workshop on 'Qualitative Methodology and the Study of Education' held at Whitelands College, London, in July 1983 and funded by the Social Science Research Council.

'Defining a subject for the comprehensive school' is an extended version of an article in BALL S.J. (Ed) *Comprehensive Schooling: A Reader*, Falmer Press, 1984.

'Becoming a school subject' first appeared in the *British Journal of Sociology of Education* in summer 1981. My thanks to Len Barton for permission to reproduce this modified version.

'The making of curriculum' was first presented as a paper at the American Educational Research Association, Easter 1985 in Chicago.

'Studying curriculum' was first presented as a paper at the American Educational Research Association, Easter 1987 in Washington.

Lastly, to The D.B. Weldon Library at the University of Western Ontario for the provision of a study in the library, wherein a good deal of this text was written.

For my wife Mary and my son Andrew
with love and thanks
and
to my mum, Lily
and
to my dad, Frederick (1903–1982)

A poor boy hobbled forth to give a reply. He was lame and humpbacked, and his wan, emaciated face told only too clearly the tale of poverty and its consequences — but he gave forthwith so lucid and intelligent a reply to the question put to him that there arose a feeling of admiration for the child's talents combined with a sense of shame that more information should be found in some of the lowest of our lower classes on matters of general interest than in those far above them in the world by station. It would be an unwholesome and vicious state of society in which those who are comparatively unblessed with nature's gifts should be generally superior in intellectual attainments to those above them in station.

Lord Wrottesley, 1860

True education is not for every man the scrap of paper he leaves school with. Dare we as teachers admit this? Dare we risk our existence by forcibly expressing our views on this? While we pause after the first phase of our acceptance, are we to rely on examinations for all to prove ourselves worthy of the kindly eye of the State? Dare we allow to leave some of our charges who have been once more neglected and once more squeezed into a heap of frustrating unimportance?

P.L. Quant, 1967

Foreword

Writing in the *Journal of Curriculum Studies* in 1983 I argued for 'the potential of curriculum history in furthering our understanding of schooling'. In that article I began, rather tentatively, 'to provide some instances of historical work which explores that potential'.[1] This book seeks to advance that project and look at the manner in which such work can broaden and deepen our understanding of schooling, in this case, state secondary schooling.

Since developing my initial ideas in 1983 a number of factors have affected the focus of my work. Firstly there have been several seminal studies of schooling which have developed an historical perspective. Most influential of all in aiding my conceptualization of curricular history was Cuban's book, *How Teachers Taught*, a study of a constancy and change in American classrooms over the period 1890–1980.[2] The book (which I discovered at a History of Education conference in Atlanta in November, 1985) served to strengthen my belief in historical methods and to establish the case for histories of pedagogy. But in addition the book indicated the limitations of histories of pedagogy and the need for (complementary) studies of the history of curriculum. Neither approach, I believe, reaches anywhere near its potential for illumination without the other.

A further historical perspective was added while I was teaching a summer school on curriculum history in 1985 at the University of British Columbia. I had gone there eagerly anticipating a dialogue with George Tomkins, the eminent Canadian curriculum historian. Unfortunately, George died tragically a few months before. His legacy was left however in the papers which became *A Common Countenance*.[3] Wrestling with Tomkins work in the summer of 1985 as I prepared for the summer school and for a symposium on curriculum history was a fascinating experience. I was able to make the connection between work that had been familiar to me for some time on the emergence and politics of curriculum and the kind of curriculum history which I had been undertaking since 1975.

But more important, I suspect than the emerging ideas on the history of schooling were the changes that were underway in the 'structuration' of schooling in the 'real world'. To live in England in the 1980s was to witness a massive initiative to restructure state schooling. The curriculum was a significant arena for this restructuring and as such the general argument for critical scholarship in 'curriculum studies' was, I think, substantially enhanced. In particular the emergence of the new 'National Curriculum' has to be historically located.

English Schooling Since 1980: Towards a National Curriculum

The essays in this volume are built around a series of case studies of English State Schooling covering the period 1965–1980. In recent years so severe has been the sense of change, not to say dislocation, in English state schooling that a belief in abrupt discontinuity might be forgiven. By this belief these case studies would be thought to have little to say about the 'new world' of Thatcher's Britain. But revolutions are seldom what they seem and continuities are often as important, if not more important, than discontinuities. So, I believe, is the case with the newly pronounced 'National Curriculum'.

In this book I have argued that the 1904 Secondary Regulations were a crucial statement about the secondary school curriculum by the Board of Education. Let me quote the full text of these regulations for they may provide believers in the new Thatcherite curriculum revolution with something of a 'shock of recognition':

> The course should provide for instruction in the English Language and Literature, at least one Language, other than English, Geography, History, Mathematics, Science and Drawing, with due provision for Manual Work and Physical Exercise, and in a girls' school for Housewifery. Not less than $4\frac{1}{2}$ hours per week must be alloted to English, Geography and History; not less than $3\frac{1}{2}$ hours to the Language where one is taken or less than 6 hours where two are taken; and not less than $7\frac{1}{2}$ hours to Science and Mathematics, of which at least 3 must be for Science.

These regulations, defined essentially by Sir Robert Morant at the Board of Education, established a clear priority for the traditional subjects of the public and grammar schools. He deliberately blocked any progress towards incorporating the more broadly vocational curriculum then being pioneered in the 'higher tops' streams of the secondary schools. The academic tradition drawn from the public schools was to provide the model for all. As Eaglesham has written: 'For the future the pattern of English culture must come not from Leeds or West Ham but from Eton and Winchester.'[4]

Yet when we look now at the revolutionary national curriculum, clear continuities can be discerned. Indeed, many commentators have noted this. The editorial in the Times Educational Supplement following the issue of the 'National Curriculum' was entitled *1904 and All That*. We are informed here that the new '8–10 subject timetable which the discussion paper draws up has as academic a look to it as anything Sir Robert Morant could have dreamed up', indeed the editor provides a clear statement of historical continuity, 'The first thing to say about this whole exercise is that it unwinds eighty years of English (and Welsh) educational history. It is a case of go back to go'.[5]

Perhaps therefore in our studies of education it is worth 'going back to go' and seeking to understand the genesis and evolution of school subjects for in the 'National Curriculum' we have the clearest possible reassertion of their primacy within state schooling.

There are always substantial dangers in drawing conclusions from past historical experiences embedded in different political and social contexts. Nonetheless, historical study of previous epochs might provide some waring to those directing the new initiatives in English State Schooling. E.G.A. Holmes, writing in 1911 about another period of substantial state intervention, the payment by results period of 1862–1895, wrote:

> The State, in prescribing a syllabus which was to be followed, in all the subjects of instruction, by all the schools in the country, without regard to local or personal considerations, was guilty of one captial offence. It did all his thinking for the teacher. It told him in precise detail what he was to do each year in each 'Standard', how he was to handle each subject, and how far he was to go in it; what width of ground he was to cover; what amount of knowledge, what degree of accuracy was required for a 'pass'. In other words, it provided him with

his ideals, his general conceptions, his more immediate aims, his schemes of work; and if it did not control his methods in all their details, it gave him (by implication) hints and suggestions with regard to these on which he was not slow to act; for it told him that the work done in each class and each subject would be tested at the end of each year by a careful examination of each individual child; and it was inevitable that in his endeavour to adapt his teaching to the type of question by which his experience of the yearly examination led him to expect, he should gradually deliver himself, mind and soul, into the hands of the officials of the Department, — the officials at Whitehall who framed the yearly syllabus, and the officials in the various districts who examined on it.

What the Department did to the teacher, it compelled him to do to the child. The teacher who is the slave of another's will cannot carry out his instructions except by making his pupils the slaves of his own will. The teacher who has been deprived by his superiors of freedom, initiative, and responsibility, cannot carry out his instructions except by depriving his pupils of the same vital qualities. The teacher who, in response to the deadly pressure of a cast-iron system, has become a creature of habit and routine, cannot carry out his instructions except by making his pupils as helpless and as puppet-like as himself.

But is not only because mechanical obedience is fatal, in the long run, to mental and spiritual growth, that the regulation of elementary or any other grade of education by a uniform syllabus is to be deprecated. It is also because a uniform syllabus is, in the nature of things, a bad syllabus.[6]

This quotation warns us that teachers are often ill-served by those who control schooling; in this book teacher groups are sometimes presented in pursuit of status and resources, of material and self-interests. This is not, however, to say that teachers are generally self-interested individuals. Nothing could be further from the truth. In my experience teachers are often the most selfless and dedicated of individuals. But the bureaucraticization and structuration of schooling leaves the groups or associations which represent teachers with little choice but to pursue status and resources. For to fail to acknowledge what one teacher calls the 'kindly eye of state' is to confirm one's colleagues and one's students to low-status and poor resources. Our scrutiny should primarily turn to the motives and aspirations of the individuals and interest groups that structure and restructure schooling. For if there is a heart to the problem, I suspect it is here.

Ivor Goodson
Professor of Education
University of Western Ontario
November, 1987

Notes and References

1 GOODSON, I.F. 'Subjects for study: Aspects of a social history of curriculum', in *Journal of Curriculum Studies*, Vol. 15, No. 4 1983, p. 393.
2 CUBAN, L. *How Teachers Taught: Constancy and Change in American Classrooms 1890–1980.* (New York: Longman 1984).
3 TOMKINS, G. *A Common Countenance: Stability and Change in the Canadian Curriculum.* (Scarborough, Ontario: Prentice Hall, 1986).
4 EAGLESHAM, E.J.R. *The Foundations of Twentieth Century Education in England.* (London: Routledge and Kegan Paul, 1967) p. 59.
5 *Times Educational Supplement*, 31 July 1987.
6 HOLMES, E.G.A. *What Is and What Might Be.* (London: Constable 1912) pp. 103–4.

I   The Search for Sources

1 Investigating State Schooling: The Search for Sources

The Search For Sources

A lot of my conversations with my father (to whom this book is partly dedicated) began with him saying 'Tell me what you're getting at'. Perhaps to be consistent I should explain what I am seeking to 'get at' in this book.

At heart the book is concerned with ways of investigating the nature of state schooling. It grows from a wish to uncover the agendas, aspirations and purposes of state schooling in general. Of necessity the focus is far more conceptually and historically specific. The later essays focus on state secondary schooling, so-called comprehensive schools primarily, in England in the period since their inception as state policy in 1965, up until 1980.

From the beginning I held the belief that a philosophical or a more narrowly sociological treatment of the issue of state schooling, whilst valuable in its own right, would not provide me with what I was after. I wanted a sense of the historical emergence of state schooling as well as its specific, contemporary realization in state secondary schooling in England. This argued for some kind of historical approach and a search for broadly based historical sources. But what kind of sources?

In focussing on recent state secondary schooling I was aware that more conventional history of education approaches might have led me to sources such as government minutes, records, administrative and legislative drafts and acts. In this way the origins of the state comprehensive schools could be clearly traced back to the second world war (and indeed much further back). Government minutes from 1941, for instance, exhibit a perhaps surprising degree of support for comprehensive schools among civil servants, though presented in abbreviated note form:

In framing policy for development of education system it was necessary to take account of political atmosphere in which that policy would be examined. There were indications that responsibility for the direction of the nation's effort in the immediate postwar years would remain in the hands of a National Government prepared to face radical changes in social and economic systems and contemplating not merely restoration or return to normality but reconstruction in a very real sense. While policy would have to command support of main elements in all parties, clear that war was moving them more and more in the direction of Labour's ideas and ideals and planning for a national 'New Order' would be more towards left than might generally be imagined.[1]

'Total' war of democracy against dictatorship emphasized essential unity of nation, common interests of its members and need for making a reality of democratic system which they professed to be defending, resulting in a greater merging of different sections of community and breaking down of social and economic barriers and privileges.

Schools would be expected to confirm and contribute to this social revolution.

This memo ends with the assertion that:

Perhaps the only satisfactory answer was the multilateral post-primary school attended by all children over 11 alike, most of whom would stay to 15, many to 16 and a few later. It might be that the difficulties of converting present system, with its comparatively small school buildings each with its own tradition of greater or lesser prestige into an organization of necessarily large units would prove insuperable. But the system should receive further and most careful exploration since, in theory at least, it appeared the only full solution to the problem of truly democratic education.[2]

In the event the difficulties did prove insuperable (or were presented and accepted as insuperable). 'Truly democratic education' was not embraced and a 'tripartite' system was developed comprising grammar, technical and secondary modern schools. The point of including these quotations is, however, to indicate what kind of history, what kind of insights on schooling, would be provided from such sources. Essentially this would be a history of the 'organization' and politics of the state educational system.

The vagueness of government records on the actual 'detail' of schooling is clear in the minutes cited above. The only mention of what is to be taught comes in the sentence:

> The ideal would be a common school for all post-primary education attended by all children alike and comprising within itself courses or 'sides' to meet all aptitudes academic and clerical, technical and modern or practical.[3]

Such sources in short offer limited help in reconstructing the detail of schooling. For plainly the common school ideal argued for above could be theoretically subverted by internal structuring of courses or 'sides' which effectively reintroduced differentiation, albeit under the same school roof. The organization of schools might change and our history of education would record this change but curriculum or indeed, individual, class or gender experiences and patterns could remain substantially unchanged. On these critical questions, about the details of schooling, a more conventional historical approach might provide limited purchase.

Historical sources would be required which would give some indication of what was taught in schools — in short which allowed some reconstruction of the detailed agendas and purposes of schools. In writing this book I was aware of Cuban's (1984) work on the history of pedagogy. I profoundly agreed with Lee Shulman's introduction which asserted that

> Those who conduct research on schooling rarely consider historical investigations germane to their work. There is a sense in which history is treated as arcane, esoteric and of little import to the concerns of practice and policy. In reading this book, I am convinced that precisely the opposite is true. Carefully conducted historical enquiry may well provide us with the most powerful guides available.[4]

However, Cuban's work left me with a sense of vicarious practice (see critique in chapter 2), a sense of schooling as organized by government but realized, in a substantially autonomous manner, by classroom teachers. Yet in English comprehensives, where local and classroom autonomy was much vaunted, I knew from my own teaching in highly reform-minded schools that the teacher was subject to many interventions. Above all the definition of curriculum and examination of curriculum seemed to me obvious yet central variables. But in Cuban's history of pedagogy these were seldom mentioned or employed as historical sources.

Other attempts at developing a history of pedagogy seemed to founder on the same point. Hamilton's (1980) essay on the origins of class teaching ends with an explicit apologia for omitting the study of the subject-based curriculum:

> The history of classing also intersects with the rise of subject teaching. After the middle of the nineteenth century the masters of method discussed whether classes would remain the same at all times, or at the other extreme whether children should be reclassified for every activity and subject. In an important sense, however, the omissions (sic) of any detailed discussion of this topic can be excused on the grounds that, as part of the pre-history of the modern management movement in schooling it too might be better tackled elsewhere.[5]

I sensed then, that in developing our understanding of schooling, a mode of study which sought only to recover and reconstruct pedagogy whilst valuable was inadequate. Alongside this work, studies of 'the making of curriculum' were required. Such studies would complement the work going on in the history of pedagogy but in some ways would extend the project of understanding schooling. This was not least because if histories of curriculum were developed alongside histories of pedagogies, then subsequently studies of the relationship between the two might be facilitated.

In the search for sources, the archives of curriculum statements and syllabuses represent a veritable treasure trove. For those seeking to understand the purposes and agendas of state schooling, these archives comprise a series of, at the least, statements of intent. Above all 'curriculum' designates a central mode by which external agencies from the state downwards have sought over time to penetrate and control the 'license' of the individual classroom. Historically, the written curriculum was partially modelled for this purpose as a result; it is a valuable source for understanding certain external intentions and agendas as they impinge on schooling. If we are to broaden our study of state schooling it is partly through studying curriculum at this level that we might gain glimpses of the relationship between external structure and internal agency.

State Schooling and the Emergence of Curriculum

In chapter 3 the emergence of curriculum is traced in some detail. For the moment it is important to note the argument that: 'If class and curriculum' entered educational discourse at a time when schooling was transformed into a mass activity in England, 'classroom system and school subjects emerged at the stage at which that mass activity became a state subsidized system'.[6] The state, when playing a part in developing schooling, was perhaps unlikely to initiate classrooms as sites of uncontrolled action; this was particularly the case as schooling moved from being an elite enterprise to a mass educational endeavour. State schooling and mass clienteles presaged detailed attempts to control the content and form of classroom life; initially through attempts (for example Kay Shuttleworth) at the definition of pedagogy and of the subjectivity of teachers, but soon by prescribing written curriculum. Curriculum, our chosen source, develops in this way, is institutionalized and, subsequently, allied to an examination system. The definition of written curriculum for subsequent classroom realization developed in a manner which provided elements and mechanisms for directing and controlling the activity of schooling. It is for this reason above all that the curriculum provides such a valuable source for the study of state schooling.

It is vital to stress that the original character of curriculum as an historical source does not argue for a replacement of more conventional history of education focussing on organizational and administrative change nor histories of pedagogy or classrooms, nor studies of school process or studies of school text. We need to recognize that, in examining state schooling, we confront a 'system' of interlinked parts which in England have been painstakingly constructed and consolidated over the past century and a half. Hence we must pursue multidimensional study; a unidimensional approach cannot suffice. We are dealing with a complex matrix of structures and factors involving a state organizational system alongside a private sector, a teacher training system, varying teacher ratios and resources, a wide range of subjects and curriculum. Each aspect has of course the capacity to sponsor improvement and change or alternatively differentiation, discrimination and privilege. Changes in political governance can disturb the balance of the matrix. Some times this 'balances out', at other times we witness the headlong pursuit of differentiation and privilege — private schooling is promoted, selective state schooling is sponsored, and significantly, the state seeks increased power over the 'fine print' of curriculum. It would seem that even though we confront an interlinked system, that curriculum retains its power to serve as a litmus test of political intervention and intention.

The written curriculum is part of the complex nature of institutional state schooling. Crucially, curriculum and classroom systems are interlinked. Whilst the classroom system established prominence in Britain after the 1830s with the gradual spread of state supported (and state-supervised) schooling 'by the twentieth century the batch production rhetoric of the "classroom system" (for example, lessons, subjects, timetables, grading, standardization, streaming) had become so pervasive that it successfully achieved a normative status'.[7] By the present day the duality of classroom and curriculum represent a successfully 'invented' tradition with normative status had the power to set standards for all other educational initiatives. From the time they became interlinked classroom and curriculum were focal keywords which together established a practice and a programme for a particular style of teaching and learning. The sequential curriculum, primarily organized in subjects has been, since the emergence of the classroom system, a vital prop in substantiating this dominant version of schooling.

To divorce studies of practice from studies of preactive curriculum definition therefore ignores the history and systemic nature of schooling. It further ignores the crucial role which such curriculum plays in defining statements of intent. 'It sets up a standard' against which educational initiatives have been and are judged. Were it only a matter of historical veracity or dispassionate 'standards' this would be of largely scholastic or philosophical interest. But it is precisely because we are dealing with a 'State system' that curriculum construction has such central significance. Patterns of resource allocation, financial distribution, status allocation and career construction are all directly related to a system where curriculum definition, particularly in 'subject' or 'basics' style, has a central position. Thus the structure of the system, and its material and concrete form, is associated with the way that particular patterns of curriculum are constructed and reconstructed. In this way, certain priorities and parameters are set for local authorities, educators and practitioners. The political economy of the curriculum particularly of the school subject, is then of vital concern for it is a 'heartland' for that patterning and prioritizing which establishes a particular 'character' for schooling.

An example might illustrate how structure and action interact. Some time ago I studied the emergence of environmental studies at secondary level as an integrated curriculum area in English schools in the 1960s and 1970s. This was a period of considerable educational innovation and rapid organizational change to a comprehensive system. But in order to attain their goals (promoting environmental studies) the innovators had to accept the existing structure, the existing 'rules of the game' if you will. To gain status and resources, they were forced to stress the academic knowledge and 'discipline' element of their curriculum when their prime purpose was to promote something practical, immediate and locally relevant. The original practitioner thrust was thereby reversed by the antecedent structures associated with the making of curriculum. The distribution of resources and graded posts through specialist subject departments, the definition of teachers' careers through such departments, the definition of external examinations of a written academic mode: all serve to promote and maintain a particular view of school curriculum form and content. Proponents of new curriculum areas face these antecedent structures as clear 'rules of the game'.[8] Thus while school practitioners are potentially spontaneous agents they are constrained by elements of the structure of schooling derived from prior actions and decisions which limit their capacity for internal school action. This is not to argue that practice (or indeed local politics) can never transcend these antecedent structures but to note that it is important to acknowledge and understand the existing 'rules of the game'. In this sense we are dealing not with laws but likely parameters to alternative views of practice and process.

So far I have argued that preactive written curriculum is: (1) an important part of a consolidated State system of schooling; (2) that it sets 'standards' and defines statements of intent; and (3) that it provides clear 'rules of the game' for educators and practitioners, parameters but not prescriptions. Once established a structure then affects subsequent action in complex ways. This moves us beyond an explanation where State schooling is seen as involving a structure which then facilitates 'domination' by dominant interest groups (see M.F.D. Young *et al*). As was argued before:

> The role of dominant groups shows perhaps most clearly in the victory of the academic tradition in the early years of the twentieth century. This victory was embodied in the influential 1904 Regulations and most significantly, the 1917 School Certificate. Once established, however, these curricular patterns (and their associated financial and resource implications) were retained and defended in a much more complex way and by a wider range of agencies. It is therefore correct to assume that initially the rules for high-status knowledge reflected the values of dominant interest groups at the time. But it is quite another issue to assume that this is inevitably still the case or that it is dominant interest groups themselves who actively defend high status curricula.[9]

There is a need to distinguish therefore between domination and structure and between mechanism and mediation. At the mediating level existing parameters are patrolled and protected. Central in such mediation are school subject groups representing existing 'traditional' subjects, particularly formal subject associations such as the Geographical Association or Historical Association. These groups act as mediators and often serve to perpetuate that curriculum form and content which normally ensures maximum resource allocation and the associated work and career prospects these entail for the relevant subject specialists. These mediating groups have a classically vested interest in the perpetuation of existing structures. For them the first line of defence of the *status quo* is the primacy of their subject, preferably as a scholarly academic discipline. The latter involves a fully developed alliance with university scholars. This often hands over a good deal of control in curriculum definition to universities.

Of course such mediations involve control over more than resource allocation. Subject associations and university departments have also the power to socialize. Hence, patterns of curriculum are defended and reproduced through socialization into the subject subculture. McLeish (1970) noted the salience of subject specialism:

> The most remarkable differences in attitudes of any in the total sample appear to be between subject specialists... Similar differences to those found in the students on entry to their courses are found and between college lecturers specializing in their main subjects.[10]

Lacey (1977) found similar patterns in University of Sussex teacher trainees:

> The subject sub-culture appears ... to be a pervasive phenomenon, affecting a student teacher's behaviour in school and university as well as their choice of friends and their attitudes towards education.[11]

School subjects are never final, monolithic entities. They are 'loose amalgamations of segments pursuing different objectives in different manners', 'more or less delicately held together under a common name at particular periods in history'.[12] We are witness to a continuing contest in one of the central heartlands of schooling. Prior actions have bequeathed a consolidated state system with clearly integrated statements of curriculum intent. Structures with their own 'rules of the game' have been developed. Over time there is mediation by interest groups such as subject associations which represent dominant coalitions within the subject. These associations socialize their members, and develop alliances with university and teacher training subject departments.

The conceptual and systemic antecedents of curriculum, the structures, the mediating and socialising groups, are then vital aspects of the social construction of schooling. They are aspects that have so far been seriously neglected in the study of curriculum and schooling.

Notes and References

1 Public Record Office Education Documents 4403, 13 January 1941, Mr. Cleary memo, items 2, 3. (University of Leeds Library).
2 *Ibid.* item 7.
3 *Ibid.* 1 February, M. Cleary, General Memo.
4 CUBAN, L. *How Teachers Taught: Constancy and Change in American Classroom 1890–1980*, (New York, Longmans, 1984) Introduction by Lee Shulman, p. vii.
5 HAMILTON, D. *On Simultaneous Instruction and the Early Evolution of Class Teaching*, Mimeo of paper given at the History Workshop Conference, (Brighton, November 1980) p. 13.
6 See chapter 3, p. 29.
7 HAMILTON, D. Adam Smith and the moral economy of the classroom system, *Journal of Curriculum Studies*, 12, 4, October–December 1980, p. 286.
8 Giddens has dealt with the problems of potential misinterpretation in relating notions of structure to 'rules' and resources. See GIDDENS, A. *The Constitution of Society*, (Berkeley and Los Angeles, University of California Press, 1984).
9 GOODSON, I.F. *School Subjects and Curriculum Change*, (London and Sydney, Croom Helm, 1983) p. 198. Republished in a revised and extended edition by Falmer Press, 1987.
10 McLEISH, J. *Students' Attitudes and College Environment*, quoted in LACEY, C. *The Socialisation of Teachers*, (London, Metheun, 1977) p. 64.
11 *Ibid.*, LACEY, C. (1970) pp. 63–4.
12 BUCHER, R. and STRAUSS, A. 'Professions in process' in HAMMERSLEY, M. and WOODS P. (Eds), *The Process of Schooling*, (London, Routledge and Kegan Paul, 1976).

2 *Studying Curriculum*

Prologue

In our studies of schooling curriculum is a 'keyword' in the full sense of Raymond Williams' definition. The use of such a word and its place in our discourse on schooling needs to be fully examined because 'like any other social reproduction it is the arena of all sorts of shifts and interests and relations of dominance'. Curriculum is a keyword with substantial potential for scholarly exhumation, examination and analysis, for the 'moral panics' over meaning are often carried out in a most public manner. As Williams (1974) comments:

> Certain crises around certain experiences will occur, which are registered in language in often surprising ways. The result is a notion of language as not merely the creation of arbitrary signs which are then reproduced within groups, which is the structuralist model, but of signs which take on the changeable and often reversed social relations of a given society, so that what enters into them is the contradictory and conflict-ridden social history of the people who speak the language, including all the variations between signs at any given time.[1]

In such a manner, the conflicts over the definition of the written curriculum offer visible, public and documentary evidence of the continuing struggle over the aspirations and purposes of schooling. For this reason alone it is important to develop our understandings of this kind of curriculum conflict. But as has been noted conflict over the written curriculum has both 'symbolic significance' and also practical significance — by publicly signifying which aspirations and intentions are to be enshrined in written curriculum criteria are established for the evaluation and public estimation of schooling. In this sense, 'ground rules' are thereby publicly established by which practice is evaluated or to which it is related. Financial and resource allocation is similarly linked to these ground rules of curriculum criteria.

The establishment of rules and criteria has significance even if practice then seeks to contradict or transcend this preactive definition. We are therefore bound by previous forms of reproduction even as we become creators of new ones.

This relationship between antecedent definitions and present potential is of enormous significance in the study of curriculum. Jackson (1968) has characterized the two elements (although in some senses this is falsely dichotomous) as: *'preactive'* definition of curriculum and *'interactive'* realization of curriculum.[2] Maxine Greene (1971) has developed a dual notion of curriculum which furthers our understanding of the distinction. She describes the dominant view of curriculum as 'a structure of socially presented knowledge, external to the knower, there to be mastered'.[3] This is to present preactive definition *as* curriculum, but against this she juxtaposes a notion of curriculum as: 'a possibility for the learner as an existing person mainly concerned with making sense of his own life world'. M.F.D. Young (1977) has used this distinction to develop two views of curriculum. The first he calls 'curriculum as fact'. He suggests that:

> The 'curriculum as fact' needs to be seen as more than mere illusion, a superficial veneer on teachers' and pupils' classroom practice, but as a historically specific social reality expressing particular production relations among men. It is mystifying in the way it presents the curriculum as having a life of its own, and obscures the human relations in which it, as any conception of knowledge, is embedded, leaving education as neither understandable nor controllable by men.

He goes on to argue that the notion of 'curriculum as practice' can equally mystify to the degree that:

> It reduces the social reality of 'curriculum' to the subjective interventions and actions of teachers and pupils. This limits us from understanding the historical emergence and persistence of particular conceptions, of knowledge and particular conventions (school subjects for example). In that we are limited from being able to situatize the problems of contemporary education historically we are again limited from understanding and control.[4]

Seen in this manner one can grasp some of the range of debate and conflict which is likely to surround the word curriculum. In a certain sense promoting the notion of 'curriculum as fact' is liable to give priority to the past intellectual and political 'settlement' as enshrined in the written curriculum. 'Curriculum as practice' rather gives precedence to contemporary action, and allows for contradictory, aberrant or transcendent action in relation to preactive definition.

This has often led reformists to seek to ignore preactive definitions, viewing this as a legacy of the past, and to try to spontaneously create new ground rules for action. In curriculum terms this is to seek to ignore that circumstances are 'directly encountered, given and transmitted from the past'. Once again let me give an example of how this works as it bears fundamentally on the thesis I shall wish to advance in this volume. In the late 1960s and the 1970s a small number of comprehensive schools in England and Wales began to seriously engage with the problem of how to devise a curriculum through which *all* children might learn. I say 'small number', not so as to deny the important work going on in all comprehensive schools but merely to remind readers that most comprehensive schools at that time continued to teach a range of curricula largely inherited or adapted from the previous tripartite system. One of the most radical of the reforming comprehensive schools was Countesthorpe Upper School in Leicestershire. The school was deeply committed to the education of all its pupils and stressed above all the 'autonomy' of its pupils. By this the staff meant:

> ... that every student should be responsible for determining the choice and direction of his own course of study with the help and support of his teachers. The task we set ourselves was to create the conditions in which autonomy could thrive. We did not intend meekly to submit to each student's passing whims and fancies, for unless teachers are ready to be positive, forceful and ambitious in their expectations of their students they cannot hope to create the conditions for a thriving autonomy.[5]

The problems encountered in the early years of the school to some extent focussed on which 'expectations' to be 'positive, forceful and ambitious' about. Here the thoroughgoing nature of the reform stumbled against preactive definitions and antecedent structures. Hence, expectations focussed on the existing disciplines:

> Our commitment (was) to the major disciplines of human thought, the traditional forms of knowledge, mathematics,

science, the humanities, the arts. We were convinced at the time, and remain convinced, that every student has the ability to pursue knowledge in all these forms, and that our task was to help each student to do so.[6]

Here then we see how the most idealistic practical aspirations normally inherit previous forms of preactive curriculum. Past and present collide: and in so doing set clear parameters for the realization of contemporary purpose.

In the Countesthorpe situation this led to some practitioners arguing for a wholesale 'reconstruction of knowledge' and to new internal experiments. Take the following prophecy in 1973:

As many kinds of subject matter are now organized it is not obvious nor easily possible to transform the teaching of them to a more self-directed and informal style of work in schools. Under these circumstances we are rather likely to fall back into the old polarities. By one party the tradition of the formal course will continue to be seen as for the most part a dreary, ineffective and superficial 'coverage' of subject matter on its way to ossification. By the other party the advocacy of resource-based learning will be seen as a denigration of both rigour and discipline in the mastery of subject matter. What I hope is this old issue be buried and that we address instead the question as to *how* wider ranges of subject matter of that stuff alluded to in curricula and syllabi, can be revived and reconstituted and extended so as to make it more diversely accessible and appealing to growing minds more interwoven in the texture of a rich school environment.[7]

In this quotation it is possible to discern the manner in which previous definitions of curriculum (as subject matter) circumscribe contemporary debate (as well as action). Unless such antecedent definitions can be rapidly replaced we fall back into the 'old polarities' (and patterns of social relationship and reproduction).

From this example it is possible to grasp the importance of understanding antecedent struggles over the preactive definition of curriculum. In such circumstances it is politically naive and conceptually inadequate to argue that 'what matters is classroom practice' (just as it is crass to talk of keeping the politics out of education). What matters also, and all too obviously in this instance, is to understand the antecedent parameters to practice. What should also be clear, however, is that it is not merely the intellectual definitions which emanate from written curriculum which have force.

The written curriculum is but the visible, public and changing testimony of selected rationales and legitimating rhetorics of schooling. As such it both promulgates and underpins certain basic intentions of schooling as they are operationalized in structures and institutions. To take a common convention in preactive curriculum, the school subject: whilst the written curriculum defines the rationales and rhetorics of the subject this is only the most tangible aspect of a patterning of resources, finances and examinations and associated material and career interests. In this symbiosis it is as though the written curriculum provides a guide to the legitimating rhetorics of schooling as they are promoted through patterns of resource allocation, status attribution and career distribution. In short, the written curriculum provides us with a testimony, a documentary source, a changing map of the terrain: it is also one of the best official guide books to the institutionalized structure of schooling.

In this book, I will concentrate on the 'making of curriculum' at the preactive level. In doing so I should wish to make two claims. Firstly, that studying the conflict over preactive definition of written curriculum will increase our understanding of the interests and influences active at this level. Secondly, that this understanding will further our knowledge of the values and purposes represented in schooling and the manner in which preactive definition may set parameters for interactive realization and negotiation in the classroom and school.

Further, in focussing on the preactive definition of written curriculum as constituting the making of curriculum I am specifically not wishing to add aid and sustenance to an exclusive notion of 'curriculum as fact'. Any progressive notion of curriculum (and of the making of curriculum) would have to work with curriculum as realized in practice as a central component. But total belief in the 'world-changing' properties of curriculum as practice is, I think, intenable (as the previous historical instance seeks to illustrate). It is a view which is encouraged by the present under-developed stage of our understandings of preactive curriculum. Understandings of the making of curriculum should help provide cognitive maps of the antecedent purposes and structures which precede and locate contemporary practice.

Curriculum as Social Conflict

Central to the project of a pervasive reconceptualization of curriculum studies are the range of arenas and levels where curriculum is produced, negotiated and reproduced. A move towards a more historical and social constructionist view of curriculum work would have to work across the full range of these arenas and levels. Plainly this is an undertaking for a whole cohort of scholars and at the moment, one can only provide or point to a few parts of the mosaic of such a reconceptualized undertaking. Curriculum is made then in a variety of arenas and at a variety of levels. Central to this variety, however, is the distinction between the written curriculum and the curriculum as classroom activity. The dangers of only studying the written curriculum are manifest, for as Rudolph (1977) has warned us:

> The best way to misread or misunderstand a curriculum is from a catalogue. It is such a lifeless thing, so disembodied, so unconnected, sometimes intentionally misleading.[8]

As I have noted this often leads on to the assertion or implication that the written curriculum is in a real sense irrelevant to practice: that the dichotomy between espoused curriculum as written and the active curriculum as lived and experienced is complete and inevitable. There are a number of versions of the complete dichotomy thesis. Some versions of 'conspiracy theory' would argue that since schooling, particularly state schooling, is intimately related to economic and social reproduction, and is compulsory and under-resourced, certain intractable features of classroom practice and life are virtually inevitable (true) and that, therefore, written curriculum 'rhetoric' is basically irrelevant (unproven). More common would be the 'wordly-wise' view. This is typified by Cuban's (1984) commentary on US schooling:

> In examining how various forces shaped the curriculum and their consequences for classrooms over the last century, I used the metaphor of a hurricane to distinguish between curriculum theory, courses of study, materials and classroom instruction. Hurricane winds sweep across the sea tossing up twenty foot waves, a fathom below the surface turbulent waters swirl, while on the ocean floor there is unruffled calm.[9]

Of course Cuban's ocean analogy does resonate with a good deal of our understanding and experience of curriculum reform attempts. Yet even within his exemplary study of how teachers taught, data emerges which hints at conflicts over 'what counts as curriculum', hints therefore at how certain apparent 'givens' in the situation were constructed.

This implies that there may have been a prior debate about what passes as curriculum (and as curriculum theory) which was resolved in one way that is now presented as a *fait accompli*, as a once and for all given. Hence, while Cuban stresses the constancy of classroom practice, the parameters of that practice with regard to different versions of curricula remain unanalyzed. This leads him to provide quotes such as:

> We have a lot of work. The curriculum is overloaded and we have so many assessments to do. So much paperwork. Yet I teach Spanish in the first grade. That's not in the curriculum. Every other Friday, we cook. That's not in the curriculum. But I feel that they need these extras.[10]

Hence, such a research view of practice, albeit a historical view, leaves major questions unanalyzed as to what counts as curriculum and as to the manner in which other potential curriculum areas simply become 'extra'. Constancy in classroom practice there may be but is not the historical conflict over these precursors to practice, the construction and reconstruction of these parameters, part of that story? Even if there is a dichotomy between written curriculum, curriculum theory and practice is not that dichotomy part of an ongoing contest, a situation that is in a sense 'achieved' rather than inevitable?

Certainly, histories of the relationship between theory and practice point to wide differentials in the gap between the two. The dichotomy far from being wide and intractable seems to be, at least partially, tractable and highly variable over time. Simon (1985) examined the relationship between theory and practice in three periods 1880–1900, 1920–1940 and 1940–1960. In the first and last periods he found 'a close relation between theory and practice'. For instance in the period 1880–1900:

> For a whole concatenation of reasons, and from a variety of motives, it was thought that the masses should be educated, or at least schooled — and they were. This whole enterprise was, as it were, powered by an ideology — or theoretical stance — which emphasized the educability of the normal child, a view underpinned by advances in the field of psychology and physiology relating to human learning.[11]

The point is that the potential for close relationship, or at the other extreme no relationship, between theory and practice or between written curriculum and active curriculum depends on the nature of preactive construction of curricula statements and theory as well as the interactive realization of curriculum in the classroom.

As currently constituted, our understandings of preactive construction are so minimal as to make any thoroughgoing study of the relationships between preactives and practices virtually unachievable. The precursor then to any study of this kind is to begin to analyze the social construction of curricula. Social constructionist study has the intrinsic value of allowing insights into the assumptions and interests involved in the making of curriculum. By furthering our understanding of the manner in which some of the parameters to practice are negotiated such work should facilitate subsequent studies of relationships between preactive construction and interactive realization.

This is not, of course, to suggest a direct or easily discernible link between the preactive and the interactive nor that on occasions the interactive might not subvert or transcend the preactive. But it is to argue that preactive construction may set important and significant parameters for interactive realization in the classroom. Unless, therefore, we analyze the making of curriculum the temptation will be to accept it as a given and look for variables inside the classroom or at least within the individual school domain. We would be accepting as 'traditional' and 'given' versions of curricula that, on closer inspection, can be seen as the culmination of long and continuing conflict.

Two final instances will substantiate this point and I hope illustrate the potential significance of analyzing the making of curriculum. Vulliamy (1976) has studied the origins of 'what counts as school music'. He concludes that the definition of school music as a curriculum subject which focusses on 'serious music' involves a clear set of social and political priorities which inevitably effect pedagogic orientation and potential realization within the classroom. The making of curriculum in this case plainly sets parameters for practice:

> My analysis of the subject perspective of music teaching suggests that with music we have a rigid stratification of knowledge and perhaps the clearest example in the school curriculum of a rigid distinction between subject-based knowledge ('serious music') which is the musical culture of the school, and everyday knowledge ('pop' music) which is the musical culture of most of the school pupils.[12]

Curriculum theory for the training of music teachers has often reinforced this dichotomy. Brocklehurst (1962) for example, is quoted as arguing that:

> The primary purpose of musical appreciation is to inculcate a love and understanding of good music. It is surely the duty of teachers to do all they can to prevent young people falling

ready prey to the purveyors of commercialized popular music.[13]

In the making of the music curriculum the conflict between serious and popular music has resulted in a clear victory for the former. We have insights into a conflict not only about the intrinsics of curriculum but about the purposes and potentials of curriculum. What sort of mass education is being pursued when that which is popular is not merely ignored but positively disvalued? Is it advisable to analyze classroom practice without consideration of this critical antecedent struggle over curriculum definition and construction? When investigation is limited to the immediate realization of subject knowledge, there is a grave danger of perpetrating a classroom myopia that inevitably obscures and mystifies a central component in the complexities of classroom life.

A further historical example might suggest an answer. In *Science for the People*, David Layton (1973) describes a movement in the initial development of the school science curriculum called the 'Science of Common Things'.[14] In this curriculum, the pupils' experiences of the natural world, of their homes, daily lives and work formed the basis of their enquiries in school science (almost by analogy like teaching music through the pupils' experience of popular music rather than through their non-experience of serious music). But the curriculum was limited to elementary schools with a predominantly working class clientele. There is clear evidence provided by Layton, and in contemporary government reports, that the science of common things allowed considerable practical success in classrooms. We would be wrong, however, to assume therefore that the problem was solved and that the science of common things provided the basis for the definition of school science. Far from it. Other definitions of school science were being advocated by powerful interests. Lord Wrottesley chaired a Parliamentary Committee of the British Association for the Advancement of Science on the most appropriate type of science education for the upper classes. Hodson (1987) argues that the report:

> reflected a growing awareness of a serious problem: that science education at the elementary level was proving highly successful, particularly as far as the development of thinking skills was concerned, and the social hierarchy was under threat because there was not corresponding development for the higher order.[15]

Wrottesley gave an instance which confirmed his worst fears:

... a poor boy hobbled forth to give a reply; he was lame and humpbacked, and his wan emaciated face told only too clearly the tale of poverty and its consequences ... but he gave forthwith so lucid and intelligent a reply to the question put to him that there arose a feeling of admiration for the child's talents combined with a sense of shame that more information should be found in some of the lowest of our lower classes on matters of general interest than in those far above them in the world by station.

He concluded:

It would be an unwholesome and vicious state of society in which those who are comparatively unblessed with nature's gifts should be generally superior in intellectual attainments to those above them in station.[16]

Soon after Wrottesley's comments in 1860, science was removed from the elementary curriculum. When science eventually reappeared in the curriculum of the elementary schools some twenty years later it was in a very different form from the science of common things. A watered-down version of pure laboratory science had become accepted as the *correct* view of science, a view which has persisted, largely unchallenged, to the present day. Science, as a school subject, was powerfully redefined to become similar in form to so much else in the secondary curriculum — pure, abstract, a body of knowledge enshrined in syllabuses and textbooks.

To begin any analysis of schooling by accepting without question a form and content of curriculum that was fought for and achieved at particular historical points on the basis of certain social and political priorities and to take that curriculum as a given is to forego a whole range of understandings and insights into features of the control and operation of the school and the classroom. It is to take over the mystifications of previous episodes of governance as unchallengeable givens. We are, let us be clear, talking about the systematic 'invention of tradition' in an arena of social production and reproduction, the school curriculum, where political and social priorities are paramount. Histories of other aspects of social life have begun to systematically scrutinize this process. Hobsbawn (1985) argues that the term 'invented tradition':

... includes both traditions actually invented, constructed and formally instituted and those emerging in a less traceable manner within a brief and dateable period — a matter of a few years perhaps — and establishing themselves with great rapidity.

Hobsbawn defines the matter this way:

> Invented tradition is taken to mean a set of practices, normally governed by overtly or tacitly accepted rules and of a ritual or symbolic nature which seek to circulate certain values and norms of behaviour by repetition, which automatically implies continuity with the past. In fact, where possible, they normally attempt to establish continuity with a suitable historic past.[17]

In this sense, the making of curriculum can be seen as a process of inventing tradition. In fact this language is often used when the 'traditional disciplines' or 'traditional subjects' are juxtaposed against some 'new fangled' innovation of integrated or child-centred topics. The point, however, is that the written curriculum is a supreme example of the invention of tradition: but as with all tradition it is not a once and for all given, it is a given which has to be defended, where the definitions have to be constructed and reconstructed over time. Plainly, if curriculum theorists, historians and sociologists of education substantially ignore the history and social construction of curriculum the mystification and reproduction of 'traditional' curriculum form and content becomes easier.

In such a situation it is quite possible to develop an ideology, as in current times, where our gaze is directed to individual classrooms and schools, since they are thought to have 'autonomy'; the search is on for efficient teaching (ie. teacher appraisal or 'incompetent teachers') for 'school effectiveness' or 'better schools'. The researcher is guided towards the individual classroom or school in a quest for the ingredients of the more successful practice. The differentials of success become paramount: ie. why is one classroom better than another?; why do parents choose one school rather than another? This all restores attention to the individual practice of school and classroom.

Conversely, our gaze is directed away from the parameters of practice, from the commonalities of success and failure in schooling: from the historical analysis of the social construction of the curriculum. Yet this is part of the story of the 'good' classroom or the 'better' school; for this is the story of how this particular range of goals were established and enshrined. In short, there has been an antecedent struggle to achieve a belief that one particular version of school should be viewed as 'good'.

As the episode of the 'science of common things' makes clear it is also the story of how other goals and values were defeated. In taking the current parameters as given and searching for better classrooms and schools of the established sort we would be foreclosing any analysis of fundamental alternatives. But research which accepts major variables as *fait accompli* is undeserving of that title: we are in the business of 'fine-tuning' or, to pursue the car analogy, 'maintenance'. The struggle over the definition of curriculum is a matter of social and political priorities as well as intellectual discourse. The history of past curriculum conflicts needs therefore to be recovered. Otherwise our studies of schooling will leave unquestioned and unanalyzed a set of inherited priorities and assumptions which should be at the heart of our intellectual understanding and practical operation of schooling.

Notes and References

1 WILLIAMS, R. *Politics and Letters*, (London, New Left Books, 1974) p. 176.
2 JACKSON, P. *Life in Classrooms*, (New York, Holt Rinehart and Winston Inc., 1968) pp. 151–2.
3 GREENE, M. 'Curriculum and consciousness', *The Record*, 3, 2, 1971.
4 YOUNG M. and WHITTY, G. *Society, State and Schooling*, (Lewes, Falmer, 1977), p. 237.
5 ARMSTRONG, M. and KING, L. 'Schools within schools' in WATTS, J. (Ed), *The Countesthorpe Experience*, (London, George Allen and Unwin, 1977) p. 54.
6 *Ibid.*
7 *op. cit.*, p. 62. Quoting D. Hawkins.
8 RUDOLPH, F. *Curriculum: A History of the American Undergraduate Course of Study since 1636*, (San Francisco, Jossey Bass 1977) p. 6.
9 CUBAN, L. *How Teachers Taught: Constancy and Change in American Class-rooms 1890–1980*, (New York, Longman, 1984) p. 2.
10 *Ibid.* p. 255.
11 SIMON, B. *Does Education Matter?*, (London, Lawrence and Wisehart, 1985) p. 49.
12 VULLIAMY, G. 'What counts as school music' in WHITTY, G. and YOUNG, M. *Explorations in the Politics of School Knowledge*, (Driffield, Nafferton, 1976) p. 24–5.
13 BROCKLEHURST, J.B. *Music in Schools*, (London, Routledge and Kegan Paul, 1962) p. 55.
14 LAYTON, D. *Science for the People*, (London, George Allen and Unwin, 1973).

15   HODSON, D. 'Science curriculum change in Victorian England: A case
     study of the science of common things', in GOODSON, I.F. (Ed)
     International Perspectives in Curriculum History, (London, Croom Helm,
     1987) p. 36.
16   *Ibid.* p. 36–7.
17   HOBSBAWN, E. and RANGER, T. (Ed) *The Invention of Tradition*,
     (Cambridge University Press, 1985) p. 1.

3 Etymologies, Epistemologies and The Emergence of Curriculum: A Speculative Essay

The problem of reconceptualizing our study of schooling can be partially illustrated in the basic etymology of curriculum. The word curriculum derives from the Latin word *currere*, which means to run, and refers to a course (or race-chariot). The implications of etymology are that curriculum is thereby defined as a course to be followed, or most significantly, presented. As Barrow (1984) notes 'as far as etymology goes, therefore, the curriculum should be understood to be "the presented content" for study'.[1] Social context and construction by this view is relatively unproblematic, for by etymological implication, the power of 'reality-definition' is placed firmly in the hands of those who 'draw up' and define the course. The bond between curriculum and prescription then was forged early; it has survived and strengthened over time. Part of the strengthening of this bond has been the emergence of sequential patterns of learning to define and operationalize the curriculum as prescribed.

From its Latin origins it is important to trace the emergence of curriculum as a concept which began to be used in schooling. According to Hamilton and Gibbons (1980) 'the words class and curriculum seem to have entered educational discourse at a time when schooling was being transformed into a mass activity'.[2] But the origins of the class/curriculum juxtaposition can be found earlier and at the higher education level. From Mir's analysis of the origins of 'classes' as first described in the statutes of the College of Montaign, we learn:

> It is in the 1509 programme of Montaign that one finds for the first time in Paris a precise and clear division of students into *classes*... That is, divisions graduated by stages or levels of increasing complexity according to the age and knowledge required by students.[3]

Mir argues that the College of Montaign actually inaugurated the Renaissance class system but the vital connection to establish however is how organization in classes was associated with curriculum prescribed and sequenced for stages or levels.

Hamilton provides further evidence from Glasgow where the Oxford English Dictionary locates the earliest source of 'curriculum' in 1633. The annexation of the Latin term for a race-course is clearly related to the emergence of sequencing in schooling but the question 'Why Glasgow?' remains. Hamilton believes that 'the sense of discipline or structural order that was absorbed into curriculum came not so much from classical sources as from the ideas of John Calvin (1509–1564).

> As Calvin's followers gained political as well as theological ascendancy in late sixteenth century Switzerland, Scotland and Holland, the idea of discipline — 'the very essense of Calvinism' — began to denote the internal principles and external machinery of civil government and personal conduct. From this perspective there is a homologous relationship between curriculum and discipline: curriculum was to Calvinist educational practice as discipline was to Calvinist social practice.[4]

We have then an early instance, if these speculations carry weight, of the relationship between knowledge and control. This works at two levels with regard to curriculum definition. Firstly, there is the social context in which knowledge is conceived of and produced. Secondly, there is the manner in which such knowledge is 'translated' for use in particular educational milieu, in this case classes but later classrooms. The social context of curriculum construction must take account of both levels.

The evidence of Paris and Glasgow in the sixteenth and seventeenth centuries has been summarized in the following quote in which we can see the interlinked nature of the emerging mode of curriculum and patterns of social organization and control:

> The notion of classes came into prominence with the rise of sequential programmes of study which, in turn, resonated with various Renaissance and Reformation sentiments of upward mobility. In Calvinist countries (such as Scotland) these views found their expression theologically in the doctrine of predestination (the belief that only a preordained minority could attain spiritual salvation) and, educationally, in the emergence of national but bipartite education systems where the

'elect' (ie. predominantly those with the ability to pay) were offered the prospect of advanced schooling, while the remainder (predominantly the rural poor) were fitted to a more conservative curriculum (the appreciation of religious knowledge and secular virtue).[5]

This quote sets up the unique significance of curriculum as it developed. For soon after as its power to designate what should go on in the classroom was realized, a further power was discovered. Alongside the power to *designate* was the power to *differentiate*. This meant that even children who went to the same school could be given access to what amounted to different 'worlds' through the curriculum they were taught.

Hamilton (1980) contends that 'the "class" pedagogies pioneered at Glasgow University had a direct influence on those adopted in the elementary schools of the nineteenth century'.[6] The general connection between 'class' pedagogies and a curriculum based on sequence and prescription is clear but to move towards the 'modern' duality of pedagogy and curriculum involves the transition from class to classroom system.

In analyzing the historical transition from 'class' to classroom system, the shift in the initial stages of the Industrial Revolution in the late eighteenth and early nineteenth century 'was as important to the administration of schooling as the concurrent shift from domestic to factory production was to the management of industry'. Indeed, as Smelser (1968) has shown the two were intimately related:

In the pre-industrial family of a craftsman, the parents themselves are responsible for teaching the child minimum occupational skills, as well as for his emotional molding during his early years. When a growing economy places demands for greater literacy and more technical skills, the pressure is for this multi-functional family to give way to a new, more complex set of social arrangements. Structurally distinct educational institutions appear and the family begins to surrender some of its previous training functions to these new institutions, having lost these functions, accordingly, the family becomes more specialized, focusing relatively more on emotional conditioning in the early childhood years and relatively less on its former economic and educational functions.[7]

In the 'domestic-putter out' system the family unit remained at home and education, albeit rather more in the guise of training and apprenticeship, could therefore take place in the home. With the triumph of the factory system, the associated break-up of the family opened up these roles to subsequent penetration by state schooling and to their replacement by the classroom system where large groups could be adequately supervised and controlled. Hence 'the change from class to classroom reflected a more general upheaval in schooling — the ultimate victory of group-based pedagogies over the more individualized forms of teaching and learning'.[8]

If we specifically turn to the development of schooling in England at this stage, the intersection of pedagogy and curriculum begins to resemble more 'modern' patterns. As Bernstein (1971) has argued, pedagogy, curriculum and evaluation considered together constitute the three message systems through which formal educational knowledge can be realized; in this sense, they constitute a modern epistemology.[9] In the 1850s, the third prong was pioneered with the founding of the first university examination boards. The centennial report of the University of Cambridge Local Examinations Syndicate (1958) reports:

> The establishment of these examinations was the universities' response to petitions that they should help in the development of 'schools for the middle classes'.[10]

Also at this time the features of curriculum mentioned earlier, the power to differentiate, was being institutionalized. The birth of secondary *examinations* and the institutionalization of curriculum *differentiation* were then almost exactly contemporaneous. For instance the Taunton Report in 1868 classified secondary schooling into three grades depending on the time spent at school. Taunton asserted:

> The difference in time assigned makes some difference in the very nature of education itself; if a boy cannot remain at school beyond the age of 14 it is useless to begin teaching him such subjects as required a longer time for their proper study; if he can continue till 18 or 19, it may be expedient to postpone some studies that would otherwise be commenced earlier.[11]

Taunton noted that 'these instructions correspond roughly but by no means exactly to the gradations of society'. (This statement could as we shall see, be equally well applied to the Norwood Report nearly a century later.) In 1868 schooling till 18 or 19 was for the sons of men with considerable incomes independent of their own exertions, or professional men, and men in business whose profits put them on the same level. These received a mainly classical curriculum. The second grade up to 16 was for sons of the 'mercantile classes'. Their curriculum was less classical in orientation and had a certain practical orientation. The third grade till 14 was for the sons of 'the smaller tenant farmer, the small tradesmen, (and) the superior artisans'. Their curriculum was based on the three Rs but taught up to a fairly high level. These gradations cover secondary schooling. Meanwhile, most of the working class remained in elementary schools where they were taught rudimentary skills in the three Rs. By this time the curriculum functioned as a major identifier of, and mechanism for, social differentiation. This power to designate and differentiate established a conclusive place for curriculum in the epistemology of schooling.

By the turn of the century the epistemology, with which we are familiar, was emerging. Thus:

> By the twentieth century, the batch production rhetoric of the 'classroom system' (for example, lessons, subjects, timetables, grading, standardization, streaming) had become so pervasive that it successfully achieved a normative status — creating the standards against which all subsequent educational innovations came to be judged.[12]

The dominant epistemology which characterized state schooling by the beginning of the twentieth century combined the trilogy of pedagogy, curriculum and evaluation. The last of the pieces in the trilogy was the establishment of university examination boards and here the side-effects on curriculum were to be both pervasive and long lasting. The classroom system inaugurated a world of timetables and compartmentalized lessons; the curriculum manifestation of this systemic change was the school subject. If 'class and curriculum' entered educational discourse when schooling was transformed into a mass activity in England 'classroom system and school subject' emerged at the stage at which that mass activity became a state-subsidized system. And in spite of the many alternative ways of conceptualizing and organizing curriculum the convention of the subject retains its supremacy. In the modern era we are essentially dealing with the *curriculum as subject*.

Whilst this system was inaugurated in the 1850s, it was established on the present footing with the definition of the Secondary Regulations in 1904 which list the main subjects followed by the establishment of a subject-based School Certificate in 1917. From this date, curriculum conflict began to resemble the existing situation in focusing on the definition and evaluation of *examinable* knowledge. Hence, the School Certificate subjects rapidly became the overriding concern of grammar schools and the academic subjects it examined soon established ascendancy on these schools' timetables. In 1941 Norwood stated that:

> A certain sameness in the curriculum of schools resulted from the double necessity of finding a place for the many subjects competing for time in the curriculum and the need to teach these subjects in such a way and to such a standard as will ensure success in the School Certificate examination.

The normative character of the system is clear and as a result of 'these necessities' the curriculum had 'settled down into an uneasy equilibrium, the demands of specialists and subjects being widely adjusted and compensated'.[13] The extent to which university examination boards thereby influenced the curriculum through examination subjects is evident. The academic subject-centred curriculum was in fact strengthened in the period following the 1944 Education Act. In 1951 the introduction of the General Certificate of Education allowed subjects to be taken separately at 'O' level (in the School Certificate blocks of 'main' subjects had to be passed); and the introduction of 'A' level increased subject specialization and enhanced the link between 'academic' examinations and university 'disciplines'. The academic subjects which dominated 'O' and especially 'A' level examinations were then closely linked to university definitions; but even more crucially they were linked to patterns of resource allocation. Academic 'subjects' claiming close connections to university 'disciplines' were for the 'able' students. From the beginning it was assumed that such students required 'more staff, more highly paid staff and more money for equipment and books'.[14] The crucial and sustained link between 'academic' subjects and preferential resources and status was therefore established.

But if this system was predominant with regard to staffing and resources for academic subjects in grammar schools, the implications for the other schools (and styles of curriculum) should not be forgotten. Echoing Taunton, Norwood in 1943 had discovered that schooling had created distinctive groups of pupils, each of which needed to be treated 'in a way appropriate to itself'. This time the social and class basis of differentiation remained the same but the rationale and mechanism for differentiation was significantly different. Before, the argument had focussed on time spent at school, now the emphasis was on different 'mentalities', each recognizing a different curriculum. Firstly, 'the pupil who is interested in learning for its own sake, who can grasp an argument of follow a piece of connected reasoning: such pupils 'educated by the curriculum commonly associated with grammar schools have entered the learned professions or have taken up higher administrative or business posts'.[15] The second group whose interests lie in the field of applied science or applied arts were to go to technical schools (which never developed very far). Thirdly, for the pupils who deal 'more easily with concrete things than with ideas' the curriculum would 'make a direct appeal to interests, which it would awaken by practical touch with affairs'.[16] A practical curriculum then for a manual occupational future. These pupils were to go to the secondary modern school.

We see then the emergence of a definite pattern of *prioritizing* of pupils through curriculum; what emerges I have called elsewhere 'the triple alliance between academic subjects, academic examinations and able pupils'. Working through patterns of resource allocation, this means a process of pervasive 'academic drift' afflicts sub-groups promoting school subjects. Hence, subjects as diverse as woodwork and metalwork, physical education, art, technical studies, book-keeping, needlework and domestic science have pursued status improvement by arguing for enhanced academic examinations and qualifications. Likewise, those schools defined as different from grammar schools, the technical schools and secondary modern schools, were also ultimately drawn into the process of academic drift both ending up competing for success through academic subject based styles of examination.

The manner in which this structure effects the definition of the school curriculum as subjects are defined, promoted and redefined is examined in some detail in the later chapters (particularly 'Becoming a school subject', chapter 10). In a way the evolution of each subject reflects in microcosm a struggle over alternatives over time, which is not dissimilar to the overall pattern discerned as state schooling is established and defined. Hence, Layton (1972) sees the initial stage as one where 'the learners are attracted to the subject because of its bearing on matters of concern to them. At this point the teachers are seldom trained as subject specialists but do 'bring the missionary enthusiasms of pioneers to their task'. Significantly at this stage, 'the dominant criterion is relevance to the needs and interests of the learners'.[17] However, as the subject 'progresses' (a subject at any point in time resembling a coalition which veneers a sub-set of warring factions) the role of the universities becomes more and more important. This is not least because subject groups employ a *discourse* where they argue increasingly for their subject to be viewed as an 'academic discipline' (thereby claiming the financial resources and career opportunities which accrue). The corollary of this claim is that university scholars must be given control over defining the 'discipline' (the aspiration to the rhetoric of 'the discipline' is related to acceptance of this hierarchical pattern of definition, so in this sense the discursive formation is critical). Jenkins and Shipman (1976) have noted that:

> One detects a certain embarrassment in teachers who not unnaturally feel the difference between forms, disciplines and subjects are in part differences of status.[18]

In effect the differences are over *who* can define 'disciplines' — essentially, this is presented as the characteristic activity of university scholars.

The progressive refinement of an epistemology suited to state schooling then embraces the trilogy of pedagogy, curriculum and examination. Until recently, the 'triple alliance' of academic subjects, academic examinations and able students have been able to enjoy a clear hierarchy of status and resources. Thus, our understanding of curriculum has to focus mainly on analyzing the dominant convention of the school subject and the associated examination by university boards. The linking of resources to 'academic' subjects places a priority on subjects that can be presented as 'academic disciplines' and this places further power in the hands of the universities. Not that the power of the universities over curriculum is unchallenged, for the challenges are recurrent. Reid (1972) has noted that a major area of conflict is between the external constraints arising from university requirements and the internal pressures which have their origins in the school:

> Schools are, however, poorly equipped to resist university pressures. To a large extent they allow the legitimacy of the university demands, and have evolved an authority structure which is linked to them.[19]

Such recurrent conflict is of course likely as the school subjects 'progresses' away from Layton's early stage where 'the dominant criterion is relevance to the needs and interests of the learners'. But as we have seen, an epistemology has been institutionalized and resourced which places the academic 'discipline' at the top of the curriculum apex. Not surprisingly, the culminating stage in the establishment of an 'academic' subject celebrates the power of scholars to define the disciplines' field. In this culminating stage, however, Layton argues that related to this change in who defines school knowledge 'Students are initiated into a tradition, their attitudes approaching passivity and resignation, a prelude to disenchantment'.[20]

The final stage of Layton's model summarizes (and comments upon) the kind of political 'settlement' with regard to curriculum, pedagogy and evaluation in operation. Plainly however, there are recurrent conflicts and the 'achievement' of this 'settlement' has been a painstaking and deeply contested process. It is important when assessing the contribution of scholars of education to establish how their work resonates with the contested nature of education generally and curriculum specifically. As always, there is a danger of accepting that which is worked for and achieved as a *fait accompli*, a given. Nothing could be further from the truth.

Antecedents and Alternatives

The epistemology and institutionalized system of state schooling briefly described above was in sharp contrast to antecedent forms of education and to the involvement of the state in schooling at this earlier stage. Rothblatt (1976), for instance, describes education in Georgian England as follows:

> The state was not interested in 'national education' — indeed the idea had not yet occurred. The Church, which was interested in education, because of its continuing rivalry with Dissent, still did not have a firm policy and left the direction of studies to local or personal initiatives, or to the forces of the market. The demand for education and the demand for particular levels of education varied radically from period to period and from group to group, depending upon social and economic circumstances, occupational distributions, and cultural values. Countless persons, lay as well as clerical, opened schools, tried out various educational experiments and programmes in an effort to retain a fickle or uncertain clientele. And home tuition, where adjustments in curricula could be made quickly and easily according to the learning ability of the pupil, certainly remained one of the most important means of elementary and secondary education throughout the nineteenth century.[21]

Such a personal and local mode of educating could well have allowed response to the experience and culture of the pupils, even in situations less ideal than home tuition 'where adjustments could be made quickly and easily according to the learning ability of pupil'. But among working class groups, certainly in the sphere of adult education, such respect for life experience in curriculum was a feature at this time and later. This contribution can be summarized as: 'the students' choice of subject, the relation of disciplines to actual contemporary living and the parity of general discussion with expert instruction'.[22] Above all there is the idea of curriculum as a two-way *conversation* rather than a one-way *transmission*.

Likewise, different patterns of education and attendance characterized the working class private school, which thrived in the first half of the nineteenth century and continued into the second half in many places even after the 1870 Act. Harrison (1984) has described these schools and the views which state inspectors held of them:

> Government inspection and middle class reformers condemned such schools as mere baby-minding establishments. They noted with strong disapproval the absence of settled or regular attendance. The pupils came and went at all times during the day. School hours were nominal and adjusted to family needs — hence the number of two- and three-year-olds who were sent to be 'out of the way' or 'kept safe'. The accommodation was over-crowded and sometimes stuffy, dirty and unsanitary. The pupils were not divided into classes, and the teacher was a working man or woman...

As well as not being arranged in classes, the curriculum was often individualized rather than sequential. Harrison describes 'Old Betty W's school' where 'On fine days the little forms were taken outside her cottage and placed under the window. The children had their books, or their knitting and the old lady, knitting herself incessantly, marched backwards and forwards hearing lessons and watching work'.[23]

These working class schools were effectively driven out by the version of state schooling which followed the 1870 Act. Thompson (1968) has argued that the watershed for such schools, certainly such styles of working class education, were the fears engendered by the French Revolution. From now on the state played an increasing role in the organization of schooling and of curriculum:

> Attitudes towards social class, popular culture and education became 'set' in the aftermath of the French Revolution. For a century and more most middle class educationalists could not distinguish the work of education from that of social control: and this entailed too often, a repression or a denial of the life experience of their pupils as expressed in uncouth dialect or in traditional cultural forms. Hence education and received

experience were at odds with each other. And those working
men who by their own efforts broke into the educated culture
found themselves at once in the same place of tension, in
which education brought with it the danger of rejection of
their fellows and self-distrust. The tension of course
continues.[24]

The disjuncture then between common cultural experience and curriculum can be estimated, for working class clienteles, as developing
after the moral panic associated with the French Revolution. From
this date on, the school curriculum was often overlaid by social control
concerns for the ordinary working populace.

For other classes at the time this overlay of closely structured,
sequenced and presented curriculum was not always deemed necessary. We learn that the public schools 'followed no common pattern
of education, though they agreed on the taking of Latin and Greek as
the main component of the curriculum. Each evolved its own unique
forms of organization with idiosyncratic vocabularies to describe
them'.[25] In so far as the curriculum depended on a learning of texts it
was not judged essential that the teacher taught the text — a highly
individualized form of curriculum was therefore possible. Moreover,
'where students were divided into "forms" (a term referring originally
to the benches on which they sat) this was done in a rough and ready
manner for the convenience of teaching and not with the idea of
establishing a hierarchy of ability or a sequence of learning'.[26]

Hence, coherent alternative forms of education and curriculum
developed in a wide range of schools for all classes prior to the
Industrial Revolution and even after industrial transformation were
retained in the public schools for the 'better classes' (and indeed for
the working class were retained and defended in pockets such as 'adult
education'). The model of curriculum and epistemology associated
with state schooling progressively colonized all educational *milieu* and
established itself some time in the late nineteenth century as the
dominant pattern. The subsequent linking of this epistemology to the
distribution of resources and the associated attribution of status and
careers stands at the centre of the consolidation of this pattern. The
assumption that the curriculum should be primarily academic and
associated with university disciplines has been painstakingly worked
for and paid for. We should beware of any accounts which present
such a situation of 'normal' or 'given'.

At root such a hierarchical system is often seen as denying the
dialectic of education, the notion of dialogue and flexibility which

some viewed (and view) as central to the way we learn. If 'subject matter is in large measure defined by the judgments and practice of the specialist scholars' and 'students are initiated into a tradition', their attitudes approach passivity and 'resignation', this mutuality is deliberately denied. The rhetoric of the 'discipline' and the academic subject might therefore be seen as characterizing a particular mode of social relations.

Educationists concerned with establishing a more egalitarian practice and curriculum are driven to constantly assert the need for dialogue and mutuality, and, with it, to argue for 'reconstruction of knowledge and curriculum'. For if the opinions cited are right, the very fabric and form of curriculum (as well as the content) assumes and establishes a particular mode of social relations and social hierarchy. Seen in this way, to argue only for changing the teaching method or the school organization is to accept a central mystification of hierarchical structure through curriculum, which would actively contradict other aspirations and ideals. Hence, where pockets of alternative practice exist they present a similar case for egalitarian practice: in liberal adult education the following argument is presented:

> All education which is worth the name involves a relationship of mutuality, a dialectic: and no worthwhile educationalist conceives of his material as a class of inert recipients of instruction — and no class is likely to stay the course with him — if he is under the misapprehension that the role of the class is passive. What is different about the adult student is the experience which he brings to the relationship. This experience modifies, sometimes subtly, and sometimes more radically, the entire educational process: it influences teaching methods, the selection and maturation of tutors, the syllabus: it may even disclose weak places or vacancies in received academic disciplines and lead on to the elaboration of new areas of study.[27]

By this view then the disciplines cannot be taught as final 'distillations' of knowledge unchallengeable and unchanging and should not be taught as incontestable and fundamental structures and texts. This would provide a deeply-flawed epistemology, pedagogically unsound and intellectually dubious, for in human scholarship 'final distillations' and 'fundamental' truths are elusive concepts. We are back with the dual face of socially contexted knowledge — both because knowledge and curriculum are pedagogically realized in a social context and are originally conceived of and constructed in such a context.

The alternatives to such a dominant view continue to surface. In more recent debates, we can find certain radical teachers pursuing the comprehensive ideal seriously and arguing that in such a milieu knowledge and curricula must be presented as provisional and *liable to reconstruction*. Armstrong (1977) writes that his 'contention is that the process of education should imply a dynamic relationship between teacher, pupil and task out of which knowledge is reconstructed, for both teacher and pupil, in the light of shared experience'.[28]

Conclusion

In this chapter some of the origins of curriculum have been speculatively scrutinized. In particular, we have seen that the notion of curriculum as structured sequence or 'discipline' derived a good deal from the political ascendancy of Calvinism. From these early origins there was a 'homologous relationship between curriculum and discipline'. Curriculum as discipline was allied to a social order where the 'elect' were offered the prospect of advanced schooling and the remainder a more conservative curriculum.

Out of these origins we have seen how this concept of curriculum became appended to a new notion of discipline (so we are to believe) 'fundamental' disciplines of 'the mind'. The juxtaposition of curriculum with (newly-defined) 'discipline' intersects with a remarkably similar social configuration. This time, the 'elect' are recruited by their capacity to display a facility for those academic 'subjects' allied to the 'disciplines'; their 'election' is signified by going on to study the 'disciplines' in the universities where they are defined and institutionalized.

Notes and References

1 BARROW, R. *Giving Teaching Back to Teachers: A Critical Introduction to Curriculum Theory*, (Brighton, Wheatsheaf and Althouse, 1984) p. 3.
2 HAMILTON, D. and GIBBONS, M. *Notes on the origins of the educational terms class and curriculum* (paper presented at the Annual Convention of the American Educational Research Association, Boston, April 1980) p. 15.
3 Quoted *op. cit.*, p. 7.
4 *op. cit.*, p. 14.

5   HAMILTON, D. 'Adam Smith and the moral economy of the classroom system; *Journal of Curriculum Studies*, Vol. 12, No. 4, October–December 1980, p. 286.

6   *op. cit.*, p. 282.

7   SMELSER, N. *Essays in Sociological Explanation*, (New Jersey, Prentice Hall, 1968) p. 79.

8   *op. cit.*, Hamilton, p. 282.

9   BERNSTEIN, B. 'On the classification and framing of educational knowledge' in YOUNG, M.F.D. (Ed), *Knowledge and Control*, (London, Collier Macmillan, 1971) p. 47.

10 University of Cambridge Local Examinations Syndicate, One Hundredth Annual Report to University, 29 May 1958, p. 1.

11 TAUNTON REPORT, Report of the Royal Commission on School Inquiry, (London 1868) p. 587.

12 *op. cit.*, HAMILTON, p. 282.

13 The Norwood Report, *Curriculum and Examinations in Secondary Schools*. Report of the Committee of the Secondary School Examinations Council, appointed by the President of the Board of Education in 1941, (London, HMSO, 1943) p. 61.

14 BYRNE, E.M. *Planning and Educational Inequality*, (Slough, NFER, 1974) p. 29.

15 *op. cit.*, Norwood Report, p. 2.

16 *Ibid.*, p. 4.

17 See LAYTON (1972), quoted in full chapter 10, p. 165.

18 JENKINS, D. and SHIPMAN, M. *Curriculum: An Introduction*, (London, Open Books, 1976) p. 102.

19 REID, W.A. *The University and the Sixth Form Curriculum*, (London, Macmillan, 1972) p. 106.

20 See chapter 10, p. 165.

21 ROTHBLATT, S. *Tradition and Change I: In English Liberal Education: an Essay in History and Culture*, (London, Faber and Faber, 1976) p. 45.

22 WILLIAMS, R. *The Long Revolution*, (London, Penguin, 1975) p. 165.

23 HARRISON, J.F.C. *The Common People*, (London, Flamingo, 1984) p. 290.

24 THOMPSON, E.P. *Education and Experience*, Fifth Mansbridge Memorial Lecture, (Leeds University Press, 1968) p. 16.

25 REID, W.A. 'Curriculum change and the evolution of educational constituencies: The English sixth form in the nineteenth century' in GOODSON, I.F. (Ed), *Social Histories of the Secondary Curriculum: Subjects for Study*, (Lewes, Falmer Press, 1985) p. 296.

26 *Ibid.*

27 *op. cit.*, Thompson, p. 9.

28 ARMSTRONG, M. 'Reconstructing knowledge: An example' in WATTS, J. (Ed), *The Countesthorpe Experience*, (London, George Allen and Unwin, 1977) p. 86.

II *The Search for Methods*

4   History of Education in England: Conflicting Paradigms

This chapter focusses on the nature of 'History of Education' as it has been institutionalized in England. As with all subjects, History of Education is far from monolithic and, as in other countries, more social and/or revisionist perspectives have been influential, especially in the last two decades. Overall however, History of Education, as institutionalized, has retained a certain 'Acts and Facts' flavour. The focus on courses in History of Education in one country provides a limited viewpoint but nonetheless allows us to scrutinize the problems posed by the 'Acts and Facts' orientation within the subject.

The first section of this chapter elaborates some of the deficiencies in this orientation to History of Education before going on to argue for the kind of history of curriculum reported in the later essays in the book. This progression is followed for both methodological and substantive reasons but, above all, because of the belief that a history of education or a history of school systems, without an analysis of the history of the school curriculum, is an inevitably partial account. Yet it remains true that innumerable histories of education never mention curriculum even though it cannot be assumed that curriculum remains stable over time. Changes in the internal nature of schooling can only be established by painstaking historical study and a central source in the historical understanding of the internal nature of schooling is the written curriculum (especially if scrutinized and developed alongside histories of pedagogy). Histories of education which fail to analyze the internal nature of schooling merely accept the school as a 'black box', unopened and unanalyzed. Our awareness of the potential for internal variety and change means we must tackle the history of curriculum as a central component in future histories of education and schooling.

'History of Education' in England

Teacher training first began systematically in the 1840s with the foundation of training colleges, of 'Queens Scholarships' which contributed towards maintenance, and of examination certificates for trained adult teachers. In the beginning the training colleges focussed on practice rather than theory. By 1914, Judd could write that 'in striking contrast with (the) emphasis on practical education is the relative neglect of education theory. One is very much impressed by the fact that in the English training colleges the whole theoretical side of pedagogy has a very meagre and abstract treatment'.[1] Whilst practical training predominated, a number of the colleges began to teach history of education. The teaching and the textbooks were normally provided by past schoolteachers rather than historical specialists. An example of such a textbook was R.M. Quick's *Essays on Educational Reformers*, first published in 1868. The limited audience expected for such work was clear from the print run of 500 copies, aimed mainly at his fellow public school masters. Later in the century, however, in 1890, when the training college courses began to expand, the book was reissued and, subsequently, reprinted a number of times.

By this time, 'university day training colleges' were also being formed and, hence, a new field for developing History of Education courses opened up. From 1890 onwards these university colleges were established, following a minority report of the Cross Commission which had recommended not just that teachers be trained in universities, but that faculties of education be established to initiate academic study and research in education. At first, the universities provided three year courses where the degree work and training for teaching were carried on alongside each other, merging theory and practice. Later, theory and practice were made more separate, with work for the academic degree in the first three years and an additional year for practical professional training. Separate university departments of education began to be formed from 1911 onwards.

The university *milieu* and the establishment of degrees encouraged a more academic and theoretical approach to the study of education. But from the beginning the History of Education courses focussed primarily on the history of educational institutions and systems and the history of educational theories and ideas. This approach to the History of Education has to be seen as reflecting contemporary notions of history itself.

History as a discipline in the universities was growing quite rapidly at this time and was primarily concerned with national constitutional and political matters. As Davis (1981) records, this meant that, for a long time, 'the basic assumption . . . was that history was narrative and national'.[2] He stresses the continuity of a subject, whose guidelines, laid down in the nineteenth century, proved remarkably resilient:

> Until the 1960s, history syllabuses in British universities con-formed to a broad general pattern of which the Oxford sylla-bus was typical. It consisted of English history from 'the beginning' to 1914, examined in three papers; a period of English Constitutional History (one paper); a period of foreign history (two papers); political theory based on Aristotle, Hob-bes, and Rousseau (one paper); . . .[3]

Following these patterns in mainstream history, History of Education developed as periodized and narrative, primarily concerned with the history of educational institutions and theories; all taught in strict chronological sequence.

Seaborne (1971) has judged that History of Education had 'two basic difficulties' in the early twentieth century. Firstly, as we have mentioned, but common to other branches of educational study, there was a lack of specialization among the lecturing staff 'which often resulted in entrusting the historical aspect to lecturers who were experienced schoolteachers, but rarely acquainted with the more general developments in historical teaching and research'. The second difficulty was more basic in that it reflected on the content and methodology of History of Education as a field of study:

> The study of this branch of education began towards the end of the nineteenth century when the constitutional aspects of history were considered to be all important, illustrating as they did the triumph of parliamentary democracy in Britain. Un-fortunately, this tendency to concentrate on the history of institutions remained dominant in the colleges and depart-ments of education . . . (where) . . . courses in what have been aptly dubbed 'Acts and Facts' continued to be inflicted on generations of students and tended to give the History of Education a bad name.[4]

As we shall see in the next sections, although a number of counter-tendencies developed in both mainstream history and the History of Education, the predominance of 'Acts and Facts' courses lasted for a very long time. The legacy was considerable and Seaborne reports that a survey of courses in the History of Education carried out

in 1967, showed that in some institutions new approaches were beginning to make an impact 'but that, at least in some colleges and
departments, the general despair which the study of 'Acts and Facts'
produced had led to the abandonment of any specifically historical
component in the education course'.[5] Likewise, in 1973, Stephens
argued that 'much work in the history of education was written in a
vacuum unrelated to a general history of economic and social change
... the entrenched educational history of the textbooks ... emphasized the Acts, individual institutions and the growth of the State
system of education'.[6]

The reasons for the dominance of 'Acts and Facts' History of
Education are numerous. Perhaps most important was the carry-over
from the general mode of historical scholarship and writing at the
time that History of Education courses were devised and institutionalized in the colleges and university departments. But the reason for this
pattern itself relates both to the general social and political context of
nineteenth century Britain and to the associated range of documentary
evidence on which history has to build its interpretations. In this sense
there is the problem of the 'selective tradition'. As Williams (1961) has
reminded us, this is a general cultural phenomenon: but it has a
particular potency when practised by historians.

> To some extent, the selection begins within the period itself;
> from the whole body of activities, certain things are selected
> for value and emphasis. In general, this selection will reflect
> the organization of the period as a whole, though this does not
> mean that the values and emphases will later be confirmed. We
> see this clearly enough in the case of past periods, but we
> never really believe it about our own.[7]

Williams tells us that 'the traditional culture of a society will always
tend to correspond to its *contemporary* system of interests and values
for it is not an absolute body of work but a continual selection and
interpretation'. For the historian, the effects of contemporary selection
and associated documentation are often conclusive. If, for instance,
there is a contemporary obsession with recording 'Acts and Facts' and
not recording evidence of conflict in classrooms, this will often present
insuperable problems for subsequent historical analyses and reconstruction.

Historians of education who search out new areas of study therefore often collide with the intractable selections of past periods.
Andrews (1983), for instance, wanted to study formal and informal

networks of educational activity in nineteenth century Preston. She found, however, that:

> Documents have differential survival rates and those which do survive do not always provide all the information required. The fundamental difference between historical research and other forms of social enquiry is the impossibility of 'going back' to ask for further explanation and elaboration. This leads to all kinds of problems. The answers to a great many questions are simply not available, since the necessary records either never existed or failed to survive.[8]

One important aspect of the documentary record for historians is provided by government reports. The 'Acts and Facts' approach is found to predominate in many of the reports — hence, we see one dimension of how the selective tradition can lead an area of study, like History of Education, in a particular direction. With such a focus, it is clear that 'the answers to a great many questions are simply not available'. But, as with all generalizations, the emphasis on Acts and Facts is greater in certain periods than in others; we are dealing in fact not with 'the selective tradition' but with a range of selectivities grounded in particular historical circumstances. In the 1920s, for instance, some government reports offer considerable historical and contextual detail. The Hadow Report, published in 1927, whilst concentrating mainly on Acts as outcomes, provides a great deal of valuable historical commentary in the four parts of the section on 'The development of full-time post-primary education in England and Wales from 1800 to 1918'.[9]

Interestingly, later reports move away from this approach. Once again the focus is narrowed back to legislation and institutional structures. Clarke (1940) has commented on how the selective tradition operated in the Spens Report of 1938:

> But it is still true that the really important facts of English education remain for the mass in the region of the 'taken for granted'. As a particularly striking example of this, the Spens Report may be quoted. There is all too much truth in the Irishism that the most significant things in the Report are the things it does not say. Yet so deep-rooted is social habit, so completely lacking is any popular philosophy of education, that the profound issues of social destiny which are implied by the Report, though never explicitly raised in it, seemed to have

escaped general notice. Discussion is concerned rather with the internals of school organization, with relatively minor steps of liberalization, and with details of adjustment of school-types.

He points out that although the Report is avowedly concerned with the whole range of secondary education, it leaves out the public schools, the most high status institutions of schooling in the country. He says:

> So little attention has been given to this omission, startling enough in any other country. So generally has it been accepted as natural and proper, that one may doubt that whether it was even intentional. How vain it is to look for the explanation of such phenomena in some formal and abstract statement of educational principle! The explanation is, of course, not educational at all in that sense, but sociological. The sources of such an attitude are to be found in the social history of England since the Revolution.[10]

The omissions Clarke refers to became very much clearer in the period following the Second World War.

Paradoxically, at precisely the time that some educationists were developing a cumulative sense of the importance of historical analysis, government reports began to omit such data. Furthermore, at a time when education became 'a proper subject for discussion and study by the general public'[11], especially before and after the 1944 Act, historical data began to disappear from government reports. We are witness to how modes of educational scholarship are to some extent constructed and influenced: in the case of history, as we have noted, the vagaries of the selective tradition pass on the preferred focus to future generations of historians. Our parameters are to some extent determined by governmental preference, as evidenced in documents where 'discussion is concerned rather with the internals of school organization, with relatively minor steps of liberalization, and with details of adjustment of school types'. We are invited to concentrate on the minutes of bureaucratic progress, on systems adjustment and on legislative intention. Our gaze is conversely directed away from the internal details of schooling and curriculum, thereby stemming the full tide of historical analysis of the conflicts and compromises which underpin bureaucratic and legislative action.

The result of the focus on bureaucratic process is instanced in the Norwood Report of 1943. With no evidence of social, political and historical process, the 'evolution of education' is seen as essentially unproblematic, a natural phenomenon. The Darwinism of Norwood leads to some stunning 'historical' commentary — for instance we learn that:

> The evolution of education has in fact thrown up certain groups, each of which can and must be treated in a way appropriate to itself. Whether such groups are distinct on strictly psychological grounds, whether they represent types of minds, whether the differences are differences in kind or in degree, these are questions it is not necessary to pursue.[12]

In this paragraph we see the manner in which history is presented. I read this as a desire for closure, a desire to present contest, conflict and compromise as 'natural evolution'. This desire for closure is plainly deeply felt, but I experience it as an incitement to historical scholarship — a different kind of historical scholarship. These may be questions 'it is not necessary to pursue', but I remain intrigued by how 'the evolution of education throws up certain groups'.

In other countries this partial 'closure' of historical scholarship seems less evident. In the United States, for instance, in the 1960s the US Bureau of Education working alongside the American Historical Society actively commissioned a three volume revision of the history of American Education (by Lawrence Cremin) and there have been a spate of revisionist histories. Similarly, in Canada, the government is currently funding some historical study of curriculum notably in the field of science education.[13] In Britain, the contrast is marked. Simon (1982) has recently noted that 'there seems a marked official reluctance to give even that prominence to the historical approach which was earlier taken for granted'. We have already noted that the Spens Report omitted many aspects which had been more fully dealt with in earlier reports, but Simon notes that matters have receded further and asks us to compare 'the historical chapter of the Spens Report of 1938 ... with the amorphous and eclectic introductory chapter in the Plowden Report of 1967 (which evaded any attempt at a historical assessment of the role and nature of primary education)'.[14]

Hence, it would seem that if we are to broaden the scope of History of Education we shall to some extent be 'working against the grain'. But this is an experience familiar to a wide range of contemporary historians and it is time we turned to the origins and subsequent work of those who seek to broaden the focus of the historical enterprise.

Alternative Paradigms in the History of Education

In characterizing History of Education in the past as predominantly Acts and Facts I have been less than fair. As with any subject History of Education has not been, and is not, monolithic. There have always been different, perhaps broader, visions at work within the subject. In seeking to formulate an alternative paradigm for the historical study of education it is important to return to the origins in the early work of the first Professors of Education. We shall see that the suggestions carried herein are far from new and, indeed, build upon a well-established and respectable lineage. Certainly, many of the early Professors of Education brought a conviction that historical studies could deepen an understanding of the educational terrain.

The first university professorships of Education, established at St. Andrews and Edinburgh in the 1870s, were in the 'Theory, History and Practice of Education'. S.S. Laurie, one of the early Professors at Edinburgh, regarded history as one of the major sources of illumination in the study of education. His early lectures were published in 1903 as *Educational Opinion from the Renaissance* and he wrote that:

> I venture to issue these lectures in the conviction that the study of the History of Education in the writings of the most distinguished representatives of various schools of thought is an important part of the general preparation of those who adopt the profession of schoolmaster.[15]

Professor J.W. Adamson, who founded the Department of Education at King's College, plainly shared these convictions and was aware of the limitations of Acts and Facts. In the Introduction to *English Education 1789–1902*, he wrote: 'While the great fact of English educational history during the period is an administrative revolution, it is of course possible to view the story from other stand points'. He then points out that 'on the political plane it is a phase of the relations existing between the State and the citizen;' and that we need to direct attention to 'the changes wrought in the curricula of all grades'.[16] Barnard (1961) judges that Adamson has an important truth to pass on: 'His message to our age is that a philosophy of education not bombinant in a vacuum but based on a sound knowledge of educational history ... may help us to apply to best effect the techniques of education'.[17]

The opinion of these early professors were shared by their contemporaries in other countries. Durkheim wrote in his *Evolution of Educational Thoughts*, based on his 1904 lectures, that 'it is only by carefully studying the past that we can come to anticipate the future and to understand the present';[18] consequently he judged 'a history of education provides the soundest basis for the study of educational theory'.

The most systematic treatment of the history of the curriculum came from Foster Watson, who was Professor of Education at the University College of Wales, Aberyswyth. He was appointed in 1894 and retired in 1913 at the age of 53 to dedicate himself to writing about education. In 1922 he produced his massive *Encyclopedia and Dictionary of Education*. Earlier, in 1909, he had produced a history of the teaching of modern subjects. In this book he argued:

> If a history of any educational subject encourages and deepens within us the habit of looking with a keener interest for educational provision to the full social, economic, political and religious needs of a community in a past period, *from the point of view of the contemporary aims and scope of knowledge of that period*, then the study justifies itself. If, further, such a study stimulates that exercise of thought on the multitudinous problems which have arisen in every period, and leads us to identify ourselves in real interest with the aims and methods of the solutions attempted to those problems, then our judgment is strengthened for forming decisions as to the educational difficulties of the present age.[19]

His concern was to provide a detailed curriculum history and he argued for both its importance and, for its time, uniqueness:

> It will be generally admitted that it is high time that the historical facts with regard to the beginning of the teaching of modern subjects in England were known, and known in connection with the history of the social forces which brought them into the educational curriculum. This is precisely what is now attempted for the first time, as far as the writer knows, within a single volume.[20]

Regrettably, both in the specific case of launching curriculum history and in the general sense of launching a more broadly conceived view of History of Education, the work of the early professors was only pursued patchily in the twentieth century. As we have noted, Acts and Facts became the dominant orthodoxy in both courses and in textbooks. The growing literature, particularly from the USA, of revisionist historians and the studies which have sought to extend or critique this work is important. Moreover, changes in mainstream history may also prove catalytic. Economic and social history have grown rapidly since the inter-war years; oral history and feminist history have developed to try to exhume the 'invisible armies' suppressed by selective traditions; the work of Thompson, Hobsbawn, Harrison, Parker and Blythe illustrates how such imposed selections can in fact be transcended, how the lived experiences in our culture can be reconstructed by historians. These new tendencies within history point to new possibilities for educational history. Perhaps, at last, the early promise of History of Education courses, as glimpsed by the first Professors of Education, can at last be retrieved and carried on. It is time the 'evolution of education' was fully embraced as a question that it is 'necessary to pursue'.

Promoting the Alternative Paradigm: Towards Curriculum History

The starting point of this book is a belief that historical studies can develop our understanding of contemporary curriculum issues and can test the elaboration of curriculum theory. The History of Education Society (founded in 1967) has begun again the process of exhuming and investigating the history of curriculum first started by Foster Watson sixty years earlier. Relating this work to contemporary or theoretical purposes has, however, been uncommon (not surprising given traditional historical orientations). For instance, writing of the work of curriculum specialists with respect to historical perspective, Marsden (1978) judges that they 'have often been deficient and can roughly be divided into those which are *a-historical* and *unhistorical*, in so far as the categories can be isolated from one another'. He defines an a-historical approach as:

> One which disregards the historical perspective, the writer perceiving it to be irrelevant and/or uninteresting... Thus work proceeds, almost naively, in a temporal vacuum.

An unhistorical approach is characterized somewhat haughtily:

> As one inconsistent both in gross and in refined terms with the accepted canons of historical scholarship, purveying inaccurate, over-simplified and otherwise distorted impressions of the past. Attention is drawn to the past, not for its own sake but as a means of sharpening a particular contemporary axe.[21]

Alongside this 'misuse' of history, Marsden places those curriculum studies in which the past is scanned for support of some broad socio-political interpretation or theory.

Historians have rightly reacted to the misuse of history for 'sharpening contemporary axes' or supporting broad socio-political interpretations or theories. In my view that reaction has gone too far (understandable though it is if placed in historical context). The result is that History of Education has often remained rigidly 'periodized' in the tradition of Acts and Facts; it has often pursued a policy of 'splendid isolation' from the messy and unresolved contemporary events.

By my view, History of Education should set as one important criterion a concern, where possible, to elucidate the precedents, antecedents and constraints surrounding contemporary curriculum and practice. Likewise, the reaction to theoretical enterprises should be conquered. Historical study has a valuable role to play in challenging, informing and sometimes aiding in the generation of theory. This role should not be emasculated through a fear of theoretical misuse by others.

A further characteristic which was mentioned earlier argues for a growing dialogue between historians and curriculum specialists. In many ways History of Education has taken an 'external' view of curriculum, focussing on political and administrative contexts and on general movements in education and schooling. Partly this is a reflection of the documents available which often relate to central government regulations, edicts or commissions on education and curriculum. This is a long way from curriculum as enacted, transacted, realized and received.

The 'externality' of much History of Education had led some scholars to argue for a major reappraisal: Franklin (1977), for instance:

> I see curriculum history as a speciality within the curriculum field, distinct from educational history. Its practitioners should be individuals whose primary training is in curriculum, not educational historians who happened to be interested in the nature of the course of study within the schools.

The reasons for the separation are made clear later: 'Because the concerns and foci of the two studies are different. Most important in this respect is that the educational historian's lack of training in curriculum will lead him to either overlook or misinterpret those issues which are of most importance to the curriculum field'. Above all this is because 'the educational historian focusses on those issues in curriculum most relevant to the general issues of education and schooling, rather than the other way round'.[22]

One would not need to follow Franklin, whose work refers to the American context of curriculum, in advocating a separation of curriculum historians and historians of education to accept his diagnosis that much of the work of the latter is 'external'. Nor is the concentration on the 'external' necessarily a problem. It depends on the aspiration. If, however, an understanding of curriculum and curriculum change is given priority then a mode of study which focusses on and analyzes 'internal' issues is of paramount importance. Partly, the crucial nature of internal factors results from the way education and schooling are structured and relate the broader economy and society. As Webster (1976) has pointed out: 'Educational institutions are not as directly nor as essentially concerned with the economic and social welfare of the community as, say, factories or hospitals. They are, therefore, particularly well equipped to weather any crisis that may be going on around them'.[23] This relative autonomy explains the peculiar force of historical traditions and legacies in curriculum change. As a result, as Waring (1975) reminds us, it is really not surprising that originality always works within the framework of tradition and that a totally new tradition 'is one of the most improbable of events'. Hence, developing a sense of history will modify our view of curriculum. Instead of the transcendent expectation of basic change, we might look for alteration followed by regression, for change attempted and aborted in one place to emerge unexpectedly elsewhere. Through history we develop a longer view and with it a different timescale of expectations and, presumably, range of strategies.

The symbiotic relationship between historical traditions and legacies and contemporary curriculum practice and action thereby hints at the requirement of a similar relationship between the educational historian and curriculum historians. The force of history is physically evident to any student of schooling and curriculum both in syllabuses, textbooks, as well as in school buildings and indeed school teachers — an overlay of generations, a time-lag of views, values and valedictions. Charlton (1968) warned that:

> The present problem of curriculum planning is itself shot through with the past and with vestiges of the past, and future solutions however radical will inevitably carry something of the past with them.[24]

Likewise Blumer (1969) has drawn attention to the problem when studying large-scale organizations, and argues a need 'to recognize that joint action is temporarily linked to previous joint action'. He warns that 'one shuts a major door to understanding any form or instance of joint action if one ignores this connection'. This 'historical linkage' is important because 'the designations and interpretations through which people form and maintain their organized relations are always in degree of carry-over from their past. To ignore this carry-over sets a genuine risk for the scholar'.[25] If anything the need to understand the past traditions and legacies 'internal' to curriculum history is even more pressing in the current spate of educational or neo-educational changes.

Curriculum History and Curriculum Change

In April 1977 a group of educationists gathered at Teachers College, Columbia University, to examine the possibility of forming an organization concerned with the study of the history of the curriculum. Significantly:

> The problem that brought them together was the ahistorical and atheoretical character of curriculum reform efforts. Witness the open classroom movement which was a recycled version of an earlier educational movement, with all the glaring mistakes of the earlier version.

At the meeting, this initial pre-occupation was 'recast as the need to address pervasive educational problems from the vantage points of curriculum'.[26]

The action-orientation and concern with contemporary relevance are characteristics which might be developed in curriculum history in this country. By this view, curriculum history is less interested in history for its own sake, much more with history for the sake of curriculum — to aid understanding of fundamental curriculum issues. This objective should stand as the 'litmus test' for those undertaking curriculum history.

What is needed is to build on studies of participants immersed in immediate process, to build on studies of historical events and periods but to develop a cumulative understanding of the historical contexts in which the contemporary curriculum is embedded. The experience of the past decade has shown the painful limitations of ahistorical or transcendent approaches, both at the level of curriculum reform and study. By developing our analysis from further back, we throw more light on the present and afford insights into the constraints immanent in transmitted circumstance.

Those studies with an action-orientation have most often been confined to the view of participants at a moment in time, to the here and now of events. Their essential omission was data on the *constraints beyond* the event, the school, the classroom and the participant. What above all is needed, therefore, is a method that stays with the participants, stays with the complexity of the social process but catches some understanding of the constraints beyond. Although the human process by which men make their own history does not take place in circumstances of their own choosing as both men and women and circumstances do vary over time, so too do the potentialities for negotiating reality. Historical study seeks to understand how thought and action have developed in past social circumstances. Following this development though time to the present affords insights into how those circumstances we experience as contemporary 'reality' have been negotiated, constructed and reconstructed over time. Stenhouse (1976) saw this need for history to provide an authenticated context for hypothetical actions'. His concern was also with:

> What might be termed the contextual inertia within which events are embedded. It is here that history generalizes and becomes theoretical. It is, as it were, the story of action within a theory of context.[27]

The historical context, of course, reflects previous patterns of conflict and power. It is not sufficient to develop a static notion of the historical contexts and constraints inherited *in tacto* from the past. These contexts and constraints need to be examined in relationship to contemporary action. Moreover, we need a dynamic model of how syllabuses, pedagogy, finance, resources, selection, the economy all interrelate. We cannot, in short, view the curriculum (and its associated historical contexts and constraints) as a bounded system. Williamson (1974) has reflected on the fact 'that it is not sufficient to be aware only of the fact that the principles governing the selection of transmittable knowledge reflect structures of power. It is essential to move beyond such suspicions to work out the precise connections'.[28] This, he argues, predicates historical study of curriculum 'if the aim is to understand power in education'. Above all, we need to develop cognitive maps of curriculum influence and curriculum constraints, for as he says:

> What is provided in schools and what is taught in those schools can only be understood historically. Earlier educational

attitudes of dominant groups in society still carry historical weight.[29]

The dangers of 'Whiggism' or 'presentism' need to be clearly faced in my argument for seeking elucidation of 'contemporary issues'. The primary focus of historians is on understanding the uniqueness and complexity of *particular* times. In this chapter I have argued, however, that 'where possible' historians should seek to illuminate contemporary issues and theories. By placing one aspiration of curriculum history as elucidating the contextual background or immanent constraints on contemporary curriculum, a number of conclusions follow. To recapitulate:

(1)   Our study should set, as one objective, the illumination of contemporary reality through historical study, not so as to 'sharpen contemporary axes' but most definitely to sharpen contemporary thought and action.

(2)   Where possible, curriculum history should also aim to scrutinize, test, or contribute to educational theory. It is at the heart of the enterprise to examine curriculum development and transformation over time: such complex undertakings cannot be elucidated by 'snapshots' of unique historical events or periods. But the recurrence of events viewed in contemporary profile can help in discerning and examining explanatory frameworks and in understanding the manner in which structure and action interrelate.

(3)   Finally, curriculum history should be concerned, perhaps above all, with understanding the 'internal' process of curriculum definition, action and change.

The emphasis on the study of historical context, partly to illuminate contemporary prospect, implies a need to develop a dialogue between historians of education and curriculum specialists. It does not, I insist, imply wholly handing over the enterprise to the latter, as Franklin (1977) argues. Rather, it implies a need for curriculum historians to accept a responsibility, wherever possible, to illuminate contemporary prospect and, again where possible, develop theoretical insights and studies of internal process (most certainly it means for any curriculum specialists undertaking the work that they must begin to learn and practise the skills of the historian).

Fortunately, in the UK there are already a number of seminal studies which follow these aspirations: Layton's (1973) *Science for the People*, Waring's (1979) study of the *Nuffied Foundation Science Teaching Project*, Harold Silver's (1983) essays in *Education as History*.[30] All of this work shares a willingness, where possible, to develop links with contemporary curriculum and with educational theory and to examine and analyze 'internal' process. In the best of this work, we have the painstaking reconstruction of an historical period and the development of an understanding of the connections between previous historical struggles and present contexts, actions and possibilities. We gain insights into the process of curriculum production.

So far studies of the history of the school curriculum have tended to resemble the pre-paradigmatic stages of disciplines. The studies have been conducted in several places at different times and have often been undertaken by non-specialists who have brought the 'enthusiasm of pioneers' to their work. Hopefully we are approaching the transition to a new stage, for clearly an increasing number of educational researchers are undertaking historical work. Macdonald and Walker (1976) have argued that in school curricula 'by extending our sense of history, we can develop a different way of viewing the species'[31] whilst Mary Waring's (1975) work has argued that:

> If we are to understand events, whether of thought or of action, knowledge of background is essential. Knowledge of events is merely the raw material of history: to be an intelligible reconstruction of the past, events must be related to other events, and to the assumptions and practices of the milieu. Hence they must be made the subject of inquiry, their origins as products of particular social and historical circumstance, the manner in which individuals and groups have acted must be identified, and explanations for their actions sought.[32]

Conclusion

A change in the focus of history of education courses might be argued for if we take a historical view of the History of Education itself: viewing it as the socio-historical product of particular periods and conditions for action. History of Education grew up at a time when history itself was highly constitutional and institutional in focus, when 'Acts and Facts' were widely supported. Moreover, in the educational domain itself, it was a time when the organization, administration and alteration of educational structures and systems seemed at the heart of attempts to improve schooling. A move towards curriculum history assumes that we now take a different view: that analysis of organizational structure must be linked to a broader analysis of the legacies of status and resources, of curriculum and examination policy, if schooling is to be analyzed and improved. Hence, a history of education which reflects only part of the kaleidoscope of schooling is itself foredoomed. We now need a history of education which aids the analysis of structures and then embraces the other side of the conundrum of educational change: the secret garden of the curriculum. For to date, it has remained as secret to historians as to others.

To a point this is merely to echo the obvious — history of education as with any subject has reflected our perceptions of the educational enterprise. At the present time, as our knowledge of the sheer complexity has shifted, so we now need a history of education which responds to our new perceptions of that complexity.

Notes and References

1 JUDD, C.M. *The Training of Teachers in England, Scotland and Germany* (Washington, USA. Bureau of Education, 1914).
2 DAVIS, R.H.C. 'The content of history', *History*, Vol. 66, No. 218, October 1981, p. 362.
3 *Ibid.*, p. 361.
4 SEABORNE, M. 'The History of Education' in TIBBLE, J.W. (Ed), *An Introduction to the Study of Education*, (London, Routledge and Kegan Paul, 1971) p. 66.
5 *Ibid.*, p. 67.
6 Quoted in WARWICK, D. and WILLIAMS, J. 'History and the sociology of education', *British Journal of Sociology of Education*, Vol. 1, No. 3, 1980.
7 WILLIAMS, R. *The Long Revolution*, (London, Penguin, 1961) p. 67.
8 ANDREWS, A. 'In pursuit of the past: Some problems in the collection, analysis and use of historical documentary evidence', paper delivered at Whitelands College Workshop on *Qualitative Methodology and the Study of Education*, July 1983.
9 The Hadow Report, *The Education of the Adolescent*, Report of the Consultative Committee, (London, HMSO 1927).
10 CLARKE, F. *Education and Social Change: An English Interpretation*, (London, The Sheldon Press, 1940) pp. 9–10.
11 GLASS, D.V. 'Education and social change in modern Britain', in HOOPER R. (Ed) *The Curriculum Context, Design and Development*, (Edinburgh, Oliver and Boyd, 1971) p. 35.
12 The Norwood Report, *Curriculum and Examinations in Secondary Schools*, (London, HMSO, 1943) p. 2.
13 e.g. The work of GASKELL, J. on Physics Curricula in British Columbia.
14 SIMON, B. 'The history of education in the 1980s', *British Journal of Educational Studies*, Vol. XXX. No. 1, February 1982, p. 90.
15 From LAURIE, S.S. *Studies in the History of Educational Opinion from the Renaissance*, quoted in SIMON, B. 'The history of education', in TIBBLE, J.W. (Ed) *The Study of Education*, (London, Routledge and Kegan Paul, 1966) pp. 118–119.

16 ADAMSON, J.W. *English Education 1789–1802*, (Cambridge 'At the University Press', 1930) p. ix.

17 BARNARD, H.C. 'Adamson, J.W.' in *British Journal of Educational Studies*, Vol. X, No. 1, November 1961.

18 DURKHEIM, E. *The Evolution of Educational Thought*, (London, Routledge and Kegan Paul, 1977) p. 8.

19 WATSON, F. *The Beginnings of the Teaching of Modern Subjects in England*, (London, Pitman, 1909) pp. vii–viii.

20 *Ibid.*, p. viii.

21 MARSDEN, W.E. 'Historical approaches to curricular studies' in MARSDEN W.E. (Ed) *Postwar Curriculum Development: An historical appraisal*, History of Education Society Conference Papers, December 1978 (1979), V. 82.

22 FRANKLIN, B.M. 'Curriculum history: Its nature and boundaries', *Curriculum Inquiry 7, 1.* (1977) pp. 73–74.

23 WEBSTER, J.R. 'Curriculum change and "crisis"', *British Journal of Educational Studies*, Vol. xxiv, No. 3, October 1976, pp. 206–207.

24 CHARLTON, K. 'The contribution of history to the study of curriculum' in KERR, J.F. (Ed) *Changing the Curriculum*, (London, University of London Press, 1968) pp. 70–71.

25 BLUMER, H. *Symbolic Interactionism: Perspective and Method*, (Englewood Cliffs, Prentice Hall, 1969) p. 60.

26 *Papers of the Society for the Study of Curriculum History* (Pennsylvania State University, Spring 1981) p. 1.

27 STENHOUSE, L. *Case Study as a Basis for Research in a Theoretical Contemporary History of Education*, (Mimeo), p. 7.

28 WILLIAMSON, B. 'Continuities and discontinuities in the sociology of education' in FLUDE, M. and AHIER, J. *Educability, Schools and Ideology*, (London, Croom Helm, 1974) p. 10.

29 *Ibid.*, pp. 10–11.

30 See especially LAYTON, D. *Science for the People*, (London, George Allen and Unwin, 1973) p. 167.

31 MacDONALD, B. and WALKER, R. *Changing the Curriculum*, (London, Open Books, 1976) p. 86.

32 WARING, M. *Aspects of the Dynamics of Curriculum Reform in Secondary School Science*, Phd, University of London (1975) p. 12.

5 Investigating State Schooling: Exploring New Methods

In chapter 1 the investigation of schooling began by undertaking a 'Search for Sources'. The written curriculum was identified as a major, yet neglected, historical source with which to develop our investigations. In the last chapter, the limitations of certain orientations within history of education were discussed. In less obsessive fashion, the next two chapters, while discussing life history methods, will consider why sociology has similarly turned aside from historical and social constructionist studies of curriculum.

It becomes clear that just as the search for sources moves us into neglected territory, so too the search for an associated mode of study will require methods seldom used or, at least, seldom integrated in the study of schooling. Methods are required which allow us to study curriculum as it impinges on individual experiences as well as on the experiences and activities of social groups. Exploring curriculum as a focus allows us to study, indeed exhorts us to study, the intersection of individual biography and social structure. For, as we have seen, the emergence of curriculum as a concept in part developed from the activities of those with a concern to direct and control individual teachers' and pupils' classroom activities. The definition of curriculum developed over time as part of an institutionalized and structured pattern of state schooling. Our methods therefore have to cover the analysis of individual lives and biographies as well as of social groups and structures.

For this reason, the essays which follow employ a range of methods from life histories of individual teachers through to histories of school subjects where the interplay of groups and structures are scrutinized. As they stand the essays provide a very partial glimpse of how a reconceptualized study of curriculum and schooling might proceed. The essays are presented as examples of the kind of work which might be pursued when using curriculum as a source for investigating schooling. As we have noted before, the limitations with regard to reconceptualized method are echoed by the specificity of the content of studies. We are dealing with some historical studies of certain subjects in English comprehensive schools in the last twenty years. The focus on subjects has been explained earlier, but future studies will be required of other notions of curriculum — themes in curriculum like technical education, the study of curriculum topics, projects and activities, the study of the primary school curriculum where subjects are often less relevant and the study of the hidden curriculum and the moral curriculum. Likewise, the focus on recent English comprehensive schools imposes severe limitations.

Fortunately, new studies are underway in a range of countries examining a variety of school systems. Some of these are reported in Goodson (1987)[1]; whilst other studies, for instance, Popkewitz (1987) report on the emergence of curriculum in a wide range of local and historical situations in the United States. Hence, the limitations of these essays are already being supplemented by new work; hopefully the momentum of a reconceptualized study of curriculum and schooling is underway.

Biography, History, Society

> Social science deals with problems of biography of history and of their intersections within social structures. That these three — biography, history, society — are the coordinate points of the proper study of man has been a major platform on which I have stood when criticizing several current schools of sociology whose practitioners have abandoned this classic tradition.[2]

What C. Wright Mills (1970) argues as the case for sociology is substantially what is followed here for studies of schooling and curriculum. The essays in this volume and, more importantly, the twelve volumes currently comprising *Studies in Curriculum History*[3] seek to provide samples of such work at the life history, collective and relational levels.

Life history method is discussed in chapter 6. The genesis of life histories can be located in anthropological work at the beginning of this century; the main take-up by sociologists occurred later in a series of urban and social studies at the University of Chicago.

For a number of reasons analyzed subsequently, this work became less and less of a priority in the Chicago studies of the city and as a result the method fell into neglect until recently. In its more contemporary usage life history work has focussed mainly on studies of deviance, crime and urban ethnography. The methodology of life history is therefore still relatively undeveloped and its use in the study of schooling only just beginning. I have argued that this omission in the study of schooling is regrettable and, moving from programmatic exhortation to empirical investigation, have employed life history data to explore the intersection between biography, history and structure with specific regard to the secondary school curriculum. The background and some of the content of this work is briefly introduced in chapter 7.

More significantly, however, the programmatic exhortation contained in this chapter (first published in 1981) was taken up in a study of teachers' careers undertaken by Sikes, Measor, and Woods (1985).[4] They were, from the beginning, aware of the substantial problems and commented that 'life histories do not present themselves to us as a fully-fledged method ready to use. There is, as yet, no substantial body of methodological literature to support life history studies.'[5] Nevertheless, their work does provide us with important insights on teachers' lives and careers. The chapters on the 'life cycle of the teacher' and on 'critical phases and incidents' echo some of the themes discussed in chapter 6 with respect to one teacher. Other work, such as Bertaux's (1981) collection *Biography and Society*[6], and Ken Plummer's (1983) excellent *Documents of Life*[7], begin the rehabilitation of life history method and the exploration of the substantial methodological and ethical problems that such work entails.

Yet, beyond problems intrinsic to the life history methods are problems of relationship to other levels and modes of analysis and investigation. As Mannheim warned in 1936 'Preoccupation with the purely individual life-history and its analysis is not sufficient'.[8] Above all, and rightly, I suspect, Mannheim is railing against individualism — what he calls 'The fiction of the isolated and self-sufficient individual'. Plainly, given the powerful legacy of individualism and of individualist assumptions present in so many epistemologies, this danger must be continually scrutinized with regard to life history work. As Mannheim says:

> The genetic method of explanation, if it goes deep enough, cannot in the long run limit itself to the individual life history and the more inclusive group situation. For the individual life history is only a component in a series of mutually intertwined

> life histories ... it was the merit of the sociological point of
> view that it set alongside the individual genesis of meaning the
> genesis from the context of group life.[9]

The relationship between individual and collective (as between action
and structure) is perennially elusive. But our studies may either
accept, or exacerbate, fragmentation or seek integration. Life history
study pursued alongside the study of more collective groupings and
milieu might promote better integration. The problem of integration is
of course partly a problem of dealing with modes and levels of
consciousness. The life history penetrates the individual subject's consciousness and attempts also to map the changes in that consciousness
over the life cycle. But at the individual level, as at other levels, we
must note that change is structured, but that structures change. The
relationship between the individual and wider structures is central to
our investigations but again it is through historical studies that such
investigations can be profitably pursued:

> Our chance to understand how smaller *milieux* and larger
> structures interact and our chance to understand the larger
> causes at work in these limited milieux, thus require us to deal
> with historical materials.[10]

The difficulties of elucidating the symbiosis of the individual and
the social structure can be seen in assessing the broad goals of curriculum or schooling. The discerning of 'regularities', 'recurrences' or
patterns, is particularly elusive at the level of the individual life (and
consciousness). Feinberg (1983) has commented that 'once we understand that a goal is identified in terms of something that is reasonably
distinctive and that establishes relevance by postulating a continuity
to otherwise discrete acts, then we can see that goals may belong to
individuals, but they may also belong to individuals as they are related
to each other in acts or institutions'. He gives the example of people in
America moving westwards, 'colonizing the west', which they did for
many reasons:

> Some went to escape debt, others to make a fortune; some
> went to farm, others to pan gold, or to sell merchandise; some
> went as soldiers, others as trappers and hunters. Whereas it is
> perfectly proper to speak about the continuity of any series of
> acts performed by an individual in terms of a goal, it is equally
> appropriate to speak of a whole series of acts performed by
> different individuals along with the acts of the government
> that supported them, such as the Homestead Act and the

building of railroads, in terms of the *general* goal of settling the west. It is this way of speaking that allows us to make sense of all these acts and to see them as forming some kind of continuous meaningful event.

The dangers of 'abstraction' to the general level are evidential and can be seen when Feinberg adds: 'Moreover, it is equally appropriate to speak of the goal as beginning with the movement of the first settlers west, even though these people may not have had a whisper of an idea about the overall historical significance of their act'.[11]

In these terms, structural change provides a facilitating arena for a range of individual actions which then feed into and act upon this initial change. Consciousness of the significance of the action differs according to the time period in question and to the level of scrutiny — hence, a series of individual 'dreams' and actions build up into a movement to 'colonize' a vast territory. Likewise, with schooling and curriculum, discerning regularities, recurrences and patterns allow analysis and assessment of goals and intentions. 'To begin to characterize these goals by looking back to the origins of the school system itself is not necessarily to claim that the goals were fully understood at the time. It is simply to say that in the light of these goals we can understand some of the major lines of continuity between the activity of the past and the activity of the present.'

Developing our studies of curriculum at individual and collective level demands that our historical analyses work across the levels of individual lives and group action and assess relations between individuals, between groups and between individuals and groups. Hence, chapter 8 follows up at school subject group level some of the emphases first examined at life history level in the foregoing chapters. The significance of organizational change to a more comprehensive school system, is viewed as it affects the actions and strategies of a subject group of association. But if the collective *milieu* embraces the subject group on the broader sense, it is equally significant at school level. Chapter 9 examines the micropolitics of subject change at school level. Here it is possible to locate individual intentions and actions in a context where the resources and status are deployed through a system which favours 'academic' subjects for 'able' pupils. This section particularly is reminiscent of Esland's (1971) early exhortations to develop frameworks 'for the analysis of the knowledge which constitutes the life world of teachers and pupils in particular educational institutions, and the epistemological traditions in which they collectively participate'. The intentions are very similar:

> ... in trying to focus the individual biography in its socio-
> historical context is in a very real sense attempting to penetrate
> the symbolic drift of school knowledge, and the consequences
> for the individuals who are caught up in it and attempting to
> construct their reality through it. [12]

Histories of the symbolic drift of school knowledge raise questions
about the patterns of evolution through which subjects pass. In Chapter 10 one example is provided of a history of a school subject,
Geography. The work is merely one example of a growing body of
work on the history of school subjects. In *School Subjects and Curriculum Change*[13] I have also looked at Biology and Environmental Studies
but other monographs in the *Studies in Curriculum History* series have
looked at Science and Technology (McCulloch, Jenkins and Layton
1985), Mathematics (Cooper 1985, Moon 1987) and Physics (Woole-
nough, 1987). In *Social Histories of the Secondary Curriculum*[14] work is
collected together on a wide range of other subjects, Classics (Stray),
English (Ball), Science (Waring, who had written an earlier seminal
study on Nuffield Science), Domestic subjects (Purvis), Religious
Education (Bell), Social Studies (Franklin and Whitty) and Modern
Languages (Radford). These studies reflect a growing interest in the
history of curriculum and, besides elucidating the symbolic drift of
school knowledge, raise central questions about past and current 'explanations' of school subjects whether they be sociological or philosophical.

Above all, these studies, as summarized in chapter 11, begin to
illustrate the historical emergence and construction of the political
economy of curriculum. The structuring of resources and finance, the
attribution of status and construction of careers are linked to a system
that has developed since the foundation of state schooling and in
particular since the establishment of secondary schooling regulations
in the early years of this century. This structure acts to impinge on
both individual intentions and collective aspirations. The latter in the
form of school subject groups and associations normally embrace the
'academic' tradition. Such a coalition of individuals and sub-groups is
then loosely held together under the common name of the subject.
But other individuals and sub-groups recurrently embrace other intentions and other traditions. Whilst the existing political economy of
curriculum prevails such individuals or sub-groups are most often
marginalized or constrained as 'minority' tendencies.

Essays and Exemplars

The essays which follow need to be seen in the context of the overall project of publishing a range of work in the field of curriculum history. The series of books *Studies in Curriculum History* was launched in 1985 and each of the books provides a monographic study of a particular episode in curriculum history. But inevitably this monographic approach takes a number of rather fundamental arguments to do with the rationale for the series for granted. The argument is far from self-evident and needs to be presented in a form that is part programmatic, part polemical and part substantial. Also the range and forms of curriculum history methods need to be analyzed and provided. The essays in this book seek to address these requirements.

In providing these exemplars of curriculum history I am aware that the data employed in three of the chapters grow out of my original work on curriculum history. Partly this allows continuity with this original work but more significantly seeks to provide broader insights from the data than were initially developed, to amplify certain themes and to illustrate a range of modalities for the study of curriculum and schooling.

Behind this is a strong belief that we must stay tenaciously with curriculum history data, given its depth and complexity, if fundamental understandings are to be elicited. In other disciplines like social anthropology or history scholars may stay with their data for many years analyzing and reformulating. Kliebard (1975) has argued that in curriculum studies 'the urge to do good is so immediate, so direct, and so overwhelming that there has been virtually no toleration of the kind of long-range research that has little immediate value to practitioners'.[15] This concern with immediacy has often led educational researchers to rush off looking for the latest 'news'. The dominance of news-gathering has led to a stigmatizing of more long-run research. I take the opposite view. By this view it is far easier to rush on to the next descriptive study leading, not to cumulation and understandings but to a collection of unique case studies.

Finally, one particular problem arises from the order in which the essays are placed. They lead from essays on life histories through a connecting essay into essays on curriculum history. The implication may be taken that life history leads sequentially and unproblematically into subject history. Chapter 5 to some extent conspires to strengthen this implication. It is not, however, intended. The combination of life history and curriculum history in chapter 5 is untypical, in a sense, altogether too neat. This is because it presents the life of one leading curriculum advocate. Whilst I think this helps in articulating the force of structural constraints on a life, it overestimates the link between life history and curriculum history. To develop the life history strategy would require, so to speak, horizontal not vertical diversification. Bertaux (1981) outlines how this would work in describing his work on bakers:

> The first life study taught us a great deal, so did the second and third. By the fifteenth we had begun to understand the pattern of sociostructural relations which make up the life of a bakery worker. By the twenty-fifth, adding the knowledge we had from life histories of bakers, we knew we had it: a clear picture of this structural pattern and of its recent transformations. New life stories only confirmed what we had understood adding slight individual variations. We stopped at thirty: there was no point going further.[16]

But to return to the point. The following essays are not arranged in a sequence of logic or method. They are each separate, as they were written and together seek to show only the range and form that histories of curriculum might take.

Notes and References

1 GOODSON, I.F. (Ed), *International Perspectives in Curriculum History*, (London and Sydney, Croom Helm, 1987).
2 MILLS, C. WRIGHT *The Sociological Imagination*, (London, Penguin, 1970) p. 159.
3 A series of books edited by GOODSON, I.F. and published by Falmer Press: (see p. ii for details).
4 SIKES, P.J., MEASOR, L. and WOODS, P. *Teacher Careers: Crises and Continuities*, (Lewes, Falmer Press, 1985).
5 *op. cit.*, p. 14.
6 BERTAUX, D. (Ed), *Biography and Society: The Life History Approach in the Social Sciences*, (London, Sage, 1981).
7 PLUMMER, K. *Documents of Life: An Introduction to the Problems and Literature of a Humanistic Method*, (London, George Allen and Unwin, 1983).
8 MANNHEIM, K. *Ideology and Utopia: An Introduction to the Sociology of Knowledge*, (London, Routledge and Kegan Paul, 1972) p. 24.
9 *op. cit.*, p. 25.
10 *op. cit.*, Mills, p. 165.
11 FEINBERG, W. *Understanding Education: Towards a Reconstruction of Educational Enquiry*, (Cambridge University Press, 1983) p. 86.
12 ESLAND, G.M. 'Teaching and learning as the organisation of knowledge'

in YOUNG, M.F.D. (Ed) *Knowledge and Control: New Directions for the Sociology of Education*, (London, Collier Macmillan, 1971) p. 111.

13   GOODSON, I.F. *School Subjects and Curriculum Change*, (Revised edition, Falmer Press, 1987).

14   GOODSON, I.F. (Ed), *Social Histories of the Secondary Curriculum: Subjects for Study*, (Lewes, Falmer Press, 1985).

15   KLIEBARD, H. 'Persistant curriculum issues in historical perspective' in PINAR, W. (Ed), *Curriculum Theorizing*, (Berkeley, McCutchan, 1975) p. 41.

16   *op. cit.*, Bertaux, p. 57.

III Essays and Exemplars

6   Teachers' Life Histories and Studies of Curriculum and Schooling

I have argued elsewhere that whilst 'the rhetoric and manoeuverings of educational politicians and subject associations may reveal a great deal about the framework of limits and possibilities within which teachers and pupils work in the classroom ... neither the teacher nor the pupils are entirely passive recipients of the "espoused" curriculum'.[1] This chapter will take the view that curriculum history must therefore encompass the manner in which the curriculum is received and enacted and that the life history provides one method for examining this process. In the case of teachers, Woods (1980) has eloquently argued that for the teacher he studied, Tom:

> A curriculum area is a vibrant, human process lived out in the rough and tumble, give and take, joys and despairs, plots and counter-plots of a teacher's life. It is not simply a body of knowledge or set of skills, nor simply a result of group activity. Tom's case shows that, to some extent at least, individuals can and do chart their own courses, and can engage with the curriculum at a deep personal level. For a full appreciation of this I have argued we need to take a whole life perspective.[2]

Origins of the Life History Method

The first life histories, in the form of autobiographies of American Indian chiefs, were collected by anthropologists at the beginning of the century. Since this date, they have been primarily undertaken by sociologists. Whilst in this chapter I am arguing they should be employed in studying schooling, in examining their fate we have to scrutinize their use to date by sociologists. For sociologists, the major landmark in the development of life history methods came several decades later with the publication of Thomas and Znaniecki's (1927) mammoth study. In exploring the experience of Polish peasants migrating to the United States, Thomas and Znaniecki relied mainly on migrants' autobiographical accounts, diaries and letters. For these authors life histories were the data *par excellence* of the social scientist:

> In analyzing the experiences and attitudes of an individual, we always reach data and elementary facts which are exclusively limited to this individual's personality, but can be treated as mere incidences of more or less general classes of data or facts, and can thus be used for the determination of laws of social becoming. Whether we draw our materials for sociological analysis from detailed life records of concrete individuals or from the observation of mass phenomena, the problems of sociological analysis are the same. But even when we are searching for abstract laws, life records as complete as possible constitute the perfect type of sociological material, and if social science has to use other materials at all, it is only because of the practical difficulty of obtaining at the moment a sufficient number of such records to cover the totality of sociological problems, and of the enormous amount of work demanded for an adequate analysis of all the personal materials necessary to characterize the life of a social group. If we are forced to use mass phenomena as material, or any kind of happenings taken without regard to the life histories of the individuals who participated, it is a defect not an advantage, of our present sociological method.[3]

Thomas and Znaniecki's pioneering work established the life history as a *bona fide* research device. The prominent position of the life history was further consolidated by the flourishing tradition of sociological research stimulated at Chicago by Robert Park. In the range of studies of city life completed under Park, *The Gang* (Thrasher, 1928), *The Gold Coast* and *The Slum* (Zorbaugh, 1929), *The Hobo* (Anderson, 1923) and *The Ghetto* (Wirth, 1928), the life history method was strongly in evidence. Life history studies reached their peak in the 1930s with publications such as Clifford Shaw's (1930) account of a 'mugger' in *The Jack-Roller* and Cornwall and Sutherland's (1937) *The Professional Thief*.[4] Becker's (1970) comments on Shaw's study underline one of the major strengths of the life history method:

By providing this kind of voice from a culture and situation that are ordinarily not known to intellectuals generally and to sociologists in particular, *The Jack Roller* enables us to improve our theories at the most profound level: by putting ourselves in Stanley's skin, we can feel and become aware of the deep biases about such people that ordinarily permeate our thinking and shape the kinds of problems we investigate. By truly entering into Stanley's life, we can begin to see what we take for granted (and ought not to) in designing our research — what kinds of assumptions about delinquents, slums and Poles are embedded in the way we set the questions we study.

From this statement Becker leads on to the assertion that Stanley's story offers the possibility 'to begin to ask questions about delinquency from the point of view of the delinquent'. So that it follows that:

If we take Stanley seriously, as his story must impel us to do, we might well raise a series of questions that have been relatively little studied — questions about the people who deal with delinquents, the tactics they use, their suppositions about the world, and the constraints and pressures they are subject to.[5]

Becker's claim for the life history in this sense reiterates those made by contemporaries of the Chicago sociologists in the 1930s. Perhaps the best attempt to analyze the methodological base of the life history method was Dollard's (1949) *Criteria for the Life History*. Foreshadowing Becker, he argued that 'detailed studies of the lives of individuals will reveal new perspectives on the culture as a whole which are not accessible when one remains on the formal cross sectional plane of observation'.[6] A lot of Dollard's arguments have a somewhat familiar ring, perhaps reflecting the influence of George Herbert Mead. He notes that 'as soon as we take the post of observer on the cultural level the individual is lost in the crowd and our concepts never lead us back to him. After we have 'gone cultural' we experience the person as a fragment of a (derived) culture pattern, as a marionette dancing on the strings of (reified) culture forms'.[7] In contrast to this, the Life Historian:

... can see his life history subject as a link in a chain of social transmission. There were links before him from which he acquired his present culture. Other links will follow him to which he will pass on the current of tradition. The life history attempts to describe a unit in that process: it is a study of one of the strands of a complicated collective life which has historical continuity.[8]

Dollard is especially good, though perhaps unfashionably polemical, in his discussion of the tension between what might be called the 'cultural legacy', the weight of collective tradition and expectation, and the individual's unique history and capacity for interpretation and action. By focussing on this tension, Dollard argues the life history offers a way of exploring the relationship between the culture, the social structure and individual lives. Thus Dollard believed that in the best life history work 'we must constantly keep in mind the situation both as defined by others and by the subject, such a history will not only define both versions but let us see clearly the pressure of the formal situation and the force of the inner private definition of the situation'. This resolution, or attempt to address a common tension, is seen as valuable because 'whenever we encounter difference between our official or average or cultural expectation of action in a "situation" and the actual conduct of the person, this indicates the presence of a private interpretation'.[9]

After reaching its peak in the 1930s, the life history approach fell from grace and was largely abandoned by social scientists. This was firstly because the increasingly powerful advocacy of statistical methods gained a growing number of adherents among sociologists, but perhaps also because among ethnographically-inclined sociologists more emphasis came to be placed on situation rather than on biography as the basis for understanding human behaviour.

Since the 1930s, little attention has been paid by mainstream sociologists to life history methods. Only recently have there been signs of rehabilitation, significantly among deviancy sociologists: studies of a trans-sexual (Bogdan, 1974); a professional fence (Klockars, 1975); and, with a fine sense of history, once again a professional thief (Chambliss, 1972). Other marginal groups re-exploring life history methods are journalists-cum-sociologists, like Studs Terkel in the USA and Jeremy Seabrook and Ronald Blythe in the UK, and a growing band of so-called 'oral historians' (Thompson, 1978).[10] Daniel Bertaux's (1981) collection *Biography and Society: the Life History Approach in the Social Sciences* marks a significant step in the rehabilitation of the approach.[11]

Among these scholars, albeit in marginal or fragmented groups, a debate is underway which promises a thoroughgoing reexamination of the potential of life history methods. But before we consider the contemporary appeal of the life history, it is important to discover why life history method was for so long eclipsed by the social survey and by participant observation. In this examination, the emphasis will be on distinguishing fundamental methodological stumbling blocks from the political and personal reasons for the decline of life history work.

Reasons for the Decline of the Life History

By 1966 Becker was able to summarize the fate of the life history method among American sociologists in this manner: 'given the variety of scientific uses to which the life history may be put, one must wonder at the relative neglect into which it has fallen'.[12] Becker notes that sociologists have never given up life histories altogether but neither have they made it one of their standard research tools. The general pattern was, and is, that 'they know of life history studies' and assign them for their students to read. But they do not ordinarily think of gathering life history documents or of making the technique part of their research approach'.[13]

The reasons for the decline of life history methods are partly specific to the Chicago department. From the late 1920s, life histories came under increasing fire as the debate within the department between the virtues of case study (and life histories) and statistical techniques intensified. Faris (1967) in his study of Chicago sociology records a landmark within this debate:

> To test this issue, Stouffer had hundreds of students write autobiographies instructing them to include everything in their life experiences relating to alcohol usage and the prohibition law. Each of these autobiographies was read by a panel of persons presumed to be qualified in life history research, and for each subject the reader indicated on a scaled line the position of the subject's attitude regarding prohibition. Interreader agreement was found to be satisfactory. Each of the same subjects had also filled out a questionnaire that formed a scale of the Thurstone type. The close agreement of the scale measurement of each subject's attitude with the reader's estimate of the life history indicated that, as far as the scale score was concerned, nothing was gained by the far more lengthy and laborious process of writing and judging a life history.[14]

Even within Chicago case study work the life history declined as against other ethnographic devices, notably participant observation. One element of the explanation of this lies perhaps in the orientations of Blumer and Hughes. These two sociologists provide a bridge between the Chicago school of the 1920s and 1930s and those Matza has termed the 'neochicagoans' such as Becker and Goffman. Blumer's symbolic interactionism places primary emphasis on process and situation, and explanations in terms of biography like those in terms of social structural forces, are regarded with considerable suspicion. Hughes' comparative approach to the study of occupations may have tended to limit interest in biography in favour of a concern with the typical problems faced by occupational practitioners and the strategies they adopt for dealing with them. An additional factor which hastened the decline of the methodological eclecticism of Chicago sociology with the life history playing a central role was the decline of Chicago itself as a dominant centre for sociological studies.

The fate of life history methods is inextricably linked to the historical emergence of sociology as a discipline. Hence the methodological weaknesses of the life history method came to be set against the need to develop abstract theory. When sociology was highly concerned with providing detailed accounts of specific communities, institutions or organizations, such weaknesses were clearly of less account. But in the life history of sociology, the pervasive drift of academic disciplines towards abstract theory has been irresistibly followed: in this evolutionary imperative, it is not difficult to discern the desire of sociologists to gain parity of esteem with other academic disciplines. The resulting pattern of mainstream sociology meant that sociologists came to pursue 'data formulated in the abstract categories of their own theories rather than in the categories that seemed most relevant to the people they studied'.[15]

Alongside the move towards abstract academic theory, sociological method became more 'professional'. Essentially this led towards a model of *single study* research defined by Becker in this way:

> I use the term to refer to research projects that are conceived of as self-sufficient and self-contained, which provide all the evidence one needs to accept or reject the conclusions they proffer... The single study is integrated with the main body of knowledge in the following way: it derives its hypotheses from an inspection of what is already known; then, after the research is completed, if those hypotheses have been demonstrated, they are added to the wall of what is already scien-

tifically known and used as the basis for further studies. The important point is that the researcher's hypothesis is either proved or disproved on the basis of what he has discovered in doing that one piece of research.[16]

The imperative towards this pattern of sociological research can be clearly evidenced in the traditions and organizational format of emergent professional sociology. The PhD student must define and test his or her hypothesis; the journal article must test the author's own or other academics' hypotheses; the research project or programme must state the generalizable aims and locate the burden of what has to be proved. But this dominant experimental model, so fruitful in analogies with other *sciences*, and hence so crucial in legitimating sociology as a fully-fledged academic discipline, led to the neglect of sociology's full range of methodology and data sources.

It has led people to ignore the other functions of research and particularly to ignore the contribution made by one study to an overall research enterprise even when the study, considered in isolation, produced no definitive results of its own. Since, by these criteria, the life history did not produce definitive results, people have been at a loss to make anything of it and by and large have declined to invest the time and effort necessary to acquire life history documents.[17]

Becker ends by holding out the hope that sociologists will in the future develop a 'further understanding of the complexity of the scientific enterprise', and that this will rehabilitate the life history method and lead to a new range of life history documents as generative as those produced by the Chicago sociologists in the 1920s and 1930s.

In the period following Becker's strictures sociology has been subject to a number of new directions which have sought to re-embrace some of the elements lost in the 'positivist', theory-testing models.[18] However, the one new direction which clearly stresses biography, the phenomenological sociology of Berger and Luckmann[19], has led to little empirical work as yet. Hence research in interpretive sociology has displayed a heavy emphasis on situation under the influence of interactionism and ethnomethodology. The paradox is that the new directions in sociology have moved away from the 'positivist' model, but directly to situation and occasion, and, as a result, life history and biography have remained at the sidelines of the sociological enterprise. For instance, interactionist studies have focussed on the perspectives and definitions emerging among groups of actors in particular situations, the backcloth to this being presented as a somewhat monolithic 'structural' or 'cultural legacy' which constrains, in a rather disconnected manner, the actors' potentialities. In over-reacting to more deterministic models, this situational emphasis most commonly fails to make any connection with historical process. Thus, while interactionists retained their interest in the meaning objects had for actors, these meanings increasingly came to be seen as collectively generated to deal with specific situations, rather than as the product of individual or even collective biography.

Viewing sociology's evolution over half a century or so provides a number of insights into the life history method. Firstly, as sociologists began to take seriously their social scientific pursuit of generalizable facts and the development of abstract theory, life history work came to be seen as having serious methodological flaws. In addition, since life history studies often appeared to be only 'telling tales', these methodological reservations were enhanced by the generally low status of this as an 'academic' or 'scientific' exercise. Paradoxically even when antidotes to the experimental model of sociology developed, these took the form of interactionism and ethnomethodology, both of which stressed situation and occasion rather than biography and background. Moreover, since these new directions had status problems of their own, life history work was unattractive on this count as well. At the conference where this chapter was originally delivered as a seminar paper a classroom interactionist rejected the exhortation to consider life history work by saying:

> We should not suggest new methodologies of this sort ...
> because of the problem of our academic careers. Christ!
> Ethnography is low status enough as it is.

Set against the life history of the aspirant academic, we clearly see the unattractiveness of the life history method.

Leaving aside the political and personal reservations over life histories, however, there are clearly important methodological problems. Two major problems underpin the opposition of sociologists to the method. Firstly, there is the problem of *representativeness* or *typicality*. The aspiration to develop generalizable insights has intrinsic as well as political justifications. Life history work cannot guarantee typicality, representativeness or, therefore, directly generate theory. At the same time, there is a second problem in that life histories are a considerable undertaking. With low guarantees of generalizable findings, then, they couple the awkward necessity for *large time commitments*.

Rehabilitating Life History: Problems and Possibilities

To rehabilitate the life history, we need to indicate its relationship to theory and alongside this to overcome the other major objection, the time-consuming nature of the exercise.

As we noted earlier, some deviancy sociologists have recently embraced life history methods and are engaged in trying to resolve the ambivalence between the method and sociological theory. Faraday and Plummer (1979) present the relationship of life history to their theoretical enterprise in three ways: in the *examination* of existing theory (as Becker says 'even though the life history does not in itself provide definitive proof of a proposition it can be a negative case that forces us to decide a proposed theory is inadequate');[20] in the *exploration* of data 'in order to generate sensitizing concepts, theories and conceptual frameworks'. In areas of enquiry in which little is known, the life history, therefore, provides 'a sensitizing tool to the kinds of issue and problems involved in the field'. Finally, life history *utilizes* theory.

> There is no intrinsic disconnection of the life history from theoretical work. It is clearly not very good at testing or validating existing theory, although it might be useful in finding a falsificatory case. It is quite good when combined with a general orientation in theory which enables one to see how the theory might make sense of that field as a whole, but in no conclusive way. It is at its best when it is being used in an exploratory fashion for generating many concepts, hunches and ideas, both at the local and situational level and on a historical structural level and within the same field and in *relationship* to other fields.[21]

In general the life history is congruent with the main theoretical assumption of interactionism that the individual life is not as clear or ordered as many social science accounts (especially those following the experimental model) would have us believe. The greatest strength of the life history is in its penetration of the subjective reality of the individual: it allows the subject to 'speak for herself or himself'. But above and beyond this, the life history 'can give meaning to the overworked notion of *process*'. In the experimental model, we might give people a questionnaire at various stages in their life and attribute a process to the changing answers at different periods. But there is a gap in such a procedure: the life history can fill that gap. The well-documented life history:

> ... will give us the details of that process whose character we would otherwise only be able to speculate about, and the process to which our data must ultimately be referred if they are to have theoretical and not just an operational and predictive significance. It will describe those crucial interactive episodes in which new lines of individual and collective activity are forged, in which new aspects of the self are brought into being. It is thus giving a realistic basis to our imagery of the underlying process that the life history serves the purposes of checking assumptions, illuminating organization and re-orienting stagnant fields.[22]

The focus of the life history is clear: personal 'reality' and process. The life historian is initially only concerned with grasping personal truth: 'on the (more important) issue of attaining universal truth he or she remains mute'. The problem of this focus, as with much of interactionism, is that the personal experience and process often gets divorced from the wider socio-historical structure. The life historian must constantly broaden the concern with personal truth to take account of wider socio-historical concerns *even if these are not part of the consciousness of the individual.* The fully researched life history should then allow us:

> ... to see an individual in relation to the history of his time, and how he is influenced by the various religious, social, psychological and economic currents present in his world. It permits us to view the intersection of the life history of men with the history of society, thereby enabling us to understand better the choices, contingencies and options open to the individual.

In rehabilitating the life history it is important to see the sociological enterprise not as monolithic but as multi-faceted. Becker's image of the mosaic is useful: 'each piece added to a mosaic adds a little to our understanding' or Levi-Strauss's analogy with the jigsaw. Seen in this way the place of life histories should become evident. The object is not to resolve the tension between experimental and interactionist models: both have a place. The questionnaire can test preselected themes but in doing so closes off avenues of exploration; in complement interactionist studies and life histories trace the personal situation and life in evolution. By rehabilitating the life history the jigsaw puzzle might finally fall into place, for there is always a better chance if all the pieces are used.

Life History and the Study of Schooling

The Contemporary Situation: A Brief Review

In reviewing the history of sociology it has been argued that the experimental model of sociological investigation, with its emphasis on single studies to test pre-selected hypotheses, whilst for long dominant, has neglected participant perspectives and interactional processes. Paradoxically, the interactionist and ethnomethodological models which have sought to explore these neglected areas have focussed on situation and occasion with the result that biography and historical background have continued to be neglected. To a great extent these patterns of development for sociology in general hold true when one reviews the sociology of schooling.

Reviewing contemporary interactionist and ethnomethodological studies of schooling, one might discern two characteristic assumptions. Firstly, because of the focus on situation and occasion, little attention has been given to the individual biography, personal views and lifestyle of teachers. Partly, this may have arisen by anthropological analogy. For instance, Philip Jackson's (1968) work on *Life in Classrooms*, although full of insight, presents teachers as a particular kind of species reproducing within busy, tiring and unchanging environments:

> Not only is the classroom a relatively stable physical environment, it also provides a fairly constant social context. Behind the same old desks sit the same old students, in front of the familiar blackboard stands the familiar teacher.[23]

As a result, in these accounts the teacher becomes depersonalized, neutral above all eminently *interchangeable*: the same old familiar teacher we know so well.

A second characteristic assumption is also epitomized in Jackson, the assumption of *timelessness*: this is at one with interchangeability — whatever the time, whoever the teacher, everything is much the same. This anti-historical approach is also a feature of interactionist and especially ethnomethodological approaches:

> A fundamental assumption of the ethnomethodological approach is that the social world is essentially an ongoing achieved world. The everyday world of social events, settings and relationships is all the time created and achieved by the members of society and these events, settings and relationships

are assumed to have no existence independent of the occasion of their production.[25]

But while there is some truth in this, the actors creating the social events which Payne (1976) describes do, nevertheless, have an existence which is independent of, and previous to, the social events in which they are involved. Such a neglect of historical and biographical background makes problematic the construction of general categories within which to situate these ethnomethodological and interactionist accounts of specific events. Hence, it would be possible for a variety of social events to be portrayed, and for their internal logic to be laid bare, without getting at any general understanding of why events differ and why what is common to certain events, in this case school lessons, recurs over time. A knowledge of personal biographies and historical background would add breadth and depth to the studies and fulfil the aspiration, indeed obligation, to develop more generalizable categories of understanding.

Two characteristic assumptions in ethnomethodology and interactionism have been discerned: those of teacher *interchangeability* and of *timelessness*. As noted, these new approaches have shared with the dominant 'positivist' model of sociology a neglect of personal biography and historical background. The existence of these two characteristic assumptions will not be proven at length in this chapter. The study of a book like *School Experience*[25] would however confirm that there are grounds for believing that these characteristic assumptions are common and influential in the direction and selection of studies of schooling by ethnomethodologists and interactionists. Similarly, that excellent study *Deviance in the Classroom*[26] although marked by an eclecticism of approach, nonetheless misses many opportunities to follow up biographical data. The authors concede that teachers often 'import' life history data into accounts of their practice but as is often the case, this data is edited out in the final version. Even the more recent work of Peter Woods (1980) displays this tendency with its focus on generalized teacher and pupil strategies.[27] Yet elsewhere Woods (1979)[28] has noted that 'The social scientist has to begin to develop a perspective that enables him to develop the connection between macro-sociological and historical processes on the one hand and individual biographies on the other'.[*] But in the absence of life history data, this can only remain a pious hope. We are left in the

---

[*] In Woods' case as noted in chapter 5 he has gone on to undertake life history work.

position of having a clearly discerned portrait and analysis of a series of differentiated teacher strategies, without any understanding of how particular teachers come to adopt particular strategies. In understanding something so intensely personal as teaching, it is critical that we know about the person the teacher is: our paucity of knowledge in this area is a manifest indictment of the range of sociological imagination.

Broadening the Qualitative Approach

To avoid wandering too far in criticizing qualitative approaches, there is the need to once again reaffirm the commitment to such approaches: many of the arguments in the introductory pages of this chapter have after all been used in the past to support participant observation. Denzin (1970) has summarized the position rather well:

> The life history parallels participant observation. Its basic difference lies in the breadth of coverage, not in causal intent.[29]

I have argued that interactionist and ethnomethodological studies of schooling have generated a predominant but implausible model of the teacher: largely interchangeable, subject to timeless problems and employing a variety of standard but apparently spontaneously developed strategies to deal with them. Whilst not wishing to argue that teachers do not have important characteristics in common, I argue that there are important distinctions in attitudes, performance and strategies which can be identified in different teachers and at different times. To understand the degree of importance of these distinctions, we have to reconnect our studies of schooling with investigations of personal biography and historical background: above all, we are arguing for a reintegration of situation with biographical and historical analyses. Through such as reintegration, we might move away from studies where the human actor is studied in a manner contrivedly divorced from his/her own biography and history of situation. A model of human action is required which points to the role of both situational and biographical/historical factors and their interrelation.

Programmatic arguments for new directions are however relatively easy. The rest of the chapter tentatively defines the major dimensions of life history investigation and then seeks to illustrate this through an example of recent work in the field. Essentially, my argument involves four claims placed below in order of ascending generality (and, possibly, difficulty):

(i)   that the teacher's previous *career and life experience* shape his/her view of teaching and the way he/she sets about it;

(ii)   that the teacher's *life outside school*, his/her *latent identities and cultures*, may have an important impact on his/her work as a teacher. This relates to 'central life interests' and commitments (as in the case of a teacher recently interviewed who burst out 'but you must understand that my whole centre of gravity is elsewhere, well outside these bloody school walls'). Becker and Geer's (1971) work provides a theoretical basis here;[30]

(iii)   that the teacher's *career* is a vitally important research focus. Bogdan and Taylor (1970)[31] have argued that in the life history 'the researcher codes the subject's words according to certain phases or periods in his or her life, what many qualitative researchers call a previous *career*'. The work of Strauss, Hughes and Becker, provides a conceptual base.[32] Also notable is Becker's (1952) study of '*The Career of the Chicago Public School Teacher*', which is premised on the belief that the concept of career is 'of great use in understanding the dynamics of work organizations and the movement and fate of individuals within them';[33]

(iv)   that we must, following Bogdan, seek to locate the life history of the individual within 'the history of his time'. Clearly there are limits to this aspiration with regard to schooling. But 'life histories' of schools, subjects, and the teaching profession would provide vital contextual information. For instance, compare Countesthorpe 1970 or William Tyndale 1975 with the same schools in 1988[*]: it is surely not possible to regard such changes in 'arena' as variables to be held constant in the study of teachers in action.

In adding this fourth investigative focus we are, Bogdan notwithstanding, broadening the traditional domain of life history to include the 'life histories' of collectives. Life historians have, however, noted the need to locate the individual life experience 'within the broader socio-historical framework'. In studies of schooling this is particularly important, and, for this reason, I have chosen examples of life history work which take this focus.

---

[*] Two innovative progressive schools in their initial stages which by 1986 had been fairly thoroughly restuctured. See 'Kensington Revisited' below.

The studies which are described in the next section and the next chapter have been chosen to illustrate how profitable life histories might be and to show that quite wide-ranging biographical and historical studies can be completed with a reasonable economy of time (all that can be presented is a short summary of the research: to do these studies justice the reader is recommended to consult the original work).

'Kensington Revisited'

Louis Smith's work in the ethnography of schooling spans the last twenty-five years. In 1968 in *The Complexities of an Urban Classroom*[34], he studied the classroom teacher in action and, later in 1971, in *The Anatomy of Educational Innovation*[35], he produced a detailed organizational analysis of one showpiece elementary school innovation, being concerned with the dynamics of educational change at work in a particular school at a specific point in time.

He has come to view this work as limited in a number of ways and has set out to remedy these limitations. This new research on the same educational institution, Kensington School, attempts to answer two questions. Firstly, what is the current structure of Kensington as an educational organization and has the school reverted to its pre-innovational pattern? Secondly, what interpretation/explanation can be made of the changes that have occurred between 1964 and 1984? Smith notes in his research proposal that 'Methodologically this will involve a special kind of case study, a mix of ethnography and recent history'. Participant observation, interviews/oral history, and primary documents, e.g. local newspapers, school records and bulletins are viewed as sources of data.

Central to Smith's research follow-up are these two questions: 'What has happened to the original staff?' and 'How do they perceive the impact of the Kensington experience on their professional lives?' He writes:

> In answering these questions the hope would be to capture each part of the school and its original faculty at a second period in time, to make comparisons and to draw inferences about innovation and its effects on the lives of a small group of people.

Smith (1980) asserts that the major concern here is 'to place the issues of educational innovation into the broader context of the individual's life'.[36]

A good deal of the research pursuing these issues deals with the individual headmasters of Kensington. Data on these key individuals was often collected by retrospective interviews with members of staff at Kensington. The impact of the different perspectives of the first headmaster, Eugene Shelby, and the second, Michael Edwards, are eloquently caught in a series of such interviews as evidenced in the following transcript:

> *Teacher:* The kids were not allowed to make any choices. (In Selby's era) they were allowed to make choices all day long. And choices in important things such as 'Do I want to go to math class today, or do I want to go out and play?' And if they wanted to go out and play, they played. The first year I was there and we divided up for classes, there were three of us, and the first morning when we changed (students) 'You go here for this class, here for that class', half of our group went out the door. I said, 'Where are you going?' I ran after them. 'We're going for fishing poles.' I said, 'No you're not. What do you want fishing poles for?' 'Oh, we're going down to the creek to fish.' And they all came back in and we started to ask questions.
>
> *Observer:* So was that tightened up then?
>
> *Teacher:* Oh yeah, right away. We simply did that. 'You may go out at recess time and we'll do that, but you don't have that choice now. We will go to maths class when it's time. We will go to social studies class when it's time.'
>
> *Observer:* Now was that Mr. Edwards' influence, or the teachers' influence?
>
> *Teacher:* Right at that point it was teachers'. We went to him and said, 'This is what happened, and this is what we did at the moment.' And I can remember the three of us talking to him about it, and he said, 'Oh no, the kids *will* have class'... Once we said to the kids, 'This is the way we're going to do it now, we're all new and this is what we've decided to do.' There was nothing else, we did it that way. And the amazing part of this, the kids never said ... or very seldom said, 'But last year we...' I always found that very amazing.
>
> *Observer:* So they adjusted and adapted quite easily.
>
> *Teacher:* Yeah, and another thing I remember is when I passed out textbooks, the kids were terribly excited, 'This is

my book?' 'Yes, it's your book.' 'All year.' They really
liked that textbook that they could keep in their desk.

As the research progressed the initial focus moved from a concern
with individual teachers' life histories to a more broadly concerned
pattern of investigation of the life history of an elementary school.
The mode of investigation is now dignified as a 'longitudinal nested
systems model'. Smith in a more recent, and as yet provisional paper,
describes the genesis of the model in this way:

> We have moved from an initial set of predictions and the
> beginnings of a new perspective into a lengthy discussion of
> Kensington's history. When we sought to explain the changes
> in the school, we found ourselves drawn into two dimensions
> or contexts, time and space. Kensington School's immediate
> geographical and social context is the Milford School District.
> It was not surprising to find both the school and the district too
> have interdependent histories. As we began exploring these
> histories, we found plots and themes that enmeshed with even
> more far ranging contexts. It was as if Kensington's history
> was circumscribed by Milford's, and these two in increasingly
> broader contexts in space and time. When we first conceived
> of returning to Kensington School, its fifteen year history
> seemed to define our task. We found that we could not explain
> the changes in this once innovative school with such a narrow
> conception. Our search for antecedents has pushed us back
> near the turn of the century and widened our view to include
> Suburban County, Midwest State, the United States, and even
> the world community. The changes we found at Kensington
> originate in the histories of each of these broader systems. Our
> notion of 'Longitudinal Nested Systems' is an effort to come
> to grips with the role of these interdependent systems in shap-
> ing the school we found on our return visit.

The 'search for antecedents' is clearly open-ended, and in such a
brief description, the focus might appear far too broad. It fact the
study does not move far away from a detailed concern with explaining
the changes at Kensington School, and the broad spectrum of potential
antecedents are closely defined and related to the school in question.
The first section of the history of the Kensington innovation is
told through the periods of each headmaster's incumbency: Shelby's
brief 'Innovative Lighthouse' 1964–66; 'The Revisionary Decade' of

Michael Edwards (first section the 'Golden Era 1966–72'); 'Marking Time' the Hawkins era 1976–1979; and the 'current period of traditional stabilization' John Wales 1979 onwards. Each era is viewed through life history data on the headmasters and personal testimony from the staff. The school superintendents of Milford School District are similarly treated within the context of a history of this district since 1910.

By broadening the focus of historical investigation from headmasters' life histories to life histories of the school and the school district the whole manner of study can be transformed. Smith concludes that he was:

> ... trying for a description and analysis of changes in the innovative Kensington School between its opening in 1964 and its current status fifteen years later in 1979–80. As a piece of contemporary empirical social science research that represents a long time period. From an historical point of view it is not only recent history but also a relatively short time period. One aspect of our metatheoretical perspective assumes that a view of the history of the Milford School District will enhance our understanding of the changes in the Kensington School. More recently, as our data has accumulated, as new directions for inquiry have arisen out of available people, documents, and themes and as analysis and interpretations have continued, we have found shifts in the very nature of the problem. Now one of our guiding questions is not so much 'How and why did this school change from 1964 to 1979? but also 'Why did the Kensington School appear at all in the Milford School District?' Such is the process of inquiry.

Essentially this historical study allows us to move to a view of 'innovation as aberration' — a perspective some way from Smith's 1971 study.

Smith's work therefore moves from an initial concern to study the impact of innovation on teachers and headmasters' lives to an attempt to locate these within the history of the district and the times. The momentum of this ascending order of study is somewhat breathless in the present account because of the need to compress our summary of his research. But Smith's work serves to illustrate the methodological dynamic at work in the pursuit of life history study.

Five years after the study began Smith and his research colleagues conceptualize the whole problem differently. They describe it this way:

The history of the changing school district and community helped us 'see' the nature of the Kensington School as an educational innovation, a specific planned change. The magnitude of this insight on change is caught in the restatement of the overall title of our study. What began as *Kensington Revisited: A Fifteen-Year Follow-Up of an Innovative School and its Faculty* has become *Innovation and Change in American Education* with the original phrasing now a subtitle.

But other changes of focus and understanding have flowed from the commitment to historical study of education. In this case it is clearly stated how the commitment to history changed the researchers' consciousness: 'our history of the "growing", "evolving", "changing" Milford School District helped us to see more clearly a related set of issues, the political context of innovation':

> If educational innovation is only one kind of change and if it is, as colloquially expressed, your or my 'baby' ie. attached to someone's political interests as often is the case, and was in Milford, then a further idea follows. At a minimum, other individuals may have other interests and ideas which they see as desirable, special, and, possibly, innovative. If their ideas are not perfectly congruent with yours or mine then we begin to see a problem of priorities, resources, power, and persuasion. In short, your or my innovation may well be just one small part of a political process. Goodness and truth may not lie in your or my project to the degree we had assumed.

The belief in historical study is related to a belief in its importance for the educational innovators whose lives were at the centre of the study:

> It is our belief that many, if not most, educational innovators do not know much educational history. We believe that this is a tragedy for them and their ideas and a tragedy for many of the individuals in the schools which they 'inflict' or 'save' with their innovations... This belief, as it relates to ourselves, is one of the major results of our study. As one of our colleagues commented, 'Now you've discovered history'. And so we have. This concern for history in general and for history of the Milford District in particular is part of a major shift in our concept of paradigms or root metaphors underlying our approach to educational research, theory and practice'.

Conclusion

In this chapter I have argued that studies of schooling have neglected personal and collective biographies and that to remedy this deficiency life history data should be collected. We have noted that even interactionist and ethnomethodological work has neglected biography, by concentrating on the occasion or the event, most notably the school lesson. These studies have been characterized by assumptions of timelessness and teacher interchangeability. To remedy these failings the life history must be rehabilitated, we must explore elements of individual difference and change through personal biography, and integrate these with historical factors by studying the evolving background of the teachers' professional lives. The latter emphasis leads us to view the individual against the broader patterns of evolution in schooling: such as the development of school innovations, school subjects, educational systems and the teaching profession itself.

In life history work, then, we gain insights into the way in which, over time, individuals come to terms with the constraints and conditions in which they work, and how these relate to the wider social structure. As a result, the fate envisaged by Hargreaves (1978) of ethnography deteriorating 'into a proliferation of unique case studies' might be avoided.[37] The life history approach has the potential to make a far-reaching contribution to the perennial problem of understanding the links between 'personal troubles' and 'public issues', a task which, as C. Wright Mills (1959) pointed out many years ago, is the essence of the sociological enterprise.[38]

Notes and References

1 GOODSON, I.F. *School Subjects and Curriculum Change*, Draft mimeo, 1982.
2 WOODS, P. 'Teachers, self and curriculum', in GOODSON, I.F. and BALL, S.J. (Eds) *Defining the Curriculum: Histories and Ethnographies*, (Lewes, Falmer Press, 1984) p. 260.
3 THOMAS W.I. and ZNANIECKI, F. *The Polish Peasant in Europe and America*, (New York, 1927) pp. 1831–1833.
4 THRASHER, F.M. *The Gang: A Study of 1313 Gangs in Chicago*, (University of Chicago Press, 1928); ZORBAUGH, H.V. *The Gold Coast and the Slum: a Sociological Study of Chicago's North Side*, (University of Chicago Press, 1929); WIRTH, L. *The Ghetto*, (University of Chicago Press, 1928); ANDERSON, N. *The Hobo*, (University of Chicago Press, 1923); SHAW, C.R. *The Jack Roller*, (University of Chicago Press, 1930); CORNWELL,

    C. and SUTHERLAND, E. *The Professional Thief*, (University of Chicago Press, 1937).

5   BECKER, H.S. *Sociological Work: Method and Substance*, (Aldine, Chicago, 1970) p. 71.

6   DOLLARD, J. *Criteria for the Life History*, (Yale University Press, 1949) p. 4.

7   *op. cit.*, p. 5.

8   *op. cit.*, p. 15.

9   *op. cit.*, p. 32.

10 See especially BOGDAN, R. *Being Different: The Autobiography of Jane Foy*, (Wiley, 1974); KLOCKARS, C. *The Professional Fence*, (London, Tavistock, 1975); CHAMBLISS, W. *Boxman: A Professional Thief's Journey*, (Harper and Row, 1972) and see especially THOMPSON, P. *The Voices of the Past: Oral History*, (Opus, 1978).

11 BERTAUX, D. *Biography and Society: The Life History Approach in the Social Sciences*, (Sage, 1981).

12 *op. cit.*, Becker, pp. 71–72.

13 FARIS, R. *Chicago Sociology*, (University of Chicago Press, 1967) pp. 114–115.

14 *op. cit.*, Becker, p. 72.

15 *op. cit.*, p. 72.

16 *op. cit.*, p. 73.

17 MORRIS, M. *An Excursion into Creative Sociology*, (Blackwell, 1977); and CUFF, E. and PAYNE, G. *Sociological Perspectives*, (Allen and Unwin, 1979).

18 BERGER, P. *Invitation to Sociology*, (Doubleday, 1963) and BERGER, P. and LUCKMANN, T. *The Social Construction of Reality*, (Allen Lane, 1967).

19 *op. cit.*, Becker, p. 67.

20 FARADAY, A. and PLUMMER, K. 'Doing life histories', *Sociological Review*, Vol. 27, No. 4., 1979, pp. 773–795.

21 *op. cit.*, Becker, p. 70.

22 BOGDAN, R. *Being Different: The Autobiography of Jane Fry*, (Wiley, 1974) p. 4.

23 JACKSON, P.W. *Life In Classrooms*, (New York, Holt, Rinehart and Winston, 1968) p. 166.

24 PAYNE, G. 'Making a lesson happen' in HAMMERSLEY, M. and WOODS, P. (Eds), *Schooling and Society: A Reader*, (Open University, 1976) p. 33.

25 WOODS, P. and HAMMERSLEY, M. (Eds), *School Experience*, (Croom Helm, 1977).

26 HARGREAVES, D., HESTER, S. and MELLOR, F. *Deviance in Classrooms*, (Routledge and Kegan Paul, 1975).

27 WOODS, P. *Pupil Strategies*, (Croom Helm, 1980) and *Teacher Strategies*, (Croom Helm, 1980b).

28 WOODS, P. *The Divided School*, (Routledge and Kegan Paul, 1979) p. 3.

29 DENZIN, N. *Sociological Methods: A Sourcebook*, (London, Butterworths, 1970) p. 70.

30 BECKER, H.S. and GEER, B. 'Latent culture: A note on the theory of latent social roles' in COSIN, B.R. *et al.*, *School and Society: A Sociological Reader*, (Routledge and Kegan Paul, London, 1971) pp. 56–60.

31 BOGDAN, R. and TAYLOR, S. *Introduction to Qualitative Research Methods*, (Wiley, 1970) p. 121.
32 BECKER, H.S. *et al.*, *Boys in White*, (University of Chicago Press, 1961).
33 BECKER, H.S. 'The career of the Chicago public school teacher', *American Journal of Sociology*, Vol. 57, (1952) p. 470.
34 SMITH, L. and GEOFFREY, W. *The Complexities of an Urban Classroom*, (Holt, Rinehart and Winston, New York, 1968).
35 SMITH, L. and KEITH, P. *Anatomy of an Educational Innovation*, (Wiley, New York, 1971).
36 SMITH, L. 'Archival case records: Issues and illustrations'. Paper presented for SSRC sponsored Case Records Conference, (York, 1980). All notes that follow came from Smith's drafts at this time. Note that the full study will be published as a trilogy of books by Falmer Press (1987, 1988).
37 HARGREAVES, D. 'Whatever happened to symbolic interactionism' in BARTON, L. and MEIGHAN, R. (Eds), *Sociological Interpretations of Schooling and Classrooms: A Reappraisal*, (Nafferton Books, 1978) p. 9.
38 MILLS, C. WRIGHT, *The Sociological Imagination*, (Oxford University Press, 1959).

7 History, Context and Qualitative Methods

This chapter follows chapter 6 in arguing for methods which rehabilitate life histories and integrate studies of historical context. In the introductory section the reasons for concentrating on life history and curriculum history data are explored by analyzing some of the inadequacies of research methods as perceived in the mid-1970s when my own work began.[1]

It should be noted that since then other studies have emerged which have also sought to address these inadequacies. Studies of teacher socialization have focussed on teacher culture and careers,[2] whilst a range of 'strategies' studies have pointed to the importance of background and biography.[3] This work has considerably extended the range and theoretical aspiration of qualitative studies but in this chapter I shall stay with the original intention of exploring the role of historical studies in redressing certain emergent tendencies within qualitative methods.

In retrospect several reasons would seem to have led to a predilection for historical and biographical work when devising a research programme:

(1) It grew out of my teaching experience. Certainly after teaching at Countesthorpe (recently described as an 'unemulated educational maverick') I was susceptible to Nisbet's (1971) arguments in *Social Change and History*. Here he argues that we are often deluded into thinking fundamental social change is taking place because we do not take account of a vital distinction between:

> readjustment or individual deviance within a social structure (whose effects, although possibly cumulative are never sufficient to alter the structure or the basic postulates of a society or institution) and the more fundamental though enigmatic change of structure, type, pattern or paradigm.[4]

To pursue this distinction demands, I think, that we undertake historical work. This holds whether we seek to understand how change is contained, as readjustment or individual deviance in particular schools like Countesthorpe or within curriculum reforms in general.

(2) The documents and statements of the curriculum reform movement inaugurated in the 1960s reveal a widespread belief that there could be a more or less complete break with past tradition. A belief in short that history in general and curriculum history in particular could somehow be *transcended*. For instance, it was asserted that the new curricula then being devised promised to 'revolutionalize' English schooling.[5] Retrospectively, there still seems something admirable, however misconceived, about such belief in contemporary possibility that history seemed of little relevance. At a time when traditional curriculum practice was thought to be on the point of being overthrown, it was perhaps unsurprising that so many reforms paid scant attention to the evolution and establishment of traditional practice. In any event, radical change did not occur. By 1975, when my research programme began, one was in a position of needing to re-examine the emergence and survival of the 'traditional' as well as the failure to generalize, institutionalize and sustain the 'innovative'.

(3) But if this was a view from the curriculum chalkface, it later became clear that the *transcendent* view of curriculum change had infected many of those involved in researching schools and curriculum. The irony is supreme but for the best of reasons. Once again it is partly explained by an historical climate of opinion where curriculum change was thought the order of the day. Parlett and Hamilton's (1972) influential paper on illuminative styles of evaluation, though claiming general application, focussed on the evaluation of *innovation*. They wanted 'to study the innovatory project; how it operates, how it is influenced by the various school situations in which it is applied; what those directly concerned regard as its advantages and disadvantages'.[6] Preoccupations with 'those directly concerned', with 'what it is like to be participating' were to characterize a major school of evaluators and case study workers. Indeed, this posture characterized those researchers both most sympathetic and sensitive to the aspirations of the innovators. Above all, they wanted to 'capture and portray the world as it appears to the people in it'. Some went even further 'in a sense for the case study worker what *seems* true is more important than what is true'.[7]

Writing later, with a strong sense of my own delusions on curriculum reform, I saw the evaluators who had studied my school as merely confirming the participants' myopia.

Focussing the evaluators' work on the charting of the subjective perceptions of participants is to deny much of its potential — particularly to those evaluators aspiring to 'strong action — implications.' The analysis of subjective perceptions is incomplete without analysis of the historical context in which they occur. To deprive the subject of such knowledge would be to condemn new evaluation to the level of social control — a bizarre fate for a model aspiring to 'democratic' intentions.[8]

(4) Yet if many of those employing qualitative methods in evaluation and case study took a transcendent view of history, they were not alone. As was noted in chapter 6, by a peculiar convergence many contemporary interactionist and ethnographic studies were similarly a-historical.

Life Histories and Curriculum History

With respect to contemporary curriculum there are three levels (though of course they are not in practice separate) that are amenable to historical study:

1   The individual life history. The process of change is continuous throughout a person's life 'both in episodic encounters and in longer-lasting socialization processes over the life history'.[9]
2   The group or collective level: professions, categories, subjects or disciplines, for instance, evolve as social movements over time. Likewise school and classrooms develop pattern of stability and change.
3   The relational level, the various permutations of relations between individuals, between groups and between individuals and groups; and the way these relations change over time.

At the time of planning my original research the blending of individual history and curriculum history had been recently explored in Mary Waring's (1975) study of Nuffield Science. For Waring, the understanding of curriculum innovation is simply not possible without a history of context:

If we are to understand events, whether of thought or of action, knowledge of the background is essential. Knowledge of events is merely the raw material of history: to be an intelligible reconstruction of the past, events must be related to

football pitches. I got that fenced off, got bits of wire and so on ... as things developed I had my class for practically everything — not quite every subject, but a good deal and I developed my ideas on this form. We built bits and pieces gradually. We built a pigsty, and the 4 Practical did the actual building of that. We built a rabbit house which we built up. Eventually we kept about two calves, about six goats, a pig and a litter; we had a poultry run and hens of course, a dairy which we fitted out, and I managed to get from Gascoynes because my father was a friend of the chairman or something dairy equipment.

Johnson taught 4F for about two thirds of their timetable; other teachers taught science and woodwork. He was much influenced by the idea of rural education as the 'curriculum hub' which his headmaster actively encouraged.

I taught them maths, English, history etc., all tied in completely, because, for example, maths I based as much as possible on the farm activities. In fact, I used a series of books which was popular then, called *Rural Arithmetic* — the other I can't quite remember the title of. They were all about problems of the land: e.g. if you were mixing things for the pigs. You didn't buy ready-made meal for the pigs. You calculated by the weight what meal they require, you broke this down, the various ingredients of the meal, you get them all out separately, weighted them up, mixed them up and it had to work out right to fourteen rations, one for every morning and evening of the week. That was a piece of arithmetic it could take two people most of the day to do.

We were fairly poorly off for books in those days, frankly, so we read a lot of literature associated with the countryside. We didn't over do this to the extent of doing nothing else. They wrote compositions. We had an English textbook which I, at any rate, kept an eye on to make sure some sort of progression of spelling was maintained. But a lot of English was straightforwardly connected with the farm. For example, they each had to write a diary every day and they had to write a summary at the end of the week. It was passed on to the next students who took on the animals. That was a good piece of English, and I had said that must be perfect — no spelling mistakes, no blots — nothing.

Johnson reckons that these were some of the happiest days of his teaching career. His own enthusiasm (and that of his wife) coupled with the interest of the children seem to have generated considerable motivation to learn:

IG: Did they respond pretty well?

PJ: They absolutely lapped it up, loved it. You'd never get absences unless the kid was really ill. You'd get kids ... often at the weekends... We had to feed them at the weekends — there was no-one else to. I can't remember any occasion when the kids didn't turn up at the weekend. It may have happened but I can't remember.

IG: So you had to spend a lot of time at weekends?

PJ: Lived up there. But Joan helped a lot too. Frankly we hadn't any money to be doing anything else in those days. Until it reached a stage when my kids were getting a bit older and I took a job during the holidays because I needed the money — pay was poor. But I still did that as well.

Johnson attributed the main influences on his developing concept of rural education to his contacts with the Kent farmworkers' family which he had married into and which he lived among.

I did a lot of walking about the orchards in Kent and talking to farm workers and I can remember lots of occasions when the attitude of these people struck me very much. I had a strong feeling that education wasn't just book-learning — that's an old phrase — it involved in fact skills in the field and commonsense applied to a problem.

Johnson feels that he dealt with many very able pupils in 4F; partly a reflection of the social structure in Kent in the early 1950s. The pupils were, with one exception (for whom he could not find a job), boys, the most able of whom today would be in the sixth forms, who went as agricultural apprentices to farms who were glad to get them. 'Good farms, good employers!' I asked, at this point, if he felt any resentment that they were forced to go on to the land:

PJ: No, first of all because I didn't know anything about 'A' levels at my level of teaching. Grammar schools were a separate world and while I knew them throughout my own background, I never associated these kids with it. It never occurred to me at the time that these kids could have got into the sixth form. It didn't occur to me at that time that they were bright.

IG: Why didn't it occur to you that these children were bright?

PJ: They were bright to me but it didn't occur to me that that meant they should have an academic education. Because I was meeting people throughout the war — meeting people then whose field of work was similar to farm workers and every bit as bright. I don't think this is true today. One of the effects of the introduction of the 11+ was to cream the working class of its bright people who went into academic jobs. You constantly hear it's happened in places like India — all being bank clerks or professionals. There were a lot of intelligent people in the working class then, who by and large are not there today. They have all been creamed off into sixth forms and professional jobs. At that time, I know there were people as simple farm workers who were highly edu-cated — not educated — but highly cultured intelligent people. I didn't find it a problem at the time, nor did the kids; it was never raised.

Secondary Modern Examinations

From the early 1950s, more and more secondary modern schools began to focus on external examinations. This posed insuperable problems for those heads and teachers in secondary moderns who were exploring new modes of curricula such as rural education.

Towards Rural Studies Examinations

As the tripartite system of education gradually emerged in the form of new school buildings and modified curricula, it became clear that rural studies and gardening were only developing in the secondary modern schools. In a questionnaire survey of gardening and rural studies teachers in Kent produced, with three exceptions, the reply from grammar and technical schools of 'subject not taught', whilst in 63 of the 65 secondary modern schools the subject was given an important position in the curriculum.[18]

Rural education having been decimated as a concept within the increasingly exam-conscious secondary moderns it now became clear that the successor subject of rural studies faced major problems. Writing in 1957, Mervyn Pritchard described the situation in this way:

> There appears to be two extremes of thought in secondary modern schools:
> 1 a concentration on external examinations
> 2 those who won't have them at any price.

> In those schools where the brighter pupils are examined it is unusual to find Rural Science as one of the subjects taken and as the pupils concentrate more and more narrowly on their examination subjects it is unusual to find Rural Science used as a social subject such as craft, art or music may be.

> Even where pupils are not examined there appears to be a concentration of the teaching of the subject in streams of classes of duller children.[19]

The concern of rural studies teachers at the deteriorating status and position of their subject led to a variety of responses in the latter part of the 1950s. Mervyn Pritchard exhorted: 'as often as possible the rural studies teacher should mix with his colleagues even if he has to kick off muddy gum boots to drink his cup of tea. Much useful interchange of knowledge and information is carried out among the staffroom gossip. Informal discussion of school policy can be helped along judiciously by the rural science teacher. Frequent contact can convince our colleagues of one's normality and value'.[20] Apart from such exhortations some teachers were concerned to develop a 'philosophy of rural studies'. In 1954, Carson and Colton produced a paper which appeared in the Kent Association Journal, and, later in 1957, in the Lincolnshire *Rural Science News*. It was a systematic attempt to think through a subject philosophy, a first, embryonic attempt to define a subject, and one equipped with a contemporary rationale. They argued:

> For this study to justify its inclusion in the school curriculum it must be shown to play a vital part in developing a fully educated citizen who is aware in his heart of his kinship with the rest of life and yet realized the unique qualities of the human spirit.[21]

Carson and Colton were editors of the *Kent Association of Teachers of Gardening and Rural Science Journal*. The 'Rural Science' appendage was added at Carson's insistence when the Association was formed in

1949. The Association was predated by an ephemeral association of rural science teachers in 1925, and by a small association in Nottingham founded in 1940, and the Manchester Teachers' Gardening Circle founded in 1941.

By 1954 the Kent Journal was beginning to define a philosophy for rural studies and soon after claimed, 'this Association has constantly sought parity of esteem with the rest of the curriculum for all rural studies'.[22]

At the same time, new rural studies associations were forming in other counties, normally to pursue the aims expressed in the Kent Journal. By now, rural studies was a specialized subject of very low status, literally fighting for its existence in the exam-conscious secondary modern schools. In 1960, the County subject association banded together to form a National Rural Studies Association with its own journal. The 1961 Journal stated in 'The Constitution':

> The aim of this association shall be 'to develop and coordinate rural studies. Rural studies includes nature study, natural history pursuits of all kinds, the study of farming and the activities of the countryside, as taught in primary and secondary schools. Rural studies should be regarded as an art, a science and a craft; a subject as well as a method of teaching.[23]

The Association soon became involved in promoting examinations in rural studies. They initiated a pilot CSE (Certificate of Secondary Education an examination aimed at secondary modern schools) project and although many practising teachers complained at the inappropriateness of written examinations, a range of new CSE's in rural studies were duly promoted.

1954–1958 Secondary Modern Certification (age 34–38)

In 1953, the headmaster at Wrotham who had so strongly promoted rural education left; his successor was more examination conscious. Johnson began to look for a new job and in the Spring term of 1954 noticed a post at Royston in Hertfordshire where a teacher was required to start an ambitious rural studies programme. On the interviewing panel was a rural studies adviser, Geoff Whitby (he was, in fact, the first rural studies adviser and was steeped in the concept of rural education in which Herfordshire had long been a pioneer).

> Whitby asked me about rural education and I described what I'd been doing in Kent, and I could see at once that I'd got the

job. I should guess he's never met anyone else who had done this sort of thing. The Head saw it differently. This was very interesting. He didn't see it as rural education in that sense because he was already thinking ahead to raising the standards of this school to what could eventually be CSE. None of this existed but he was thinking in terms of this. Although I understood when I got there I could have the same set up as in Kent, with three top classes and I could have anyone who wanted to volunteer for the subject, it never in fact worked out. The classes were streamed; I only ever got the lower of the three streams. While at first I could do what I liked with that bottom stream, and I did the same sort of thing as in Kent, over the next few years this was whittled away from me, and more specialism invaded the curriculum and these kids eventually spent practically no time in running the farm. Whereas in Kent they did the whole operation of running the farm in lesson time, in Herts they had to do it before school. So it never really got going.

The problems were in fact both internal and external to the school. Inside the school there was streaming and a belief that it was vocational training for agriculture. Outside the school the community remained hostile to the whole concept, partly a result of the very different social structure of Hertfordshire compared with Kent. In Kent farm workers were better paid and treated and respected because their job was skilled.

In Hertfordshire there was a long history of poverty on the land going back to Arthur Young's travels. If you meet any of the farm workers in this area, there are tales of great poverty even in this day. So there was a feeling that going on the land here was nothing but condemnation ... nothing but ploughing and sowing, no other skills, very little mixed farming, no orchards.

But beyond the different social structure of the new locality Johnson had moved towards an awareness that 'society was changing'.

The concern was that selection was important, children were getting into grammar schools and other people were beginning to see what was happening to them. Therefore they wanted their children to do as well academically as possible in order to get better jobs ... certainly the atmosphere was different.

Johnson's disillusionment with his new school grew as he realized he would only ever be given the problem children and those stigmatized as less able. In 1956, his third year, he had a series of interviews with the head:

> I had arguments with Young. I made my case and he was adamant that this was not what was required today. They gave a school leaving certificate, and they required qualifications in other things. In my opinion he never really saw what I was up to.

At the time, he felt a deep sense of professional betrayal. After all, in Kent, he had seen a working model of rural education as an integrated 'eminently satisfactory situation of mixed ability type'. Again and again in his retirement interviews, he returns to this critical point when as he puts it 'my dream faded', 'my vision of educating children faltered'. However, at the time, although disappointed there were other goals:

> My ambition was to be a head, and I had long talks with Young about how I could get to be a head. It became increasingly obvious to me that as a rural studies man I wasn't going to get a look in.

1958–1979 Rural Studies and Environmental Studies Advisor (age 39–59)

In 1958 Johnson was asked by the Rural Studies adviser who had brought him to Hertfordshire if he would like to take over his job.

> I didn't think twice when Whitby asked. I thought an opening like this, I'll do something good in this. I started off in '58 with part-time, half my time, and he worked the other half for a year and then he retired, and I got his job. By this time, I'd really given up hope of getting rural studies seen in the way I'd taught it in Kent. Then I saw it as a specialist subject which had certain weak links. For the first two–three years, I did two things; I read all about the rural education tradition in the papers Whitby gave me on his background, etc. At the same time, I was visiting the secondary school teachers and stimulated them to get themselves organized to try and get any kids other than the least able, to get them better facilities in their schools. I spent the first three–four years with this aim.'

At this stage in his life Johnson was enthused by the prospect of using his influence as an adviser to change things. Initially this enthusiasm carried him over the loss of 'hope of getting real rural education' for by now it was clear that, whatever his preference, the specialist subject was taking over.

IG: What kind of people were they, as you travelled round in 1958–60?

PJ: They were pre-war teachers of gardening who'd come back, and there were people of my own generation living through the war who came into teaching. Gradually then we began to get the post-war younger teacher coming in and the colleges who specialized in rural studies from the 1960s onwards. Before that, they were the older chaps generally.

IG: So what did you decide would be your strategy? By then you were involved in the national association?

PJ: No, we started the national association in 1960. I called the first meeting in the name of the Herts Association. We knew there were various other groups around the country. I have no idea how we found that out.

IG: What was the thinking behind calling this meeting?

PJ: It was quite definitely to raise the standard of rural studies as a subject and the status of it because we decide that until it was raised nationally we wouldn't be able to do much in Herts. 'If you're not given a proper classroom refuse to teach this subject in any old place, and as adviser call me in', was what I told my teacherrs, and I will say 'this chap is entitled to a classroom just the same as anyone else.' To some heads this was a bit of a shock. They'd never been faced with this problem. If it rained they all just sat in the bicycle shed. We had Broad who was sympathetic to ideas … we produced that report, and as a result every school from 1960 onwards where I was adviser, we got minimal provisions called the rural studies unit in Herts.

From this point on, Johnson became a leading campaigner for rural studies as a subject — self-promotion and subject promotion became finally and inextricably linked. This pursuit of subject promotion over time was reflected upon in an article he wrote in 1963 for the Rural Studies Association Journal. It begins with the polarity that teachers actually have two duties: 'one to their classes and one the educational climate in which they worked'. It was argued that the subject had to respond to these 'changing climates' to ensure influence and resources.

> During the next few years considerable changes are likely both in the framework of our school system and in the curricula within school if rural studies is to retain its influence, then those teachers who believe in the subject must be clear about their aims and ready to adapt their methods to new conditions.

He concluded:

> Thus the climate is changing continually, now perhaps more rapidly than ever before. But rural studies teachers are used to British weather. Have we not all got a lesson up our sleeves for the sudden downpour or the unexpected fine day? Within the educational climate too. We are ready with new ideas to meet whatever the weather has in store![24]

In fact what the weather had in store at this time was the new Beloe CSE examinations for secondary moderns. Rural studies became one of the pilot studies for the new examination and despite a range of evidence that it was ill-suited to written examination, subject opportunism demanded a positive response to the changing climate. As a result, CSEs in rural studies were promoted wherever possible. This embracing of examinations was pursued obsessively when the comprehensive system was launched. Rural studies then, Johnson thought, had to 'adapt or perish'. Again the response was opportunistic. Rural studies changed into Environmental studies, and a new 'A' level in the subject was launched, for as Johnson says 'this way, you got more money, better kids, better careers'.

The Alternative Vision: A Retrospect

Although during the period when he was building his career Johnson embraced the notion of his subject as an examinable specialism, in later years doubts surfaced. On his retirement he stated quite clearly that it was the embrace of the specialist curriculum and subject examination that killed his educational vision. 'This was when my dream began to fade. I was not aware of it at the time'. For him now his alternative vision, his dream, is all powerful:

> My alternative vision was that in more general terms and I'm still convinced this is true, a lot of kids don't learn through

paper and pencil and that we do far too much of this. A lot of kids could achieve success and use all the mental skills that we talk about in the classroom such as analyzing and comparing through physical activities. Through such things as building the school farm, looking after animals. I used to talk about the fact that the real reason for keeping the farm wasn't to teach farm work. With the farm it was a completely renewing set of problems and the fact it was a farm was incidental. You were thinking in educational terms of process with these kids. That's the sort of dream I was well aware of giving up, and talked about it a number of times. I always felt dissatisfied since and I've met many teachers who have come across the same realization, not in quite such explicit terms as they'd never had the chance of doing it, whereas I had. I meet them now in schools . . . a teacher whom I met today knew that the teaching she was doing with these less able girls was not the right way to educate the girls, but what was the right way she couldn't think. Well, I know what is the right way. The right way is the sort of thing we were doing in '47 whether it's using the farm or whatever. The attitude is that you use your hands. You don't always sit at a desk necessarily. You are facing problems of a three dimensional kind at an adult level. You use terms like man's problems; and this is no longer feasible in a school situation. I couldn't tell that girl today to do that sort of thing; she wouldn't succeed at all.

To my mind, one of the tragedies of education in my life, and I would call this the secondary modern ethos — maybe it's one of many, but I don't know — was that the best thing that secodary moderns did was to promote this idea that it's just as good to be a skilled craftsman as, say, a white collar worker, and that you get as much satisfaction and challenge from it at your own level. This was what was really behind what we were doing in Kent. The fact that this is no longer recognized in schools at all is, I think, responsible for the problems we have in school today, both academically with the less able and with the anti-school group and the apathetic group.

Conclusion

This episode in a subject teacher's life illustrates the way that the collection of life histories and elucidation of the historical context can combine.

Above all, the strength of beginning curriculum research from life history data is that *from the outset* the work is firmly focussed on the working lives of practitioners. Other researchers have commented in similar manner on the peculiar force of this kind of data as the initial strategy in a research programme:

> When one conducts a life history interview the findings become alive in terms of historical processes and structural constraints. People do not wander round the world in a timeless, structureless limbo. They themselves acknowledge the importance of historical factors and structural constraints (although of course, they would not use such pompous language). The analysis of life histories actually pushes one first of all to the problems of constraints bearing down upon the construction of any one life. . .[25]

In articulating their response to historical factors and structural constraints, life story tellers provide us with sensitizing devices for the analysis of these constraints and the manner in which they are experienced. We are alerted to historical legacies and structural constraints and can pursue understanding of aspects such as in the instance given, strategies for self and subject promotion and career construction.

Certainly in the life of Patrick Johnson we gain insights into him wrestling with imperatives in the social structure. From his early professional life he develops a vision of how schools might be, this vision is challenged and defeated as subject specialism and examinations invade the early secondary modern schools; we see how self-promotion and subject promotion interrelate; and we see how one educational ideology is initially replaced by another as the teacher's career is constructed; the ideological renunciation only follows his retirement at the end of his career. Our attention is, therefore, left on the link between the structuring of material interests, strategies for career aggrandisment and the acceptance of particular educational ideologies.

A combination of life histories and curriculum histories should then offer an antidote to the depersonalized, ahistorical accounts of schooling to which we are only too accustomed. Above all, we gain insights into individuals coming to terms with imperatives in the social structure. From the collection of a range of life stories located in historical context we can discern what is general within a range of individual studies. We can thereby develop our understanding from a base that is clearly grounded within personal biography and perception.

Critical Questions

In this chapter I have taken the view that a combination of life history and curriculum history data can both broaden and deepen our accounts of schooling and curriculum. But a range of critical questions remain. Certain problems are specific to life history data, others specific to curriculum history and a further set of questions arise from the relationship between the two.

The first range of problems turns on the relaionship between life stories as told by the subjects themselves, retrospectively recounting episodes in their life, and life histories where those stories are supplemented by other data and placed in their historical context. If we seek a full retrospective life story then we come at the stage Vonnegut has described so well in his most recent novel. He argues that sociologists have ignored the fact that:

> 'We all see our lives as stories... If a person survives an ordinary span of sixty years or more, there is every chance that his or her life as a shapely story has ended; and all that is to be experienced is epilogue. Life is not over, but the story is.'[26]

But John Mortimer (1983) has summarized the problems of writing an autobiography at this stage. In the last paragraph he says:

> That is how it was, a part of life seen from a point of view. Much more happened that I cannot tell or remember. To others it would be, I am quite sure, a different story.[27]

At root the problem is to retain and defend the authenticity of the participant's account. But to do this such problems of lapsed memory or partial or selective recall must be faced. We only get a part of the picture, to be sure a vital part, but we need to push for more of the picture, more bits of the jigsaw.

In part the problem is addressed by triangulation through collecting a range of life stories, and by developing an associated documentary history of the context. But the development of research which moves across a range from life stories through to curriculum history concentrates the focus of the work; arguably in a way which challenges the authenticity of the accounts and certainly in ways which effect the relationship between the life story teller and the researcher. By moving from life story to curriculum history control is passing irrevocably to the researcher. In addition, the life story data is being concentrated onto particular issues and themes. In this case the linkage with the history of a subject could well have led, in spite of the range of life stories gathered, to an overconcentration on the career conscious, upwardly-mobile teachers. Once again, there is the danger of an over-emphasis on the unrepresentative.

I explore later the relationship of the work to theory. But in this respect it must be noted that as with life histories, so with curriculum histories, the specificity of their focus can act against their capacity for generalization. The curriculum history of Rural Studies is investigated further in the next chapter in an attempt to discern more general insights.

A further question is the nature of interpretation, the role of the commentary. As Bertaux has reminded us, moving from the personal life story to wider histories involves considerable questions of methodological reliability:

> What is really at stake is the relationship between the sociologist and the people who make his work possible by accepting to be interviewed on their life experiences.[28]

This question if deeply significant both at the ethical and procedural level.

The ethical and procedural questions relate closely to the relationship between life story teller and researcher and the potential for mutuality. This is further related to the question of 'audience'. If the earlier contention that life story data placed in a historical context offers the opportunity for research which 'engages' teachers is correct, then the prospects for mutuality are enhanced. In developing life histories, teachers could be involved in work which would illuminate and feed back into the conditions and understandings of their working lives.

Notes and References

1   GOODSON, I.F. *Curriculum Conflict 1895–1975* unpublished, D. PHIL, Sussex 1980 and *School Subjects and Curriculum Change — Case Studies in Curriculum History* (London, Croom Helm, 1983).

2   For instance LACEY, C. *The Socialization of Teachers*, (London, Methuen, 1977).

3   For instance Peter Woods' work or POLLARD, A. 'A model of coping strategies', *British Journal of Sociology of Education*, Vol. 3, No. 1, (1982).

4   NISBET, R.A. 'Social change and history' (1969) quoted in WEBSTER, J.R. 'Curriculum change and crisis', *British Journal of Educational Studies*, 3, October 1971, pp. 204–205.

5   KERR, J. 'The problem of curriculum reform' in HOOPER, R. (Ed), *The Curriculum: Context, Design and Development*, (Edinburgh, Oliver and Boyd, 1971) p. 180.

6   PARLETT, M. and HAMILTON, D. '*Evaluation as illumination: A new approach to the study of innovatory programs*', Occasional paper 9, Edinburgh Centre for Research in Educational Sciences, (1972).

7   WALKER, R. 'The conduct of educational case study' in *Innovation, Evolution, Research and the Problem of Control: Some Interim Papers*, SAFARI Project, Centre for Applied Research in Education, University of East Anglia, (1974).

8   GOODSON, I.F. 'Evaluation and evolution' in NORRIS, N. (Ed), *Theory in Practice*, SAFARI Project, Centre for Applied Research in Education, University of East Anglia, (1977), p. 160.

9   BLUMER, H. quoted in HAMMERSLEY, M. and WOODS, P. *The Process of Schooling*, (London, Routledge and Kegan Paul, 1976) p. 3.

10 WARING, M. *Aspects of the Dynamics of Curriculum Reform in Secondary School Science*, Phd., University of London (1975), p. 12.

11 WARING, M. *Social Pressures and Curriculum Innovation: A Study of the Nuffield Foundation Science Teaching Project*, (London, Methuen, 1979) p. 12.

12 *Ibid.*, p. 15.

13 YOUNG, M.F.D. 'Curriculum as socially organized knowledge' in YOUNG, M.F.D. (Ed), *Knowledge and Control: New Directions for the Sociology of Education*, (London, Collier-MacMillan, 1971) p. 23.

14 WILLIAMS, R. *The Long Revolution*, (Pelican, 1965) pp. 145–146.

15 DENZIN, N.K. *The Research Act*, (Chicago, Aldine), 1970.

16 GLASS, D.V. 'Education and social change in Modern England' in HOOPER, R. (Ed), (1971), p. 35.

17 GIBBERD, K. *No Place Like School*, (London, Michael Joseph, 1962) p. 103.

18 PRITCHARD, M. 'The rural science teacher in the school society', *Journal of the Hertfordshire Association of Gardening and Rural Subjects*, No. 2, September 1957, p. 4.

19 Survey by Herfordshire Association of Teachers of Gardening and Rural Subjects, (1957).

20 *Ibid.*, Pritchard, p. 5.

21 *Rural Science News*, Vol. 10. No. 1, January 1957.

22 *Kent Journal*, No. 4, 1954.

23 *National Rural Studies Association Journal*, (1961) p. 5.

24 'The changing climate', *National Rural Studies Association Journal*, (1963), pp. 14–15.

25 FARADAY, A. and PLUMMER, K. 'Doing life histories', *Sociological Review*, Vol. 27, No. 4, (1979), p. 780.
26 GLENDENING, V. 'Slaughterhouse epilogue', *Sunday Times*, 20 February 1983.
27 MORTIMER, J. *Clinging to the Wreckage*, (London, Penguin, 1983), p. 256.
28 *op. cit.*, BERTAUX, p. 9.

8 Defining a Subject for the Comprehensive School

'The Elimination of Separatism'

One of the episodes in the emergence of comprehensive schooling in England and Wales that has been relatively neglected is how school subjects weathered the transition from the tripartite* to the comprehensive system. The subjects taught in the grammar schools were normally distinctively different in content and pedagogic orientation to those taught in the secondary moderns. Hence for the comprehensive ideal to be implemented substantial curriculum renegotiation might have been envisaged and major curriculum reforms initiated. The belief that broad-based curriculum reform, with a range of associated political and pedagogical implications, was indeed underway was commonly held in the early era of comprehensivization following the 1965 circular. Professor Kerr asserted in 1968 that 'at the practical and organizational levels, the new curricula promise to revolutionalize English education'.[1] Likewise in 1972, following ROSLA, Rubinstein and Simon envisaged a range of curriculum reforms which effectively married the characteristics of the best secondary modern and grammar school curricula to provide a new synthesis suitable for the comprehensive school:

> The content of the curriculum is now under much discussion, and comprehensive schools are participating actively in the many curriculum reform schemes launched by the Schools Council and Nuffield. The tendency is towards the development of interdisciplinary curricula, together with the use of the

---

* A system comprising grammar schools, technical schools and secondary modern schools.

resources approach to learning involving the substitution of much group and individual work for the more traditional forms of class teaching. For these new forms of organizing and stimulating learning mixed ability grouping often provides the most appropriate method; and partly for this reason the tendency is towards the reduction of streaming and class teaching. This movement in itself promotes new relations between teachers and pupils, particularly insofar as the teacher's role is changing from that of ultimate authority to that of motivating, facilitating and structuring the pupils' own discovery and search for knowledge.[2]

The 1965 circular had sought to 'eliminate separatism in secondary education'.[3] But a close reading of the circular implies that the major concern, perhaps understandably at the time, was with eliminating separatism in the form of different school types and buildings. What was unclear and unspoken was whether the logic of providing a comprehensive education for all in the common school would be pursued into also providing a common curricula.

The grammar schools and secondary modern sectors designated 'two nations' of school children, and this was to be eliminated as it was thought unfair. But the differentiation into 'two nations' took place both by designation into separate schools and by designation of separate curricula. On the 'elimination of separate' curricula the 1965 circular was silent.

Indeed, there were clear indications that far from expecting a new synthesis of curricula along the lines defined by Rubinstein and Simon the main concern in 1965 was to defend and extend grammar school education. The House of Commons motion which led to circular 10/65 was fairly specific:

> This House, conscious of the need to raise educational standards at all levels, and regretting that the realization of this objective is impeded by the separation of children into different types of secondary schools, notes with approval the efforts of local authorities to reorganize secondary education on comprehensive lines which will preserve all that is valuable in grammar school education for those children who now receive it and make it available to more children.[4]

This hardly hints at a new synthesis of common and comprehensive curricula — was there nothing valuable in secondary modern education to be preserved and merged? 'Grammar school education for *more* children' but not *all* children. What about the children still left out-side? The concern, it seemed, was rather with spreading grammar school education a little more widely.

Even at the time, some commentators were warning that the new curriculum initiatives summarized by Rubinstein and Simon might merely facilitate a new 'curriculum for inequality'. The preserva-tion of grammar school education for some (although 'more') pupils implied that the new curricula would be essentially aimed at the 'other' pupils. This interpretation was fostered by the close association of many of the reforms with the new pupil clienteles arising from ROSLA and with the 'new sixth form' groups unsuited to the tradi-tional courses.

Marten Shipman read a paper before the British Sociological Association in 1969 which argued that the curriculum reforms were in danger of perpetuating the two nations approach inside the education-al system, what he called a 'Curriculum for Inequality'. He spoke of the 'unintended consequences of curriculum development'.

> Coming less from actual content than from the introduction of new courses into a school system that is still clearly divided into two sections, one geared to a system of external examina-tions, the other less constrained. The former is closely tied to the universities and is within established academic traditions. The latter has a short history and is still in its formative stages. It is the consequences of innovation into these two separate sections rather than the curricula themselves which may be producing a new means of sustaining old divisions.[5]

The connecting traditions are elucidated later in the paper:

> One is firmly planted in revered academic traditions, is adapted to teaching from a pool of factual knowledge and has clearly defined, if often irrelevant subject boundaries. The other is experimental, looking to America rather than our own past for inspiration, focusses on contemporary problems, groups subjects together and rejects formal teaching methods.[6]

He summarized the distinction into two notions of curricula in that 'one emphasizes a schooling within a framework of external examina-tions, the other attempts to align school work to the environment of the children'.

The long legacy of a dual curriculum stretched back to the origins of the state system in the nineteenth century and beyond. There had always been not only separate schools but separate curricula. Eliminating separate schools would not then of itself eliminate separate curricula. Indeed, the Norwood Report which inaugurated the tripartite system had been quite clear on the link between separate school types and separate curricula.

The Norwood Report of 1943 had argued that, in England three clear groups could be discerned. Firstly:

> The pupil who is interested in learning for its own sake, who can grasp an argument or follow a piece of connected reasoning; who is interested in causes, whether on the level of human volition or in the material world; who cares to know how things came to be as well as how they are; who is sensitive to language as expression of thought; to a proof as a precise demonstration; to a series of experiments justifying a principle; he is interested in the relatedness of related things, in development, in structure, in a coherent body of knowledge.

These pupils form the continuing clientele of the traditional subject-based curriculum for, as Norwood states, 'such pupils, educated by the curriculum commonly associated with the grammar school, have entered the learned professions or have taken up higher administrative or business posts'.[7] The needs of the intermediate category, 'the pupil whose interests and abilities lie markedly in the field of applied science or applied art' were to be fulfilled by the technical school. Finally, Norwood states with a very partial view of educational history, 'There had of late years been recognition, expressed in the framing of curricula and otherwise, of still another grouping of occupations'. This third group was to provide the clientele for the new secondary modern schools.

> The pupil in this group deals more easily with concrete things than with ideas. He may have much ability, but it will be in the realm of facts. He is interested in thing as they are; he finds little attraction in the past or in the slow disentanglement of causes or movements. His mind must turn its knowledge or its curiosity to immediate test; and his test is essentially practical.[8]

The implications for the school curriculum are hinted at later when Norwood notes that:

> . . . as the kind of education suitable for them becomes more clearly marked out and the leaving age is raised, the course of education may become more and more supple and flexible with the result that particular interests and aptitudes may be

enabled to declare themselves and be given opportunities for growth.

This curriculum 'would not be to prepare for a particular job or profession and its treatment would make a direct appeal to interests, which it would awaken by practical touch with affairs'.[9]

But if a government report had so recently identified different curricula for different pupil types such pervasive features could hardly be wished away by gathering all the categories under one roof through comprehensive reorganization.

The question remained as to how the different curricula and associated pupil clienteles would be merged or prioritized in the comprehensive school. On Norwood's analysis academic 'O' and 'A' level subjects were best suited only to the minority entering elite positions. Following Shipman Dennis Marsden (1971) had warned what would happen if the 'academic category' were given priority:

> If we give the new comprehensive the task of competing with selective schools for academic qualifications, the result will be remarkably little change in the selective nature of education. Selection will take place within the school and the working class child's education will suffer.[10]

To understand how the curriculum was negotiated and devised for comprehensive schools after 1965, the following case study looks at one curriculum area: rural studies. As we saw in the previous chapter, rural studies were closely allied to 'attempts to align school work to the environment of the children', and, in 1965, were beginning to face the challenge of the new comprehensive schools. A case study should provide valuable insights into the process whereby the categories of curricula and pupil clientele, identified by Norwood, were merged or prioritized in the comprehensive system. Rural studies had a long history of involvement in Norwood's category three, and were primarily found in secondary modern schools. The whole history of the subject had proceeded through 'a direct appeal to interests, which it would awaken by practical touch with affairs'.[11] Rural studies then hardly seemed fertile ground on which to sow the fears expressed by Marsden about a take-over by 'academic qualifications'. A curriculum case study in this area should provide evidence of how one subject was 'translated' from one sector of the tripartite system to the comprehensive. By viewing this process of translation in evolutionary profile, we can assess the curriculum values and pupil categories which were to achieve primacy in the comprehensive system.

Rural Studies: A Case Study

The Origins of Rural Studies

The origins of rural studies are both conceptually and chronologically widely spread. It is possible to distinguish two paramount themes. Firstly, were those advocates who stressed the *utilitarian* aspects of education allied to husbandry and agriculture. For instance, in 1651 Samuel Harlib proposed in his 'Essay for Advancement of Husbandry Learning' that the Science of Husbandry should be taught to apprentices.[12] Later, alongside Britain's 'agricultural revolution' in the eighteenth and early nineteenth centuries, a number of private schools began to teach agriculture. In the early nineteenth century a school at Tulketh Hall near Preston, run by G. Edmundson, included the subject, as did A. Nesbitt's School at Lambeth, then situated in London's rural environs.[13]

The second group advocated the use of the rural environment as part of an educational method: they were concerned with the *pedagogic* potential of such work. Rousseau summarized the arguments in his book *Emile,* written in 1767. He believed that nature not the classroom teacher with his formal methods should teach the child. The pedagogic implications of Rousseau's thesis were first explored practically in 1799 by Pestalozzi in his school at Burgdorf in Switzerland, and later by Froebel and Herbart in Germany.

In England where the major influence of ideas on rural reeducation was seen in the elementary schools and in their curricula, the utilitarian rather than pedagogic tradition was followed. The tradition emerged in the schools of industry set up in the last decade of the eighteenth century and related to the Poor Law system.[14] The curriculum of these schools included gardening and simple agricultural operations amongst other activities, such as tailoring and cobbling for the boys, and lace making for the girls. They were seen as vocational schools for the poorer classes.[15]

The Board of Education did later show some interest in rural studies but in 1904, when the secondary school curriculum was established by the issue of the 'Regulations', rural studies was omitted. Rural education was still taken seriously within the elementary sector with emphasis on those pupils not expected to proceed to secondary education. In keeping with this view, secondary examinations (from 1917 known as 'School Certificates') did not include rural studies.

Sample courses in rural education for elementary schools were prepared. In 1905, the Board of Education's *Handbook of Suggestions for*

Teachers produced a guide to school gardening and in 1908, a pamphlet entitled *Suggestions of Rural Education* offered specimen courses in nature study, gardening and rural economy intended to replace earlier draft courses prepared in 1901 and 1902.

The publication of a memorandum on the *Principles and Methods of Rural Education* by the Board of Education in 1911 stressed that the movement to implement rural education was designed to make teaching in rural schools:

> ... more practical, and to give it a more distinctly rural bias; to base it upon what is familiar to country children and to direct it so that they may become handy and observant in their country surroundings.[16]

The Board of Education's statistics evidence a substantial growth in school gardens:

1904–5	551 schools
1907–8	1171 schools
1911–12	2458 schools

In the latter year, twenty 'departments' of gardening or rural education are recorded.[17] Further, some counties had appointed expert instructors to organize horticulture teaching in schools, and other counties offered help for teachers to go on courses of instruction at Colleges and Institutes of Agriculture and Horticulture.[18] Alongside these developments, 'nature study' began to spread into many elementary schools. In 1902 a Nature Study Exhibition in London stimulated the growth of the subject and in the same year a Nature Study Society was formed which still exists.

The pre-war growth of rural studies in school was summarized as '... an attempt to use education to further the interests of rural industry in ways similar to those in which it was being used in the city'.[19] The most obvious methods of supporting rural industry was to retain the labour force that emerged at the age of thirteen from the elementary schools. Many of these children joined the 'drift from the land' which seriously threatened the viability of the rural economy. Fabian Ware (1900) argued that developing an interest in his natural environment through education '... would not only make a better worker of the agriculturalist, but would strengthen him morally against, at any rate, the lower attractions of town life'.[20]

This theme was reiterated in the inter-war years. In the influential circular on 'Rural Education' of May 1925, which inaugurated a new series of national and local circulars on the subject, the Board of

Education stressed that 'liking and aptitude for practical rural work are dependent on early experience, and an education which tends to debar children from gaining such experience has a definitely anti-rural bias and is liable to divert them from rural occupations.'[21]

Rural Studies in the Tripartite System

After the Second World War, two influences were particularly important in redefining rural studies, but significantly, the impact was confined to the secondary moderns. Firstly, 'stimulated by the thinking that had produced the 1944 Education Act and the secondary modern schools, teachers began to search again in our rural heritage for whatever might be used educationally to advantage'.[22] Alongside this search, 'the effect of the 1944 Act was to alter the school organization so that teaching in secondary schools became largely specialist in nature'.[23] At first, the changes in secondary organization did not radically alter the inter-war potential which rural studies had exhibited. Teachers and educationists continued to search for new educational methods of using the rural environment, and certain schools continued in focussing their whole curriculum around investigations of this environment. In 1950, A.B. Allen saw rural studies at the centre of the curriculum in country schools:

> Taking Agriculture and Horticulture as our foundation subjects, we see the inter-relationship within the curriculum. Agriculture leads into Elementary Science, General Biology, Nature Study, World History and World Geography. It also leads into Mathematics with its costing problems, mensuration and balance sheets. Horticulture leads into Elementary Science (and so is linked with Agriculture), and Local History.[24]

At the same time, the Central Advisory Council for Education (1947) was exhorting teachers: 'The first and rather obvious point is that what a school teaches should be connected with the environment. That is, the curriculum should be so designed as to interpret the environment to the boys and girls who are growing up in it.'[25] In some of the early secondary modern schools this vision of rural studies as the 'curriculum hub' connecting school to environment and life had a marked influence.

As the tripartite system of education gradually emerged in the form of new school buildings and modified curricula, it became clear that rural studies and gardening were developing solely in the secondary modern schools.

In 1957, the Hertfordshire Association of Teachers of Gardening and Rural Subjects, worried by the loss of status and influence of the subject, carried out a survey. Questionnaires were sent only to secondary modern schools. The financial treatment of rural studies showed clearly that by this time the priorities of secondary modern headmasters had moved away from rural studies towards other subjects. 'It is surprising to learn ... that some schools allow the Rural Studies department no money at all while others are so small that the financial pinch entails great worry to the teacher.'[26]

Of the thirty-nine schools that returned questionnaires, fifteen had no classroom allotted for rural studies. 'Generally the standard of provision for rural subjects appears to be below that of other practical subjects. Few schools are equipped satisfactorily with the items required for a good horticultural or agricultural course at secondary school level'.[27] Of the fifty-three teachers involved, 26 were unqualified in gardening or rural studies.[28]

Promoting the Subject: Early Initiatives

From the late 1950s onwards rural studies' position in the secondary moderns rapidly deteriorated (as illustrated in the 1957 survey). This was largely because of the take-up of specialist examinations within secondary moderns, more parents began to realize that certification led to better jobs, teachers found examinations a useful source of motivation and heads began to use examinations as a means of raising their schools' reputation and status.

For some heads, support for GCE may have stemmed from an initial rebellious non-acceptance of the whole tripartite philosophy. But soon 'success in this examination started a national avalanche'.[29] By 1961–63, when Partridge studies a secondary modern school, the competitive nature of the 'examination race' was clearly apparent: 'With the public demand for academic attainments, reflecting the fact that education has become the main avenue of social mobility in our society, GCE successes would immeasurably enhance the repute of such a school, and hence the standing and status of the headmaster.'[30]

The take-up of GCE and a wide range of other examinations in secondary moderns led to an exhaustive inquiry by the Ministry of Education which culminated in the Beloe Report. As a result of the

Report's recommendations in 1965 the CSE (Certificate of Secondary Education) was inaugurated. The growing emphasis of specialist subject examinations and their effects on rural studies in the secondary modern are a harbinger of the patterns which emerged later in the comprehensive schools. But the debates which finally pushed the subject towards specialist examination took place in the mid-sixties when the comprehensive system was being rapidly developed.

By this time rural studies teachers were beginning to respond to the dual challenges posed by the spread of specialist examinations and the prospects of comprehensivization. The first response was the formation of a National Rural Studies Association to promote rural studies as a specialist subject worthy of 'parity of esteem'. The inaugural meeting was in 1960 when six County Associations that had been formed previously met together to form the Association. By 1961, eleven new County Rural Studies Associations had been formed and affiliated.

The second response was to scrutinize the whole question of examinations, particularly the new CSE. By 1962, Carson had realized that the National Association could never get 'parity of esteem' for the subject without accepting external examinations. The spread of the CSE drew attention to the dilemma that faced advocates of rural studies. A good deal of the energies of the association centred on gaining more facilities, time and better qualified staff for the subject. But in the increasingly exam-conscious secondary moderns, little success could be hoped for in a non-examinable subject. To break out of the cycle of deprivation faced by the subject the only way forward seemed to be in defining an examinable area. By 1962, Carson had realized the cul-de-sac which the National Association's efforts had entered:

> We never forgot our aims were to see this subject get taught to *all* children ... that facilities should be better, etc. Then it became increasingly obvious to me and one or two others, that it wasn't going to get anywhere! That however many good ideals we might have, in fact it was not going to be realized.

As a result the Association initiated a major experiment by which to test a new rural studies exam. The experiment was reported in the Herts journal:

> Following a meeting of representatives of Rural Study Associations, the panel of HM Inspectors for Rural Studies and Dr. Wrigley of the Curriculum Study Group of the Ministry of

Education, a joint experiment has been held in schools in North Hertfordshire, Nottinghamshire, Staffordshire, Lincolnshire and East Sussex to test the validity of sections of our examination scheme. This is being evaluated by the Ministry of Education's Study Group.[31]

Sean Carson was involved in the experiment:

It was an attempt to find out whether exams were a good thing. We were trying to find out whether we should remain outside or whether we should have anything to do with them.

The moves to devise an examination in the subject posed a number of problems for rural studies. For behind the rhetoric of the advocates and subject associations, and apart from a few innovatory schools and teachers, most rural studies teachers continued in basing their work on gardening. The subject's essentially practical assignments were not easily evaluated by written examinations.

Preparing for the Comprehensive School

The formation of a national association for the specialist subject of rural studies and the scrutiny of external examinations were to be the watershed in the development of Rural Studies. Sean Carson, who had set up the meeting which founded the National Association, had now emerged as a leading spokesman for the subject and, in 1958, was appointed as organizer for Rural Education in Hertfordshire.

In embracing the specialist subject the National Association played a symbolic role:

The object of that (forming the association) was really to raise the status of rural studies and get the facilities for the subject which other subjects got. For example, we used to constantly compare what was given to cookery, metalwork and woodwork, and we had got practically nothing whereas they had properly equipped classrooms...

This is what we set out to do and we achieved it to a certain extent, but the situation was never there to achieve any more than that it was specialism in a school and should be adequately supported.

Carson's final sentence here summarizes the situation which rural studies had come to occupy by 1957. As the Kent Journal noted, 'with the building of large secondary schools within the last few years, full-time specialists are needed'.[32] Rural studies was just one of a range of specialisms in the secondary modern schools. Moreover, it was of low status and historically poorly organized.

But if the fact of becoming a specialist subject was now inevitable the kind of subject was still the matter of urgent debate among rural studies teachers, advisers and the Inspectorate. In this debate we see the potential utilitarian and practical (and to some extent the optimistically pedagogic 'rural education') traditions within the subject facing the implication of joining in the process of academic certification. The whole genesis, evolution, intentions and practice of rural studies made the subject uniquely ill-suited to playing this role whether in the secondary moderns or in the comprehensive school.

The early reports were outspokenly frank about this. The first report on the possibility of a CSE in rural studies stated that: 'Rural studies teachers are by nature opposed to the competitive and restrictive aspects of examinations in school'. But more specifically a practical subject like rural studies was utterly unsuited to a mode of written examination borrowed from academic grammar school subjects. To set examinations of this sort amounted to a renunciation of the very intentions of the subject and of the pupil clientele for whom it had historically catered. The reports drawn up by rural studies teachers put the problem of the renunciation of subject tradition as diplomatically as possible: 'Few examinations included much practical work and rarely was there any assessment of the candidate's practical ability and achievement over a period of time'.[33] These examinations produced 'unfavourable backwash effects in the teaching of rural studies': 'In order to produce candidates who would be successful in the written examination, teachers felt that they had to concentrate on written work to the neglect of practical activities which are the essential features of rural studies'.[34]

Following the 1965 circular, the pace of comprehensive reorganization began to quicken. With respect to examinations the debate was speedily transformed from an uncertain response to the suitability of written examination at CSE to a realization that in fact only an even more basic reorientation to 'O' and even 'A' level would ensure survival.

Confined within the secondary modern school sector, rural studies was especially vulnerable to comprehensive reorganization. In 1966 the NRSA Journal carried its first report on the 'The Place of Rural Studies in the Comprehensive System', produced by a working party set up at the Spring, 1966 Conference of Wiltshire Teachers of Rural

Studies. The report began by explaining why such a working party had been thought necessary:

> There are many reasons. At the present time schools are facing reorganization. The eleven plus examination is rapidly being swept away: the Plowden report is imminent, and the primary school age-range may be extended to 12. The secondary school, as we know it today, will merge into a comprehensive school from 12 to 18 years, giving greater opportunities for rural and environmental studies of a scientific nature and the opportunity to examine measures needed for the full enjoyment of the countryside, and the protection of its natural beauty.
>
> Some grammar schools are still tied to rather rigid 'O' and 'A' level Biology syllabuses, and these changes may well provide the opportunity to break away from old concepts and embrace a more liberal approach through practical experience in rural studies in accordance with the ideals of the Nuffield Schemes.
>
> The need for more and well-trained rural studies teachers is greater than it has ever been. It depends, therefore, on the interest aroused in young people in grammar and comprehensive schools as to whether the college of education and universities receive the right type of student to undertake this quite specialized training.

For these reasons the Wiltshire teachers concluded rural studies 'has much to offer as a subject in its own right in the comprehensive system of education'.[35]

Within the report, there is some evidence that the Wiltshire teachers were extremely concerned about the fate of their subject in the comprehensive school. The change to comprehensives was taking place against a background of decline in the subject which had begun in some areas in the late 1950s.[36] By the early 1960s, Sean Carson saw the decline setting in in Hertfordshire: 'it was already happening inside some schools. Where a teacher was leaving, they didn't fill the place, because they gave it to someone in the examination set up'. In 1966, the Wiltshire teachers were advising:

> The urgent necessity is for us to persuade teachers and Education Authorities that the omission of the facilities for teaching rural studies in new schools and in buildings which are being

adapted to a comprehensive form of education would be a mistake.[37]

The problem was partly explained by the fact that:

> ... as many of the new heads of comprehensive schools were being appointed from grammar school backgrounds these heads had little or no experience of the value of rural studies in the education of the secondary child. Because of this lack of knowledge, rural studies as an examination subject was being equated with rural biology, agricultural science or even pure biology. In addition there was little demand for rural studies as a post 'O' level subject.[38]

The teachers themselves saw clear evidence of broad-based decline and, by November 1967, one was writing of a 'general air of defeatism among rural studies teachers'.[39] A Hertfordshire teacher recalled this period:

> A few years back, rural studies was being phased out ... it was getting itself a poor name ... it was ... you know, losing face ... it was being regarded as not the subject we want in this up-and-going day and age. And we had awful difficulty in getting examining boards and universities to accept it at 'O' level and 'A' level ... mainly because of its content ... I could see that I was going to have to phase out rural studies because the demand for it in the school was going down ... it was being squeezed out in the timetable and the demand for it at options level in the fourth year was going down.[40]

Not only was rural studies less in demand but those areas of the curriculum where the subject may have expanded were being taken over the other subject specialists. In the comprehensives, rural studies was often not included or was being confined to the 'less able'. In a position of rapidly falling demand and closing options, rural studies was faced with extinction, certainly in those countries where comprehensive education was rapidly pursued. Carson, in Hertfordshire, was convinced that rural studies was 'a dead duck', 'it would rapidly have disappeared' and Topham, who was later to devise an 'A' level, thought that at this time rural studies 'was finished'.

Whither Rural Studies: Practical Subject or Academic Discipline?

The inauguration of CSE's and the rapid changeover to comprehensive schooling meant that rural studies was engulfed by a rapidly changing situation which threatened the very survival of the subject. On one point, those seeking subject promotion now began to focus: what was needed was not just a new 'emphasis' or even a specialist subject, but a discipline. The rhetorical requirement of a discipline symbolized the dual purpose of redefinition — a new synthesis of knowledge but also one which afforded higher status and could be offered to a new clientele covering a higher ability spectrum than the previous clientele for whom CSE was the highest aspiration.

Sean Carson, whose research at Manchester was initially concerned with the CSE, began in the autumn of 1966, to perceive the need for 'a discipline' of rural studies for the following reasons:

> The lack of a clear definition of an area of study as a discipline has often been a difficulty for local authorities in deciding what facilities to provide and more recently in having rural studies courses at colleges of education accepted for the degree of BEd. by some universities. It has been one of the reasons for the fact that no 'A' level courses in rural studies exists at present.[41]

Further, in commenting on the Report of the Study Group on Education and Field Biology, he noted: 'because rural studies was not recognized as a discipline at any academic level, even at 'O' level, the Group were prevented from giving it serious consideration'.[42]

Carson's judgments were passed on to the Schools Council Working Party on Rural Studies set up in 1965 who reiterated them in the report to the Council of June, 1968. The working party perceived 'the need for a scholarly discipline'. The discipline would spread 'across the present system of specialization' and might 'take the form of an integrated course of study based upon environmental experience in which rural studies has a part to play'.[43] This recommendation hinted at a change of title from rural studies to environmental studies which was to emerge later.

The most common pattern for defining new 'disciplines' of knowledge in the essentially hierarchical education system in England has been through the work of university scholars. Unfortunately, at this time, there was very little academic activity in this field for the rural studies advocates to build upon.

Since a new disciplinary definition of rural or environmental studies was not forthcoming from scholars in the higher education sector the process of definition had to be undertaken at the secondary level as an 'A' level subject. One of the pioneers of the 'A' level syllabus later claimed that the process of curriculum development undertaken:

> ... is schools-based and is the result of initiatives taken together by practising teachers with the support of their local authority. Such self-generated work offers a viable way of developing an area of the curriculum.[44]

Thus, in the schools-based model the academic discipline is developed because classroom teachers perceive the need for a new area of knowledge and then set about involving academics in its construction.

The growing perception of such a need among rural studies teachers can be discerned from the beginning of 1967. In February, 1967, Mervyn Prichard as Secretary of the Research and Development Sub-Committee of the National Rural Studies Association reported that: 'There was some difficulty in impressing the intellectual content of the subject', and that the sub-committee: '... wanted to discover how rural studies experience can help students with gaining entry to colleges of education, and what value post 'O' level qualifications in rural studies would have for this purpose'. In the discussion which followed this report, John Pullen, HMI, said 'Several questions required answering', among them:

> Do we consider an 'A' level course should be included in rural studies?

> What do we do about the reaction, 'We do not want people with 'A' level in rural studies?

> What parts of rural studies should be treated as aspects of other disciplines?

At the same meeting the Policy Committee reported that a subcommittee had been formed 'to find existing curricula for able children, leading to at least 'O' level in the rural studies field' and 'To produce evidence that there is a need for rural studies up to 'O' level, ie. to show that the subject is of benefit to able pupils'.[45]

In March, a 'statement of evidence' was presented by the National Association to the Schools Council Working Party on Rural Studies. The definition of rural studies advocated was almost identical to that established in Carson's Manchester research:

The study of the landscape, its topography, geology and pedology, the ecological relationship of the plants and animals naturally present, together with the study of man's control of this natural environment through agriculture, horticulture and forestry.[46]

In advocating this definition of rural studies and adding as an objective 'The development of an awareness and appreciation of the natural surroundings' the National Association contended:

There is a growing demand for examinations at 'O' and 'A' level based upon the studies described ... we are certain that if such examinations are introduced they will be used increasingly.

Finally, they asserted that the content which they had defined 'provides a unified and clear area of study and a valuable academic discipline'.[47]

At this time, a small group of HM Inspectors interested in rural studies, among them John Pullen, also saw a need for a discipline of rural studies in schools. They argued (1967) in an article published in the house journal, *Trends*:

A broad interpretation of rural studies in school should mean that pupils will have experienced work which calls for disciplined study to acquire a structured body of knowledge about the countryside, entering into many of the familiar subjects of the curriculum.[48]

The HMI's saw such rural studies work as potentially examinable at 'A' level:

Work now being attempted at many schools could justifiably claim to reach this level. It is true that some schools with strongly developed rural studies courses find, as one might expect, that older pupils turn very naturally and successfully to 'A' level courses in chemistry, biology and geography and often gain university entrance on the standards they have achieved. Nevertheless, the time appears to be ripe for the introduction of 'A' level courses in agriculture, agricultural science, and in the wider field of rural studies.[49]

The changeover to comprehensives precipitated a number of teachers who had previously worked with CSE to define rural studies at 'O' and 'A' level. The 1968 NRSA Journal noted that schools in Yorkshire, Nottinghamshire and Hertfordshire were campaigning for such exams.[50] Reporting on 'Rural Studies in the Comprehensive School', Topham argued that 'Rural studies should be so organized within the comprehensive school that no child, boy or girl, of whatever ability, is denied the opportunity to participate'.[51] The rural studies teachers in a comprehensive school should aim to offer:

(a) a course leading to an 'O' level GCE
(b) a course leading to CSE
(c) an integral course
(d) to participate in a general studies course
(e) a course leading to the 'A' level GCE and when established to a certificate of further secondary education.

Consequently, 'in a large comprehensive school one can envisage generous allocation of staff to the department'.[52]

The Schools Council Working Party on Rural Studies had reported that one of the paramount problems facing teachers of the subject was dealt with in the section on 'status': 'there is no doubt that a substantial proportion of rural studies teachers do find themselves in a difficult position because of the demanding nature of the task the lack of ancillary help, and the attitude which regards the subject as a sublimating exercise for the less able'.[53] Elsewhere the report noted: 'The old concept of the subject predominantly as gardening, often gardening for the backward boys only, did not die easily'.[54] The remedy for this situation was clearly perceived: 'Examinations in rural studies have helped to improve the image of the subject and to give it a certain status in the eyes of the pupils and their parents. Acceptable 'A' levels could raise the status still further'.[55]

By the late 1960s, rural studies faced a dilemma: the choice was clear but bitter in its implications. Within the comprehensive schools the subject was in sharp decline, its very survival turning on whether it could be presented and accepted as a valid academic qualification. But its practitioners were in large majority trained and aligned to a concept of rural education which was above all practical in orientation. To embrace academic examination meant a stark renunciation of the very intentions of the subject, a renunciation of its traditional pupil clientele. In effect, its teachers were being asked to renounce their priority commitment to this style of learning and to this group, Norwood's category 3, in favour of a style of examination suited to a different mode of learning and pupil clientele, Norwood's category 1. To not renunciate would be to face extinction.

The period is so fascinating because of the wealth of evidence that at the time the teachers knew precisely what was at stake: they knew the renunciation that was being demanded. The following short article written in 1967 for the *Hertfordshire Rural Studies Journal* by Mr. P.L. Quant of Baas Hill Secondary Modern School summarizes the stark reality of the choice and speaks for significant sections of rural studies teachers who saw the implications of the suggested changes:

> What has been forgotten in our exuberance to thrust forward rural studies as an examinable subject is the mainspring of its very creation. This is the joy, experience, and most of all, the practical and useful scientific logic which is gained during the release from far-sighted concepts which many other subjects tend to involve themselves in. Many will agree with me in saying that the children who gain most of all from rural studies are the academically less-able. Many have little concern about the world they are about to enter and fumble without understanding about the usefulness of schooling.
>
> These are the children who can be intrigued by practical and concrete concepts, the only things in which they show real signs of involvement. Lesson material is quite often spontaneous, and is the basis of asking by the teacher — 'But what would happen if —?' and a scientific line of related research is born.
>
> But there is no doubt that in our efforts to maintain our status in the looming inevitability of the comprehensive school — indeed our very existence — we have dragged the 'Science is our Leader' concept out of the cut and thrust of rural studies teaching to replace it by a syllabus of scientific detail which is chaining us down. Once again, we can see the unwanted children of lower intelligence being made servants of the juggernaut of documented evidence, the inflated examination.
>
> However, I must give credit to the examination as far as it deals with the more able child. The strict division according to intelligence at 11+ is not justifiable, and our secondary schools are shining in their ability to produce pupils apt enough to gain academic credit in many recognized academic studies, and who do credit also to rural studies, from an examinable standpoint. Indeed, many schools are showing what a good subject rural studies can be for these children. Long may it remain so.

> But I do not think my fears are entirely groundless. The state needs to tap the resources of schools with increasing urgency, and consequently the new schools will be expected to fill their halls at speech day with the successes they have turned out. But what praise for the unintelligent now? Are we to make a mockery of our Mode three liberty in order to gloss over the realities of this urgent problem?
>
> True education is not for every man the scrap of paper he leaves school with. Dare we as teachers admit this? Dare we risk our existence by forcibly expressing our views on this? While we pause after the first phase of our acceptance, are we to rely on exams for all, to prove ourselves worthy of the kindly eye of the state? Dare we allow to leave some of our charges who have been once more neglected and once more squeezed into a forgotten heap of frustrating unimportance?
>
> My knowledge of rural studies teachers leads me to say how lively and stimulating they are in their enthusiasm for the subject. Then let us not shirk from the sum total of our responsibility towards *all* our children.[56]

In fact the points made by Quant were privately conceded by the main advocates of academic examinations who were so influential in causing the National Rural Studies Association to move rapidly to embrace the academic discipline route to better resources and status. Topham, whose course became the model for the 'A' level in environmental studies, said at the time 'I firmly believe that success in examinations is not really indicative of the value of any subject and this is especially true of rural studies.' Likewise, Carson felt 'by embracing academic examinations we forever abandoned the aim of education for *all'*.

Embracing the Academic Examinations: The Price of Comprehensivization

From the acknowledgement among rural studies advocates advisers, the Inspectorate and Schools Council that a 'scholarly discipline' was needed, events moved rapidly. A range of 'O' levels in rural and environmental studies were devised and accepted by a number of examination boards. Other initiatives aimed to develop 'A' levels in rural studies, most notably in Hertfordshire and Wiltshire.[57] The Hertfordshire 'A' level began in Shepalbury School in Hertfordshire in 1967 where the rural studies teacher, Paul Topham, with the strong support of the head, Dr. Jack Kitching set about devising an 'A' level. Both felt rural studies had outlived its usefulness. The headmaster had not previously encountered the subject and saw little use for such a practical subject aimed only at the less able. By now in this new comprehensive: 'everyone was very much concerned with achievement and what bit of paper was going to unlock the golden gate to college, university and employment'.[58] Topham devised a prospective 'A' level course which was circulated in February 1967 to universities, colleges and professional bodies. Initially, the response was rather unfavourable but the proposal gained new momentum when Paul Topham became an advisory teacher under Sean Carson. By this time Carson was convinced that rural studies could achieve new status by aligning itself with the new 'environmental lobby'. The National Rural Studies Association had that year, very much at Carson's initiative, embraced the new title environmental studies (in 1971 it became the National Association of Environmental Education). The new title, like the aspiration to become a scholarly discipline, summarized the desire to leave for ever the low status enclave of traditional rural studies in favour of a new well-financed niche as an 'A' level subject.

Topham and Carson developed a strategy for an environmental studies 'A' level using Topham's original rural studies 'A' level Proposal. Topham was clear on the rationale for this:

> Well, at that point I think we had got to prove a lot of things. I think that we had got to prove that environmental studies was something that the most able of students could achieve and to do something with it . . . if you started off there all the expertise and finance that you put into it will benefit the rest — your teaching ratio goes up, etc. and everyone else benefits — the side effects that people don't mention sometimes.[59]

To establish environmental studies in this way a new strategy was evolved:

> So we decided we should be at 'A' level . . . that we should think up the right syllabus and then that we should being together the teachers of Hertfordshire, examine it, critically examine it, develop it . . . take advice from people . . . so we did this, there was the first meeting of the Working Party.[60]

Sean Carson adds a number of reasons for the founding of the Working Party of Hertfordshire teachers:

> In talking to Paul, we decided that the only way to make progress was to get in on the examination racket ... we must draw up an examination... We decided that the exam was essential because otherwise you couldn't be equal with any other subject. Another thing was that comprehensive education was coming in. Once that came in, no teacher who didn't teach in the fifth or sixth form was going to count for twopence. So you had to have an 'A' level for teachers to aim at.[61]

The Hertfordshire Working Party duly completed the construction of an 'A' level syllabus after detailed consultation with a range of academics, advisers, inspectors and examination board officials. The proposed 'A' level now encountered fierce opposition from the Geographers in particular. Their opposition was mounted both within the examination boards to whom the 'A' level was submitted and then in Schools Council subject sub-committees. Above all, the opposition turned on whether Environmental Studies was really a 'discipline', especially as it had no subject scholars based in universities:

> With no prospects of a scholarly discipline of environmental studies coming from the universities, the Hertfordshire advocates were even forced into attempting to define 'a discipline' from school level. This allowed opponents of the new subject, whilst broadly conceding its value to the young and less able, consistently to deny that it could be viewed as in any sense a 'scholarly discipline'.[62]

The result of the subject opposition was to deny environmental studies 'A' level any chance of broad-based take-up. In the event two 'experimental' 'A' levels were agreed but they were not to be taken with geography. The subject groups 'filibuster' delayed acceptance until 1973 when much of the momentum of the environmental lobby had passed.

The rural studies advocates, having finally indicated their willingness to renunciate their practical origins in favour of 'O' levels and especially 'A' levels in environmental studies, were thereby blocked at the last hurdle. The new subject was left somewhat in limbo with the range of new 'O' levels, which had been accepted, but without the unequivocal 'A' level status that would have finally ensure the finance, resources and high-status careers that were so urgently sought.

Comprehensive Schools, Divisive Exams

The evolution of rural studies presents us with a range of insights into the curriculum values and pupil categories which achieved primacy in the comprehensive school. The subject moved from utilitarian and practical origins through a similar pattern in the early secondary modern period (alongside a small minority of innovative schools built on the practical tradition to develop an integrated model of rural education) towards an embrace of academic examinations in the comprehensive school. The sudden renunciation of the practical and utilitarian heritage of rural studies and its traditional pupil clientele was because 'if you didn't, you wouldn't get any money, and status, and intelligent kids!'[63]

Within the comprehensive schools, a clear hierarchy of school subjects developed. The hierarchy was based on the primacy of grammar school subjects which were naturally given priority by the grammar school staff who largely took over the headships and head of department posts. But the hierarchy was crucially underpinned by patterns of resource allocation. As was mentioned in chapter 3, Byrne (1974) has shown how this took place on the basis of assumptions that 'academic' subjects are suitable for 'able' students whilst other subjects were not. She noted that the primacy of academic grammar school subjects was not challenged after comprehensivization. There was, she said, 'little indication that a majority of councils or chief officers accept in principle the need for review and reassessment of the entire process of allocation of resources'.[64] Hence, the 'academic' grammar school subjects and 'able' pupil clienteles continued to enjoy financial priority after comprehensive reorganization. Separatism of buildings was eliminated, separatism of curricula maintained.

The curricular implications of this academic dominance can be readily viewed in the case of rural studies. Rural studies advocates were persuaded by the structuring of material interests and career prospects to renunciate their practical, utilitarian origins and traditional clientele. The promoters of rural studies showed no inclination or interest in defining a new common curriculum for all abilities of pupil. There was no effort to develop an 'alternative road' leading in an integrated manner from the practical to the academic. From the beginnings of comprehensive reorganization, rural studies was in flight from its practical origins and clientele towards as new 'academic scholarly discipline' that would ensure finance, resources, the subject's survival and the teachers' careers. For the teachers, the renunciation of their traditional pupil clientele was the price for survival and status improvement in the comprehensive school.

But for many pupils the domination of all comprehensive curricula by academic examination subjects was to have severe implications. Paradoxically the secondary moderns, though rooted in the realities of the class structure, training working class children for working class jobs did have considerable freedom in the curricular means they employed. The ends were clear, the means more variable. In the comprehensives both ends and means were closely structured and defined. The secondary moderns, on balance, provided more potential for identity and commitment for Norwood's category 3 than was ever to be allowed in the comprehensive. The comprehensive schools' embrace of the meritocratic vision of academic hierarchy postulated, as rural studies shows, instant renunciation for Norwood's category 3.

Ongoing governmental concern for the 'bottom forty per cent' responds to a situation which arises less from intrinsic pupil problems than from the systematic production of an under-class by the curriculum structures embraced by comprehensive schools:

> For lower ability children, the majority of whom would have been attending in the past incorporative secondary moderns, the new comprehensives have, clearly, been a different experience. Except for some of those in the middle third of the ability range that may have been enticed into acquiescence and acceptance of the comprehensives through the schools' promise of examination success, these lower ability pupils would have been experiencing an atmosphere more alienating than in the secondary moderns ... they are likely to experience higher levels of coercive strategies, such as physical punishment, and are also likely to experience strict rule enforcement.[65]

Clearly the examination structure exacerbates the problem. Examinations not only distort the curriculum but also increase problems because examination groups get more than their fair share of resources. Sorting pupils into examination and non-examination groups early in their secondary career leads to disaffection among the non-exam pupils which shows itself in absenteeism, disruptive behaviour and lack of motivation.

As in the tripartite system, so in the comprehensive system, academic subjects for able pupils are accorded the highest status and resources. The triple alliance between academic subjects, academic examinations and able pupils ensures that comprehensive schools provide similar patterns of success and failure to previous school systems. For the teachers who have to cater for all kinds of pupils this concentration on a particular kind of pupil and a particular kind of educational success poses the same dilemma voiced by the rural studies teacher in 1967 in the face of the 'looming inevitability of the comprehensive school': 'True education is not for every man the scrap of paper he leaves with. Dare we as teachers admit this? Dare we risk our existence by formerly expressing our views on this?' This case study of rural studies provides a definitive answer to his questions.

Notes and References

1 KERR, J. 'The problem of curriculum reform' in HOOPER, R. (Ed), *The Curriculum Context, Design and Development*, (Edinburgh, Oliver and Boyd, 1971).

2 RUBINSTEIN, D. and SIMON, B. *The Evolution of the Comprehensive School 1926–1972*, (London, Routledge and Kegan Paul, 1975).

3 DES *Organisation of Secondary Education*, Circular 10/65, (London, HMSO, 1965) p. 1.

4 *Ibid.*

5 SHIPMAN, M. 'Curriculum for inequality', in HOOPER, R. (Ed), (1971), pp. 101–102.

6 *Ibid.*, p. 104.

7 The Norwood Report, *Curriculum and Examinations in Secondary School*, (London, HMSO, 1943) p. 2.

8 *Ibid.*, p. 3.

9 *Ibid.*, p. 6.

10 MARSDEN, D. *Politicians, Equality and Comprehensives*, T. 411, (London, Fabian Society, 1971) p. 26.

11 *op. cit.*, The Norwood Report, p. 6.

12 ADAMSON, J.W. *Pioneers of Modern Education 1600–1700*, (1951) pp. 130–131.

13 HUDSPETH, W.H. *The History of the Teaching of Biological Subjects including Nature Study in English schools since 1900*, (M.Ed. Thesis, University of Durham, 1962) pp. 69–70.

14 The Poor Law Act was passed in 1834.

15 CARSON, S. *The Use and Content and Effective Objectives in Rural Studies Courses*, (M.Ed. Thesis, University of Manchester, 1967) p. 4.

16 BOARD of EDUCATION Memorandum on the *Principle and Methods of Rural Education*, (1911) p. 7.

17 BOARD of EDUCATION *Report for 1904–1939*, (London, HMSO, 1939).

18 BOARD of EDUCATION *Report for 1910–1911*, (London, HMSO, 1911).

19 SELLECK, R.J.W. *The New Education: The English Background 1870–1914*, (Melbourne, Pitman, 1968) p. 150.

20 WARE, F. *Educational Reform*, (London, Methuen, 1900) p. 62.

21 BOARD of EDUCATION *Rural Education* Circular 1365, (London, HMSO, 1925).
22 CARSON, S. and COLTON, R. *The Teaching of Rural Studies*, (London, Edward Arnold, 1962) p. 3.
23 SCHOOLS COUNCIL WORKING PAPER 24: *Rural Studies in Secondary Schools*, (London, Evans/Methuen Education, 1969) p. 5.
24 ALLEN, A.B. *Rural Education*, (London, Allman and Sons, 1950) p. 16.
25 Report of the Central Advisory Council for Education, *England School and Life*, (London, HMSO, 1947) p. 35.
26 Report on *Rural Subjects and Gardening in Secondary Schools in Hertfordshire*, (Mimeo, 1957).
27 *Ibid.*
28 *Ibid.*
29 GIBBERD, K. *No Place Like School*, (London, Michael Joseph, 1962) p. 103.
30 PARTRIDGE, J. *Life in a Secondary Modern School*, (Harmondsworth, Pelican, 1968) p. 68.
31 *Hertfordshire Teachers Rural Studies Association Journal*, October 1963.
32 *Journal of the Kent Association of Teachers of Gardening and Rural Science*, April 1953, September 1958, p. 1.
33 Rural Studies Draft Report: *The Certificate of Secondary Education Experimental Examination*, (Mimeo).
34 *Ibid.*
35 *National Rural Studies Association Journal*, 1966, pp. 31–32.
36 *Ibid.*, p. 36.
37 *National Rural Studies Association Journal*, 1961–1970.
38 *Ibid.*
39 George Wing to Sean Carson 12 November, 1965.
40 Interview with Gordon Battey, Hertfordshire teacher, 8 November 1975.
41 *op. cit.*, Carson.
42 *op. cit.*, p. 135.
43 *op. cit.*, Carson, M.Ed., p. 61.
44 CARSON, S. (Ed), *Environmental Studies. The Construction of an 'A' Level Syllabus*, (Slough, NFER, 1971) pp. 7–8.
45 *op. cit.*, NRSA.
46 *op. cit.*, Carson, p. 369.
47 *op. cit.*, NRSA. (1968) p. 38.
48 *Trends in Education*, (London, DES, October 1967), (article on 'Rural Studies in Schools').
49 *Ibid.*
50 *op. cit.*, NRSA, p. 44.
51 *Ibid.*, p. 45.
52 *Ibid.*, p. 46.
53 *op. cit.*, Schools Council Working Paper 24, p. 15.
54 *Ibid.*, p. 5.
55 *Ibid.*, p. 12.
56 QUANT, P.L. 'Rural studies and Newsom courses', *Hertfordshire Rural Studies Journal*, (1967) pp. 11–13.

57 *op. cit.*, Carson (Ed), 1971.
58 Interviews with Paul Topham, 1975, 1976.
59 *Ibid.*, Topham.
60 *Ibid.*, Topham.
61 Interviews with Sean Carson, 1975, 1976, 1977.
62 GOODSON, I.F. *School Subjects and Curriculum Change*, (London, Croom Helm, 1983) p. 97.
63 *op. cit.*, Carson interview.
64 BYRNE, E.M. *Planning and Educational Inequality*, (Slough, NFER, 1974).
65 REYNOLDS, D. and SULLIVAN, M. 'The comprehensive experience' in BARTON, L. and WALKER, S. (Eds) *Schools, Teachers and Teaching*, (Lewes, Falmer Press, 1981) p. 44.

9 The Micropolitics of Curriculum Change: European Studies

European Studies: The Micropolitics of Curriculum Evolution

Whilst the foregoing chapters in the book have focussed on individual teacher's careers and life histories and on the history of curriculum conflict at subject group or university level, this chapter examines such conflict at school level. Many innovations are schools-based and attempts to generalize them and to create a wider 'structure' of change have to grapple with the problems experienced and perceived at school level. If such problems are substantial, innovations are often 'contained' within the school and curriculum conflict remains local and idiosyncratic. One example of a new curriculum 'subject' which developed in the 1960s was European Studies. Its subsequent development offers an opportunity to scrutinize the history of a 'contained' school innovation over two decades.

The concern in this chapter is less with the historical understanding of how European Studies was structurally contained but more with how this containment was received and perceived by teachers of the subject. This pattern of reception and perception is, of course, part of the story of containment — for hostility at individual school level (and associated problems at personal career level) can defuse attempts to achieve broader structural changes in curriculum.

European Studies: Historical Background

European Studies emerged as a fashionable curriculum innovation in the 1960s and originated from two quite unconnected events. Firstly, the growth of a movement aiming to develop European unity and

European consciousness. In the forefront of this movement were agencies like the European Commission and the Council of Europe. For instance a resolution passed by the Ministers' Deputies of the Council of Europe in October 1966 stated that 'at a time when Europe is becoming a reality it is the imperative duty of secondary education to inculcate into its pupils an awareness of European facts and problems'.[1] Essentially the messiahs of the new Europe were concerned to encourage an awareness of the Common European heritage. The European governments associated with the European Cultural Convention in 1966 were exhorted to 'do everything within their power to ensure that all disciplines concerned — for instance history, geography, literature, modern languages — contribute to the creation of a European consciousness'.[2]

Secondly, the re-organization of the English secondary school system and associated changes in the curriculum encouraged the growth of European Studies. The 1960s were a time of rapid change with the spread of the comprehensive system throughout the country. Interdisciplinary and integrated approaches were an important element in the curriculum reforms initiated in the 1960s to meet the new pedagogical demands of the comprehensive schools and the associated changes to mixed ability to ROSLA (1972).

As a solution to the problems engendered by the didactic teaching of traditional subjects in these new comprehensive classes curriculum reform groups such as the Goldsmiths team advocated organizing schemes of work around interdisciplinary enquiries:

> We suggest ENQUIRY as the basic concept. We suggest this not merely as a technique but as the essence of the curriculum. Subject teaching to a syllabus restricts enquiry by the pupils. It is the teacher who has been creative, in making up the syllabus; what he has created then becomes the content of the syllabus, which is then *taught to* the class. Even if the teacher demonstrates the interrelationships of his subject with others at particular points it is he who is being creative, not the children. The children are merely being *taught*.

> Teaching a theme embracing a number of subjects, despite its greater freedom, has the same limitations. It does not do what is essential to shift the emphasis from *instructing* to *active exploring*.[3]

Another curriculum project aimed at young school leavers underlined both the need to reappraise 'subjects' and to clearly define new pedagogic relationships. The Humanities Curriculum Project (HCP) began in 1967 with Lawrence Stenhouse as its director. HCP pursued the pedagogic implications of curriculum reform through the notion of 'neutral chairmanship'. This meant: 'that the teacher accepts the need to submit his teaching in controversial areas to the criterion of neutrality ... ie. that he regards it as part of this responsibility not to promote his own view', and further that: 'the mode of enquiry in controversial areas should have discussion, rather than instructions as its core'.[4]

   Alongside new definitions of pedagogy were new strategies for their implementation. Most commonly, 'team teaching' was seen as a mechanism for conducting enquiry-based or thematic, integrated studies. David Warwick's (1972) book *Team Teaching* states that 'team teaching' and 'integrated studies' are very closely linked and argues that a new organizational format is replacing the subject-based curriculum:

> Most subjects have two or three single periods each week. They cannot spare the time for ... experimentation and if they could, forty minutes is totally inadequate. The practice of one man, one class, inevitably leads to departments often even individual teachers, working in complete isolation...
>
> ... A whole new approach is coming into being. It entails complete afternoons given over to realistic fieldwork of all kinds, the availability of two or more members of staff simultaneously involved in one project: a breaking away from the conventional form of classroom divisions; and a 'blocking' of the school timetable to give the facilities and space required. It is a process that seeks to cast off the concept of the teacher as the '2-4-7 man' — someone most at home within the two covers of a text book the four walls of a classroom and the seven periods of a school day.[5]

   At the very time European Studies teachers were seeing integrated or interdisciplinary courses as the strategy for establishing their subject, other voices were warning of the dangers inherent in the curriculum forms then being pursued. In 1969, Marten Shipman was warning about a new 'curriculum for inequality'[6], but a year later at the British Sociological Association conference, Michael Young extended Shipman's analysis, linking his two 'traditions' to status patterns inside the educational system. The academic tradition represented 'high-status knowledge' and the newer traditions 'low-status knowledge'. High status knowledge tended to be 'abstract, highly literate, individualistic and unrelated to non-school knowledge'. Low status knowledge was organized in direct contradiction to this pattern and was normally available only 'to those who have already 'failed' in terms of academic definitions of knowledge'.[7]

Languages and the Comprehensive School — the Genesis of European Studies

The continuing division in British curricula between the two notions of 'the able' and the 'less able' is strongly in evidence when considering the emergence of European Studies. A Department of Education and Science Survey in April 1974 showed that 80 per cent of European Studies courses in secondary schools in this country came under the aegis of modern languages departments. The most recent regional survey carried out in East and West Sussex confirmed that 'the majority of teachers responsible for European Studies are modern linguists'.[8]

With the introduction of the comprehensive system, modern language departments were faced by an enormous challenge: how to teach their subjects to the whole ability range. In the past three-quarters to four-fifths of the school population had gone to secondary modern schools. The 1963 Newsom Survey noted that 'just under a third of the modern schools provided some foreign language teaching, mainly in French and largely confined to the ablest pupils. Thus, for the section of the comprehensive school population, somewhere over half the intake, defined as 'less able' learning a modern language was to be very much a new experience.[9]

From the beginning it was clear that the low motivation to learn traditional academic subjects of 'the less able' was unusually potent in modern languages, Gardner and Lambert (1975) have noted that:

The young person from a less advantaged background, without parental support, with relatively poor abilities and low achievement orientations is very likely to do poorly in academic work, including the study of Language.

What was needed, they argued, was to inform these pupils about the background and lives of the foreign people whose language was to be studied. Thereby the 'less able's' interest might be engaged and their motivation to learn enhanced. In educational jargon, they put it like this:

> An integrative and friendly outlook toward the other group whose language is being learned can differentially sensitize the learner to the audiolingual features of the language making him more perceptive to forms of pronunciation and accent than is the case for a learner without this open and friendly disposition.[10]

A number of teachers have tested out Gardner and Lambert's assertion. Though in a sense these teachers represent a 'second wave' in the introduction of European Studies, since their efforts are well documented they throw light on the general position of Modern Languages pioneers introducing the new subject. Basically, they confirm Michael Williams' (1977) contention that:

> Many European Studies courses have begun with the feeling of modern language teachers that a small 'pill' of language will be taken by weak pupils if it is strongly dissolved in a heavy surfeit of jam ie. non-language study.[11]

William also argues that:

> Without doubt the teaching of European Studies to pupils in the first two years of comprehensive schools has become part of the debate over equality of curricula opportunity. If French is to be taught to one child then some would argue it should be taught to all. To make it palatable to the academically weaker pupils, especially when they are taught in mixed ability groups, much time must be spent arousing their interest, motivating them to learn the language, by using non-language studies.[12]

The desire to use European Studies as a vehicle for motivating the less able in languages lessons inevitably inverts the process by which school subjects are defined. In the traditional manner the 'intellectual disciplines' of the subject are defined and the pedagogic strategies with which to teach these disciplines are then formulated. European Studies, introduced because pedagogic strategies to teach language could *not* be formulated, in desperation invoked pupil interest as the major criteria for content selection.

In each school we were of course dealing with separate subject ideologies. For French departments, the effect (if not the stated intention) was often to quickly identify and displace the non-linguists (to use common school parlance) in language departments. As a result the French teacher was then left with a small group of linguists to instruct for examination courses. European Studies was the other side of this coin: dependent on traditional subject fall-out for recruits.

Perceptions and Receptions 1979–84

The historical location of the origins of European Studies within the new comprehensive schools and with the focus on less able students of a traditional discipline point up the similarities with environmental studies. The latter, analyzed elsewhere, was able to mount a substantial challenge to the traditional discipline from below.[13] In European Studies this has not happened to the same extent and hence we have to focus our studies on the individual schools if we are to understand the history of 'containment'.

Teachers' contemporary perceptions of European Studies focus on a range of episodes and constraints. It is possible to group these in the following manner: (i) views developed as the European Studies courses were initiated; (ii) responses of colleagues; (iii) 'career' problems and possibilities; (iv) external opinions — parents, employers and universities.

Teachers' Perceptions of European Studies

The dominant perception amongst teachers recalling the beginning of their courses in the 1960s and 1970s was of haphazard and idiosyncratic reasons for introducing European Studies. The following comment is rather typical:

> At the time I was head of Geography in the Faculty of Social Studies. In the Summer the headmistress suddenly decided we would have European Studies. It was to be non-exam only.

Here we see two of the most common features: the rapid and essentially 'reactive' nature of the initiative and the concern for non-academic, non-examination pupils. In the English context of resource allocation the latter factor was of critical import from the earliest stages. The following comments extend the dual characteristics of European Studies Courses:

> In my school languages were going down badly with whole sets of kids. The Deputy Head decided something new was needed ... for the 'C' set anyhow...

> My head of languages gave me the responsibility for devising it (The European Studies Course). He wanted something fairly broad fairly wide for the non-exams. Something to be taught from Macdonalds Atlas ... that was the only book we had that was of any use... There were mutinies in the ranks ... the teachers had seldom seen this band of kids. He introduced it just like that on the first day of September.

> I think it came from the staff originally, I mean the Head was very keen on it to start with and there were certain members of departments like myself, (ie. liberal studies), History and Modern Languages and Geography... Basically we were at the staff meeting talking about the less able students ... saying 'we've done this for 'n' years and it's running down' and that was the situation, universal apathy reigned and we just felt like giving them something else ... and European Studies came up, at the same time the Head was very helpful indeed and was looking for an expansion of the sixth form option thing ... we've got you know a very wide range of 'A' level students and we wanted one year courses for the people who had a lot of free time...

A number of teachers described their awareness of the dangers which flowed from hasty considerations of what to do with the less involved pupils. In several instances this led to the development of a more positive view of the potentialities and position of European Studies:

> Well you see ... I think as far as we are concerned this was a conscious turning away from what was beginning to develop and that was people starting to say 'what are we going to do with the youngsters who are not learning French or German ... From the point of view of timetable convenience they ought to be doing something associated ... let them learn about Germany, you know and what you have for tea in Brussels or something ... we were so frightened that this was what European Studies was going to become some sort of dustbin ... I think we have consciously turned away from that the although I think we haven't got to lose sight of it eventually, I think we've got to come back to terms with this after we've done the other things ... I think we've got to go

ahead from our middle school into our sixth form first and get that thing right and get the subject established with status ... then we may be able to add on these less able youngsters.

The origins of European Studies as an impulsive, haphazard response to problems of involving 'less able' linguists meant that many courses were ephemeral, changing from year to year in opportunistic response to the character of pupil cohorts and reactions as well as to other institutional and timetable pressures. The most common teacher descriptions were of the following sort:

> Well, it may well be that in various years depending on the staff there one of the CSE unit options will be a European Studies course with geography, history and all the rest of it ... but very hotchpotch and off-the-cuff.

> Well, when I became Head of Humanities they also made me Head of European Studies ... which had been taught on and off for several years to the 'dumbos' in languages... So I organized a meeting to discuss it as a subject — only the young assistant teachers were interested. I went to the Head and asked for money, I was given £150.

> We drafted out a syllabus based on 'what can we reasonably do with them' — we then worked out a few aims ... mainly based on bits of the local environment, like the ferries, identity cards ... we were fighting to make it broad but sometimes we had to draw the line ... glacial deposits, that was too technical. I didn't mind much what went on as long as the teachers could make it work. We built up our course mainly on the basis of what had worked in the first 'panic' year.

Once again, we see the genesis of European Studies as a response to the problems of what to do with 'them', 'the dumbos'. There seems solid evidence to substantiate some of Shipman's claims listed earlier of a development of a 'curriculum for inequality'.

Responses of Other Teachers

The responses from teachers of related disciplines were commonly the most hostile. As with environmental studies geographers were reportedly highly resistant to the new subject but so also were historians. Often this was expressed as a defence of the 'department':

> In a place like this departments are huge and they like to keep their legality. It's all a problem of trying to cross barriers which have been there for a long time. However well you get on with people it's still a thought in the back of their mind that their empire could be being chipped away at. Interdisciplinary studies are always going to be in that situation.

Often this emotional defence of 'subject' and 'department' has a rational basis for in fact new subjects will reduce numbers and hence resources. A deputy headmistress confirmed the point, 'I don't see why European Studies shouldn't be out on its own but it would mean that probably history and geography numbers would go down. Fewer children would opt for them'.

The territorial defence of departments and subjects increases sharply in the fourth year with the defining of examination groups. These groups are closely related to the distribution of resources and graded posts in schools: subject interests and material interests now converge. For many of the integrated subjects which are happily conceded space lower in the school the dilemma is acute. A member of the school hierarchy put it this way:

> I see the strength of Bob's argument that European Studies doesn't tread on history's and geography's toes in the 2nd and 3rd years so why suddenly discriminate at this level.

The micropolitics of subject defense move beyond special lobbying of heads and deputy heads. A good deal of interpersonal negotiation goes on between colleagues. The proponents of new subject contenders like European Studies have to put up with a good deal of 'sniping'.

A head of a very successful European Studies department who was subsequently promoted listed the responses in the following manner:

Type		*Response*
1	Hostile	'You're building a nice little empire'
		'Here comes Mr. Euro Studies'
2	Skeptical	'That sounds NICE'
		'Not more education'
3	Comparative	'It's not better than what we've got'
		'Other things are far more valuable'
4	Ignorance	'But we do French already'
		'I suppose it'll help with their geography'

5	Personal	'It's beyond me'
		'I'm a mathematician, not a social scientist'
6	Apathetic/ Lethargic	'It sounds a good idea but I'd rather not'
7	Suspended	'I really am too busy, you know'
		'If you do get it off the ground then I might join you next year'
8	Situational	'How are you going to fit it in?'
		'I can't see parents wanting their children to get a CSE in this!'
		'Where are you going to get the money?'[14]

Career Problems and Possibilities

The school subject is, of course, the major reference point in the work of contemporary secondary schools. The information and knowledge transmitted in school is normally organized and defined through subjects. This centrality of the subject is crucial for the teacher's career because of the internal organization of the school's curriculum. A number of teachers are usually required to teach each subject; these teachers are then grouped in a subject department. These departments provide the teacher with the *milieu* in which his or her career is pursued. Departments have 'graded posts' for special responsibilities and for acting as head of the department. In this way, the teacher's subject defines the means whereby salary is decided, and career structure delineated.

But further the status of the subject is crucial in deciding the allocation of resources and posts to the department. 'Academic' 'O' and 'A' level subjects normally gain the most generous allocation and hence provide the best career routes.

New subjects have to battle against the vested interest and established examination status of 'traditional subjects'. The battle is heavily loaded against new contenders:

The problem is that the children who adapt best to European Studies in the Lower School are the humanities-type children who obviously do history and geography. In the Upper School they can get 'O' levels in History and Geography so they're obviously going to opt for them. I can see that an 'O' level is going to be of far more use to them than a CSE which they can get for European Studies so we're stuck between the devil and the deep blue sea.

One teacher of European Studies, Bob, detailed his worries about the subject's status and survival. His comments typify those expressed by many European Studies teachers:

> Really now we're held up by the exam boards because they haven't produced any worthwhile syllabuses. The subject has established itself ... most schools now have European Studies departments, but even so I'm still skeptical about its survival simply because there are not public examinations to keep it moving. (...) We've got a CSE syllabus in the sixth form. It's a super syllabus but again it doesn't carry any weight.

The link between exams and the high or low status of a subject was more bluntly stated by the deputy headmaster:

> I have every sympathy with Bob's need to get high status for the subject. The problem is the cash value of a subject. How marketable a subject is depends on the cashable value of its qualifications. The children are very aware of this.

The problem of being associated with a 'low-status' subject has career implications which have become painfully clear to Bob himself:

> I'm very disillusioned about my own future. Well it hasn't given me a future after five years so I can't see that it will suddenly give me a future in the next few years. I don't think I could have done much more than I have done. I got involved with the County syllabus, had a lot of contacts with the European Resources Centre, one thing and another, and I thought this can only be of benefit to my career. But it's been going on and I've been doing things and doing things and it's done me no good whatsoever. You know I'm still where I was when I came here and that was seven years ago! I just don't know really ... obviously I've become disillusioned, disheartened. I may have to move out of the subject altogether ... go back to geography or the pastoral side. But it's not what I really want to do. (...) If you go looking for a job and say you've been head of European Studies you don't get very far!

Because of his own experience, Bob is rather pessimistic about the future of European Studies not only in his own school but in general:

> European Studies is always going to survive here I think ... as long as I'm here, but I'm very doubtful about its future unless

it becomes a common core subject. There's a lot of curiculum change going on at the moment and the possibility of the Common core is very much the in-thing. European Studies appeared at a time when the rationale was for high, wide-open options which we still operate here as a matter of fact. The number of subjects available here is incredible yet they can only choose six to follow. As things start being chiselled down as it were, I think European Studies has got to find its place as a free option soon otherwise it will disappear. I don't think it's got a tremendous future, if only because it won't be accepted by other departments ... it's sort of ... tainted in some way. It's got the mark on it (Laughter) ... the voodoo sign!

Bob's situation and his comments highlight what perhaps is the crucial factor militating against any large-scale future development of European Studies: that being associated with a subject which has not achieved full academic respectability and comparability with the established disciplines can adversely affect a teacher's career prospects and consequently his or her morale. This could result in the most energetic, committed and enthusiastic teachers such as Bob, reluctantly abandoning a subject they have painstakingly built up to return to former specialisms which seem to hold greater chances of future advancement.[15]

External Opinions

New subjects to promote their case beyond the confines of the individual school have to persuade a wider 'external constituency'[16] made up of parents, employers and the universities.

All teachers involved in the introduction of European Studies referred to the important role played by parental opinion. One of the problems consistently faced by new subjects in the secondary school is parental unfamiliarity and distrust:

Well just to confirm the fact that there are difficulties to start with because when we offered this subject at first there was considerable resistance. Parents saying my child is not doing this new-fangled invention...

Several teachers speculated on the reasons for parental distrust:

I think that people are suspicious you know ... I think that they think this is not going to be academically acceptable ... this is something that somebody had dreamt up, this is an artificial thing, contrived ... it isn't something I can easily understand like Geography or History, French and things...

And I think another thing. I think people are tired of hearing things with studies on the end. I think we'll end up teaching something with a better title ... we could do with a new term.

The most common problem I had was parents saying my child is not doing this because it is a CSE and the fact that Grade 1 is equivalent to 'O' level doesn't cut any ice...

Above all the parents judge what's going on at school from their own experience and their own experience was the three 'Rs' plus if they were lucky drawing in the afternoon ... and anything that's outside of that is extravagant.

Partly the parental opposition to innovational curricula was shared by the employers, partly indeed the parents' opposition derives from an awareness of employers' likely antipathy.

Our local employers have got a built-in prejudice against CSE — they want 'O's and 'A's to prove the child is good.

Several of the teachers appreciating the crucial importance of gaining parental support, opted for a policy of positive canvassing:

I campaigned in the third year at the Parents Open Meeting ... the Head always talks, not usually the staff ... anyhow I stood up and talked about the new subject. I said it will offer an 'O' level pass for suitable candidates[*] in the option scheme beginning in the fourth year.

I went to the parents evening with copies of the aims and objectives of my European Studies Course. I handed it out at the door ... well I had to make it sound attractive ... the staff all made jokes said it was the 'hard sell' ... but it must have worked, I got twenty-six children and at the time it was badly paired ... 'A' band had 'O' level History paired against it.

---

[*] This school, an East Anglian High School, offered the AEB exam.

European Studies as a 'Scholarly Discipline'

Many studies of school subjects have highlighted the substantial importance of the universities both (i) as 'customers' and 'recruiters' of those trained in a range of subjects at school and (ii) as definers of 'overarching disciplines' with high status.

These two aspects are often juxtaposed as the following quote illustrated. The university in question initially set up its own School of European Studies but:

> After the mid-seventies once the attraction of 'new' universities started to decline we suffered a year by year decline in applications and in quality of applicants. We eventually changed the name of our school of European Studies as a result of a new range of language-based courses. But we were influenced in reaching this decision by our own survey in selected secondary schools which almost universally demonstrated the 'low status' of European Studies both amongst teachers and pupils. Our fortunes in both quantity and quality of applications have changed dramatically for the better since that time.[17]

As was noted in the case of environmental studies there was almost a chicken and egg game being played with regard to status. Essentially until the university develops a disciplinary definition of a new subject, it will be perceived as an idiosyncratic school-based synthesis and hence of low status. This early stage can only be transcended if university scholars aid in the definition of a new synthesis. But as we can see in the quote above the initial stages of low status often act to 'warn off' such university scholars.

The conclusions of the state of the art with regard to European Studies in higher education were recently drawn as follows:

> Certainly there is no single definitive model of a European Studies course in universities, colleges and polytechnics although it is easy to identify the subjects which characteristically contribute most to such courses: languages, social sciences and history. There are in fact a number of different course models: European Studies can for example provide a whole organizing structure within which main degrees are provided (Sussex); it can be an integrated scheme composed of tightly focussed units deriving from European themes and leading to a single European Studies aware (UMIST); it can be based on

different subjects rather than themes, emphasize basic skills and have a vocational bias (Bath, Bradford), Several other models can be identified.

The range of possibilities, which is inevitable because of the scope of the subjects, led one speaker at a UACES conference in Lancaster in 1981 to refer to European Studies as a 'Humpty Dumpty' subject; ie. it can mean whatever people choose it to mean. Another participant pointed out that this can lead to the provision of too many course options which may not necessarily compose a coherent whole.[18]

The haphazard and idiosyncratic nature of European Studies in higher education at the current time is clearly evident. The reasons for this whilst partly related to social and 'political' factors also involve intellectual and epistemological considerations which are not dealt with herein. The important factor is that the implications of having no overarching 'scholarly discipline' definitions are crucial at school level. With such a vacuum at the 'top' effective change from the bottom is 'contained'. The universities in this case can act as final 'gatekeepers' and serve to ensure that restructuring innovations at subject level do not enter the educational system.

Without the prospect of any general definition and legitimation of a new subject at university level, the new contender for subject status is left fighting a series of encapsulated battles within individual schools. Over time, the micropolitical issues and perceptions summarized in this chapter will serve to ensure the initiative is not sustained over time. With no prospects of broadening the base beyond individual school definitions or isolated examination courses teachers draw negative 'conclusions' about the subject's viability and it's career-enhancing potential. A micropolitical 'war of attrition' leads to subsequent defeat for the new contender.

Acknowledgement

This chapter arises from work carried out on the Europe in the School Project. My co-worker on this, Dr. V. McGivney, shared the work on this project and is, in a real sense, a co-author of this chapter.

Notes and References

1   Civics and European Education, Resolution adopted by Minister Deputies at the Council of Europe, 6 October 1964.

2   JOTTERAND, R. *Introducing Europe to the Senior Pupils*, (Council for Cultural Cooperation of the Council of Europe, 1966).

3   *The Raising of the School Leaving Age*, Second Pilot Course for Experienced Teachers, (University of London, Goldsmiths College, 1965) p. 5.

4   *The Humanities Project: An Introduction*, (London, Heinemann, 1972) p. 1.

5   WARWICK, D. *Team Teaching*, (University of London Press, 1972) pp. 26–27, NB the 1982 edition has two misprints in the sector quoted.

6   SHIPMAN, M. 'Curriculum for inequality' in HOOPER, R. (Ed) *The Curriculum: Context, Design and Development*, (Edinburgh, Oliver and Boyd, 1971) pp. 104–105.

7   YOUNG, M.F.D. Curricula as Socially Organised Knowledge, YOUNG, M.F.D. (Ed), *Knowledge and Control*, (London Collier Macmillan, 1971) p. 40.

8   *European Studies in E. and W. Sussex*, (LEA Survey) 1977.

9   *Half our Future*, Report of the Central Advisory Council for Education, (London, HMSO, 1963).

10 LAMBERT, G. and GARDNER, N. *Attitudes and Motivation in Modern Language Learning*, quoted in LAWRENCE, F. (Ed) *Modern Languages and European Studies*, (University of Sussex, 1975).

11 WILLIAMS, M. *Teaching European Studies*, (London Heinemann, 1977) p. 18.

12 *Ibid.*, p. 19.

13 See GOODSON, I.F. *School Subjects and Curriculum Change*, (Beckenham, Croom Helm, 1983).

14 See chapter 11 and the work of John Meyer as reformulated for the English context by REID W.A. 'Curricular topics as institutional categories: Implications for theory and research in the history and sociology of school subjects' in GOODSON, I.F. and BALL, S.J. (Eds) *Defining the Curriculum: Histories and Ethnographies*, (Lewes, Falmer Press, 1984) pp. 67–75.

15 GOODSON, I.F. and McGIVNEY, V. *Europe in the School*, Research Project, (University of Sussex 1982, Mimeo).

16 *Ibid.*

17 *Ibid.*

18 *Ibid.*

10 *Becoming a School Subject*

Sociological and Historical Perspectives

Contemporary accounts of school subjects arise from two major perspectives — the sociological and the philosophical. Sociological accounts have followed a suggestion made in 1968 by Musgrove that researchers should:

> ... examine subjects both within the school and the nation at large as social systems sustained by communication networks material endowments and ideologies. Within a school and within a wider society subjects as communities of people, competing and collaborating with one another, defining and defending their boundaries, demanding allegiance from their members and conferring a sense of identity upon them ... even innovation which appears to be essentially intellectual in character, can usefully be examined as the outcome of social interaction.[1]

Musgrove remarked that 'studies of subjects in these terms have scarcely begun at least at school level'.

A more recent influential work in the field of the sociology of knowledge was the collection of papers in *Knowledge and Control* edited by Young in 1971. The papers reflect Bernstein's contention that 'how a society selects, classifies, distributes transmits and evaluates the educational knowledge it considers to be public, reflects both the distribution of power and the principles of social control'.[2] Young likewise suggests that 'consideration of the assumptions underlying the selection and organization of knowledge by those in positions of power may be a fruitful perspective for raising sociological questions about curricula'.[3] The emphasis leads to general statements of the following kind:

Academic curricula in this country involve assumptions that some kinds and areas of knowledge are much more 'worthwhile' than others: that as soon as possible all knowledge should become specialized and with minimum explicit emphasis on the relations between the subjects specialized in and between specialist teachers involved. It may be useful therefore, to view curricular changes as involving changing definitions of knowledge along one or more of the dimensions towards a less or more stratified, specialized and open organization of knowledge. Further, that as we assume some patterns of social relations associated with any curriculum, these changes will be resisted insofar as they are perceived to undermine the values, relative power and privileges of the dominant groups involved.[4]

The process whereby the unspecified 'dominant groups' exercise control over other presumably subordinate groups is not scrutinized although certain hints are offered. We learn that a school's autonomy in curriculum matters 'is in practice extremely limited by the control of the sixth form (and therefore lower form) curricula by the universities, both through their entrance requirements and their domination of all but one of the school examination boards'. In a footnote, Young assures that no direct control is implied here, but rather a process by which teachers legitimate their curricula through their shared assumptions about 'what we all know the universities want'.[5] This concentration on the teachers' socialization as the major agency of control is picked up elsewhere. We learn that:

The contemporary British educational system is dominated by academic curricula with a rigid stratification of knowledge. It follows that if teachers and children are socialized within an institutionalized structure which legitimates such assumptions, then for teachers high status (and rewards) will be associated with areas of the curriculum that are (1) formally assessed (2) taught to the 'ablest' children (3) taught in homogeneous ability groups of children who show themselves most successful within such curricula.[6]

Young goes on to note that it 'should be fruitful to explore the syllabus construction of knowledge practitioners in terms of their efforts to enhance or maintain their academic legitimacy'.

Two papers by Bourdieu in *Knowledge and Control*[7] summarize his considerable influence on English sociologists of knowledge. Unlike many of the other contributors to *Knowledge and Control*, Bourdieu has gone on to carry out empirical work to test his theoretical assertions. His recent work — though concentrated at university, not school, level — looks at the theme of reproduction through education and includes an important section on 'the examination within the structure and history of the educational system'.[8] Young (1977) also has come to feel the need for historical approaches to test theories of knowledge and control. He wrote: 'one crucial way of reformulating and transcending the limits within which we work, is to see ... how such limits are not given or fixed, but produced through the conflicting actions and interests of men in history'.[9]

Certainly the most undeveloped aspect of *Knowledge and Control* in respect to school subjects is the scrutiny of the process whereby unspecified dominant groups exercise control over presumably subordinate groups in the definition of school knowledge. Moreover, if the dominant groups in question are related to the economy, one would expect high status knowledge to be of the sort Apple (1978) refers to 'for the corporate economy requires the production of high levels of technical knowledge to keep the economic apparatus running effectively and to become more sophisticated in the maximization of opportunities for economic expansion'.[10] In fact high status groups have tended to receive 'academic' rather than 'technical' knowledge: a point that maybe contributes to the continuing dysfunctionality of the UK economy. We need to explore how this apparent contradiction developed and has been maintained in the school curriculum. Young's work, lacking in empirical evidence, develops horizontally in this exploration, working out from theories of social structure and social order to evidence of their application. Such macro-sociological theorizing is very different, although far from inimical, to studying social groups actively at work in particular historical instances. In this respect, the examination of the process of 'becoming a school subject' should generate useful historical insights.

The second school of explanation, which might almost be called the 'establishment view', is essentially philosophical and has preceded and stood in contradiction to sociological perspectives. The philosophical view has been attacked by Young because, he argues it is based on 'an absolutist conception of a set of distinct forms of knowledge which correspond closely to the traditional areas of the academic curriculum and thus justify, rather than examine, what are no more than sociohistorical constructs of a particular time'.[11] Even if we largely accept Young's critique, however, it is important to know that in fact school subjects themselves represent substantial interest groups.

To view subjects as 'no more than sociohistorical constructs of a particular time', whilst correct at one level, hardly serves to clarify the part played by those groups involved in their continuance and promotion over time.

The philosophical perspective is well summarized by the work of Hirst and Peters, and also Phenix. Hirst's position begins from a series of convictions that he defined in 1967 in a Schools Council Working Paper:

> No matter what the ability of the child may be, the heart of all his development as a rational being is, I am saying, intellectual. Maybe we shall need very special methods to achieve this development in some cases. Maybe we have still to find the best methods for the majority of the people. But let us never lose sight of the intellectural aim upon which so much else, nearly everything else, depends. Secondly it seems to me that we must get away completely from the idea that linguistic and abstract forms of thought are not for some people.[12]

Hirst argues that 'the central objectives of education are developments of mind' and that such objectives are best pursued by the development of 'forms of knowledge' (a definition later broadened to include 'fields' of knowledge). From these forms and fields of knowledge so defined, school subjects can be derived and organized. Hence, what is implied is that the intellectual discipline is created and systematically defined by a community of scholars, normally working in a university department, and is then 'translated' for use as a school subject.

This interpretation of Hirst's and Peters' work is commonly drawn, although not by the authors themselves. Other philosophers are more explicit. Phenix (1964) for instance states that: 'the general test for a discipline is that it should be the characteristic activity of an identifiable organized tradition of men of knowledge, that is of persons who are skilled in certain specified functions that they are able to justify by a set of intelligible standards'.[13] The subsequent vision of school subjects as derived from the best work of specialist scholars, who act as initiators into scholarly traditions, is generally accepted both by educationists and laymen. It is a view supported by spokesmen for governmental and educational agencies, subject associations and, perhaps most significantly, the media.

In questioning the consensus view that school subjects derive from the intellectual disciplines or forms of knowledge, it is again important to focus on the historical process through which school subjects arise. This investigation may provide evidence of a considerable disparity between the political and philosophical messages which seek to explain and legitimize the 'academic tradition' of school subjects and the detailed historical process through which school subjects are defined and established. Once a discipline has established an academic base it is persuasively self-fulfilling to argue that here is a field of knowledge from which an 'academic' school subject can receive inputs and general direction. This version of events simply celebrates a *fait accompli* in the evolution of a discipline and associated school subject. What is left unexplained are the stages of evolution towards this position and the forces which push aspiring academic subjects to follow similar routes. To understand the progression along the route to academic status it is necessary to examine the social histories of school subjects and to analyze the strategies employed in their construction and promotion.

Closer analysis of school subjects uncovers a number of unexplained paradoxes. First, the school context is in many ways starkly different from the university context — broader problems of pupil motivation, ability and control require consideration. The translation from discipline to school subject, therefore, demands considerable adaptation and as a result, 'many school subjects are barely disciplines let alone forms of thought. Many are unclear about their most fruitful concepts, forms of explanations and characteristic methodology'.[14] Secondly, school subjects are often either divorced from their discipline base or do not have a discipline base. Many school subjects therefore, represent autonomous communities. Esland and Dale (1972) have noted:

> Teachers as spokesmen for subject communities are involved in an elaborate organization of knowledge. The community has a history, and, through it, a body of respected knowledge. It has rules for recognizing 'unwelcome' or spurious matter, and ways of avoiding cognitive contamination. It will have a philosophy and a set of authorities, all of which give strong legitimation to the activities which are acceptable to the community. Some members are accredited with the power to make 'official statements' — for instance, editors of journals, presidents, chief examiners and inspectors. These are important as 'significant others' who provide models to new or wavering members of appropriate belief and conduct.[15]

The degree of isolation or autonomy of the school subject can be seen on closer analysis to be related to the stages of the subjects' evolution. Far from being derived from academic disciplines, some school subjects chronologically *precede* their parent disciplines: in these circumstances, the developing school subject actually brings about the creation of a university base for the 'discipline' so that teachers of the subject can be trained.

Layton (1972) has analyzed the development of science in England from the nineteenth century, suggesting a tentative model for the emergence of a school subject in the secondary school curriculum. He has defined three stages in this process. In the first stage:

> The callow intruder stakes a place in the timetable, justifying its presence on grounds such as pertinence and utility. During this stage learners are attracted to the subject because of its bearing on matters of concern to them. The teachers are rarely trained specialists, but bring the missionary enthusiasm of pioneers to their task. The dominant critierion is relevance to the needs and interests of the learners.

In the interim second stage:

> A tradition of scholarly work in the subject is emerging along with a corps of trained specialists from which teachers may be recruited. Students are still attracted to the study, but as much by its reputation and growing academic status as by its relevance to their own problems and concerns. The internal logic and discipline of the subject is becoming increasingly influential on the selection and organization of subject matter.

In the final stage:

> The teachers now constitute a professional body with established rules and values. The selection of subject matter is determined in large measure by the judgments and practices of the specialist scholars who lead inquiries in the field. Students are initiated into a tradition, their attitudes approaching passivity and resignation, a prelude to disenchantment.[16]

Layton's model warns against any monolithic explanation of subject and disciplines. It would seem that, far from being timeless statements of intrinsically worthwhile content, subjects and disciplines are in constant flux. Hence, the study of knowledge in our society should move beyond the ahistorical process of philosophical analysis towards a detailed historical investigation of the motives and actions behind the presentation and promotion of subjects and disciplines.

In examining the historical process of becoming a school subject, the next section provides a brief case study of geography. The subject's development is traced largely through the publications of the Geographical Association, which means that the focus of the study is on one aspect of the 'rhetoric' of subject promotion rather than on the 'reality' of curriculum practice. The elucidation of the relationship between 'rhetoric' and 'reality' remains one of the most profound challenges for future curriculum histories. (In one sense this relates to the broader problem of the historians' dependence on written and published documentary sources). This argues that subsequent studies are required to examine how far promotional activity effects the 'small print' of examination syllabuses and the content and practice of classrooms. Earlier work has, I think, evidenced that the promotional rhetoric employed by rural studies to validate its claims to be an academic discipline substantially modified the small print of an 'A' level syllabus.

The Establishment and Promotion of Geography

In the late nineteenth century, geography was beginning to establish a place in the curricula of public, grammar and elementary schools. The subject was emerging from the initial birth pangs when it appears to have been little more than a dreary collection of geographical facts and figures which MacKinder contended 'adds an ever-increasing amount to be borne by the memory'.[17] This early approach (which clearly precedes the somewhat idealized version of Layton's stage one), has been called the 'capes and bay' period. Very soon, however, the subject began to attract more inspired teachers, as a former pupil recalls: 'Later, however, in a London secondary school "capes and bays" were dramatically replaced by "homes in many lands" and a new world opened to us, through our non-graduate "specialist teacher"'.[18]

The non-graduate label was, at this time, inevitable as geography remained outside the universities. It was partly to answer this problem that one of the founding fathers of geography, MacKinder, posed the question in 1887 'How can geography be rendered a discipline?' MacKinder was aware that the demand for an academic geography to be taught in universities could only be engendered by the establishment of a more credible position in schools. Essentially, it was in the public and grammar schools that geography needed to establish its intellectual as well as pedagogical credibility.

In these schools, without full-fledged academic status, the subject's position as an established part of the curriculum remained uncertain. As a Rochester headmaster noted 'the over-crowding in the school timetable makes it impossible to give more than one and at most two lessons per week in geography'.[19] In the elementary schools, geography was rapidly seen as affording utilitarian and pedagogic possibilities in the education of the children of working people. Hence, the take-up of the subject grew considerably in the period following the 1870 Education Act. In 1875 'elementary geography' was added to the main list of class subjects examined in elementary schools.

Given the limited base in the elementary and secondary school sector, the promoters of geography began to draw up plans for a subject association. Hence in 1893 the Geographical Association was founded 'to further the knowledge of geography and the teaching of geography in all categories of educational institutions from preparatory school to university in the United Kingdom and abroad'.[20] The formation of the Association in 1893 was extremely well-timed and it rapidly began to operate as a vocal lobby for the subject. Two years later, the Bryce Commission reported and its recommendations were built into the 1902 Education Act. Further, the 1904 Secondary Regulations effectively defined the traditional subjects to be offered in secondary schools; geography's inclusion in the regulations was a major staging-post in its acceptance and recognition and in the broad-based take-up of external examinations in geography in secondary schools. The emergence of external examinations as a defining factor in secondary curricula around 1917 is clearly reflected in the sharp increase in the Association's membership around this date. At this stage, geography was included in many Examination Board regulations both at School Certificate and Higher School Certificate as a main subject. Certain Boards, however, included geography only as a 'subsidiary subject'.

For those teachers involved in promoting geography the founding of a subject association was only a first stage in launching the subject; what was also required was an overall plan aimed at establishing the subject in the various educational sectors mentioned in the constitution. At a discussion on geographical education at the British Association in September 1903, MacKinder outlined a four-point strategy for establishing the subject:

> Firstly, we should encourage university schools of geography, where geographers can be made...

> Secondly, we must persuade at any rate some secondary schools to place the geographical teaching of the whole school in the hands of one geographically trained master...

Thirdly, we must thrash out by discussion and experiment what is the best progressive method for common acceptation and upon that method we must base our scheme of examination.

Lastly, the examination papers must be set by practical geography teachers.[21]

This strategy reads very much like a plea for monopoly rights or for a closed shop. The geography teacher is to set the exams and is to choose exams that are best for the 'common' acceptation 'of the subject, (there is not even the facade that the pupils' interest should be the central criterion); the teaching of geography is to be exclusively in the hands of trained geographers and the universities are to be encouraged to establish schools of geography 'where geographers can be made'.

In the immediate period following this pronouncement, the Geography Association continued the earlier rhetoric about the subject's utility; a changeover was only slowly implemented. Thus in 1919 we learn that: 'In teaching geography in schools we seek to train future citizens to imagine accurately the interaction of human activities and their topographical conditions... The mind of the citizen must have a topographical background if he is to keep order in the mass of information which he accumulates in the course of his life and in these days the background must extend over the whole world'.[22] Eight years later, we hear that 'travel and correspondence have now become general; the British dominions are to be found in every clime and these facts alone are sufficient to ensure that the subject shall have an important place in the school timetable'.[23]

Alongside the utilitarian and pedagogic claims, as we shall see, the Geographical Association began to mount more 'academic' arguments. But the problems of the more utilitarian and pedagogic emphases had by now surfaced. Thus, in the 1930s, the Norwood Committee was concerned by the way geography appeared effortlessly to change direction and definition, thereby intruding on the territory of other subjects and disciplines. Above all, the committee was concerned with the temptation afforded by what it called the 'expansiveness of geography', for 'environment is a term which is easily expanded to cover every condition and every phase of activity which makes up normal everyday experience'. Hence, 'enthusiasts for geography may be inclined sometimes to extend their range so widely as to swallow up other subjects; in so doing they widen their boundaries so vaguely that definition of purpose is lost, and the distinctive virtues inherent in other studies closely pursued are ignored in a general survey of wide horizons'.[24]

The results of such 'expansiveness' in school geography were later reported by Honeybone who argued that, by the thirties, geography 'came more and more to be a "world citizenship" subject, with the citizens detached from their physical environment'. He explained this partly by the spread 'under American influence' of 'a methodology, proclaiming that all education must be related to the everyday experience of children'. Hence, 'in terms of geography, they insisted that the approach must always be through life and the work of men. This is a premise with many teachers of geography will agree. But when put in the hands of people untrained in geography or trained without a proper sense of geographical synthesis, it frequently meant that geography in school started with the life and work of man and made no real attempt to examine his environment'. Thus, through the work of those teachers untrained or badly trained in the subject, 'by 1939 geography had become grievously out of balance; the geographical synthesis had been abandoned; and the unique educational value of the subject lost in a flurry of social and economic generalizations'.[25]

The central problem, therefore, remained the establishment of departments in universities where geographers could be made and the piecemeal changes in pursuit of pupil relevance and utility could be partially controlled. To further this objective, the Geographical Association began to promote more academic arguments for the subject. This increasingly academic presentation of the school subject provided more pressure on the universities to respond to the demand for the training of geography specialists. As a past president of the Geographical Association has noted, 'the recognition of our subject's staus among university disciplines . . . could never have been achieved without remarkable stimulus and demand injected from out of schools'.[26] The contention, whilst correct, contains the origins of the status problems geography has encountered in universities. As David Walker (1975) has noted, 'some senior members of our ancient universities can still be found who dismiss it as a school subject'.[27] As a result, until recently, geographers remained a frustrated university profession because of what Wooldridge described as 'the widespread belief among our colleagues and associates that we lack academic status and intellectual respectability. What has been conceded is that geography has a limited use in its lower ranges. What is implicitly denied by so many is that it had any valid claim as a higher subject'.[28]

Wooldridge hints, however, that acceptance at the lower level is the main threshold to cross: 'It has been conceded that if geography is to be taught in schools it must be learned in the universities'.[29] The relevance of the school 'base' to university geography is well illustrated by St Catherine's College, Cambridge. The college has produced so many professors of geography for the country's universities that a conspiracy might be alleged. David Walker disagrees: 'In fact, to dispel the conspiracy, the reasons for this academic configuration are down to earth. St Catherine's was one of the first colleges to offer awards in geography: it established a network of contacts with sixth form teachers, many of whom later were its own graduates, and with particular schools like the Royal Grammar Newcastle'. Walker (1975) points to the personal nature of subject induction. 'Since the Second World War, moreover, many of the St Catherine's geographers who went on to become professors, readers and lecturers were taught by one man, Mr. A.A.L. Caeser, now the senior tutor'.[30]

The period following 1945 does seem to have been critical in geography's acceptance and consolidation within the university sector. Professor Alice Garnett explained in 1968 why this period was so important: 'Not until after the Second World War was it widely the case that departments were directed by geographers who had themselves received formal training in the discipline, by which time most of the initial marked differences and contrasts in subject personality had been blurred or obliterated'.[31] At this point, geography departments were established in most universities and the subject had a recognizable core of identity. By 1954, Honeybone could write a summary of the final acceptance and establishment of geography as a university discipline:

> In the universities, there has been an unparalleled advance in the number of staff and scope of the work in the departments of geography. In the University of London alone, there are now six chairs, four of them of relatively recent creation. Students, both graduates and undergraduates, are greater in number than ever before. Many of the training colleges and university departments of education are taking a full part in the progress; employers are realizing the value of the breadth of a university training in geography; and the Civil Service has recently raised the status of geography in its higher examinations. In fact, on all sides, we can see signs that, at long last, geography is forcing its complete acceptance as a major discipline in the universities, and that geographers are welcomed

into commerce, industry and the professions, because they are well educated men and women...[32]

So by the mid-1950s, geography had achieved Layton's third stage in the acceptance of a subject. The selection of subject matter being 'determined in large measure by the judgments and practices of the specialist scholars who lead inquiries in the field'; the definition of the subject was increasingly in the hands of specialist scholars. The context in which these scholars operated was substantially divorced from schools; their activities and personal motivations, their status and career concerns were situated within the university context. The concerns of school pupils, thereby unrepresented, were of less and less account in the definition of this well established academic discipline. The situation within the schools themselves soon became clear. In 1967, the report on *Society and the Young School Leaver* noted that its young subject felt 'at best apathetic, at worst resentful and rebellious to geography ... which seems to him to have nothing to do with the adult world he is soon to join'.[33] The report adds:

A frequent cause of failure seems to be that the course is often based on the traditional belief that there is a body of content for each separate subject which every school leaver should know. In the least successful courses this body of knowledge is written into the curriculum without any real consideration of the needs of the boys and girls and without any question of its relevance.

The threat to geography began to be appreciated at the highest level. A member of the Executive and Honorary Secretary of the Geographical Association recalls: 'Things had gone too far and geography became a too locally based regional thing ... at the same time the subject began to lose touch with reality ... geography got a bad name'.[34] A college lecturer, David Gowing (1973), saw the same problem facing the subject and argued: 'One must recognize the need to take a fresh look at our objectives and to re-examine the role and nature of geography in school. It is not difficult to identify the causes of increasing dissatisfaction. Pupils feel that present curricula have little relevance to their needs and so their level of motivation and understanding is low. Teachers are concerned that the raising of the school leaving age and some forms of comprehensive reorganization may exacerbate the problems'.[35]

The increasing definition of geography by the university specialists plainly posed problems for the subject in schools. To recapture the sense of utility and relevance of earlier days the subject would have needed to focus more on the needs of the average and below average school student. However, geography still faced problems of academic status within some universities and also among the high status sections of the secondary sector.

The advances in university geography after the Second World War partly aided the acceptance of geography as a subject suitable for the most able children, but problems remained. In 1967, Marchant noted: 'Geography is at last attaining to intellectual respectability in the academic streams of our secondary schools. But the battle is not quite over'. He instanced the continuing problem: 'May I quote from just two reports written in 1964, one of a girls' grammar school and the other on a well-known boys' independent school. First, 'geography is at present ... an alternative to Latin, which means that a number of girls cease to take it at the end of the third year ... there is no work available at 'A' level'. Or second, perhaps a more intriguing situation: 'In the 'O' level forms, the subject is taken only by those who are neither classicists, nor modern linguists, nor scientists. The sixth form is then drawn from this rather restricted group with the addition of a few scientists who failed to live up to expectations'.[36]

To seal its acceptance by the universities and high status sixth forms, geography had to embrace new paradigms and associated rhetorics. The supreme paradox is that the crisis in school geography in the late 1960s led not to change which might have involved more school pupils but to changes in the opposite direction in pursuit of total academic acceptance. This push for university status centred around the 'new geography', which moved away from regional geography to more quantitative data and model building. The battle for new geography represented a major clash between those traditions in geography representing more pedagogic and utilitarian traditions (notably the fieldwork geographers and some regionalists) and those pushing for total academic acceptance.

'New Geography' as an Academic Discipline

At the Madingley Lectures in 1963, which effectively launched the era of 'new geography', E.A. Wrigley contended: 'What we have seen is a concept overtaken by the course of historical change. "Regional" geography in the great mould has been as much a victim of the industrial revolution as the peasant, landed society, the horse and the village community, and for the same reason'.[37] To this problem Chorley and Haggett (1965) proposed an 'immediate solution' through 'building up the neglected geometrical side of the discipline'. They noted:

> Research is already swinging strongly into this field and the problem of implementation may be more acute in the schools than in the universities. Here we are continually impressed by the vigour and reforming zeal of 'ginger groups' like the School Mathematics Association which have shared in fundamental review of mathematics teaching in schools. There the inertia problems — established textbooks, syllabuses, examinations — are being successfully overcome and a new wave of interest is sweeping through the schools. The need in geography is just as great and we see no good reason why changes here should not yield results equally rewarding.[38]

The messianic nature of their appeal is shown when they argue that it is:

> Better that geography should explode in an excess of reform than bask in the watery sunset of its former glories; for in an age of rising standards in school and university, to maintain the present standards is not enough — to stand still is to retreat, to move forward hesitantly is to fall back from the frontier. If we move with that frontier new horizons emerge in our view, and we find new territories to be explored as exciting and demanding as the dark continents that beckoned any earlier generation of geographers. This is the teaching frontier of geography.

The Madingley Lectures proved a watershed in the emergence of the subject. Two years before, E.E. Gilbert (1961) had stated that he regarded new geography in the universities as an 'esoteric cult'.[39] After Madingley, this was no longer the case, as a college lecturer who was secretary of his local Geographical Association recalled: 'After Madingley my ideas were turned upside down... That's where the turn around in thinking in geography really started'.[40] But as Walford (1973) later noted, Madingley was 'heady to some, undrinkable brew to others'.[41] Following the second Madingley Conference in 1968, Chorley and Haggett sought to consolidate the changes they were advocating by a new book entitled *Models in Geography*.[42] By this time opinions were becoming progressively polarized about the 'new geography'. Slaymaker (1966) wrote in support of the book:

In retrospect, a turning point in the development of geographical methodology in Britain. After the exploratory and
mildly iconoclastic contents of the first Madingley lectures,
recorded in *Frontiers in Geographical Teaching*, a more substantial statement of the methodological basis and aims of the
so-called 'new geography' was required ... with the publication of this book [it is demonstrated that] the traditional clas-
sificatory paradigm is inadequate and that in the context of the
'new geography' an irreversible step has been taken to push us
back into the mainstream of scientific activity by process of
model building. The discussion of the relevance of new conceptual models in geographical research and teaching should
serve as a stimulus to participation in methodological debate to
which, with notable exceptions, British geographers have
made a disproportionately small contribution. It is therefore a
major publication, both in achievement and potential.[43]

Teachers of the subject received less enthusiastic advice from their
journal, *Geography* and its anonymous reviewer 'PRC'(1968):

What ... is its object, and to whom is it addressed? These
questions are avoided wih perverse skill and in the absence of
guidance, the conviction gradually takes root that, in fact, the
authors are writing for each other! This may explain, though it
does not excuse, the use in some papers of a barbarous and
repulsive jargon. Is it then a joint expression of faith on the
part of the New Geographers? This would indeed have been
welcome but a new faith is hardly likely to be attained by a
frenzied search for gadgets which might conceivably be turned
to geographical ends. The nature of those ends calls for solid
thought, a task which cannot be delegated to computers.[44]

A year later, the president of the Geographical Association pursued a
similar opposition with a more explicit statement of the fears which
new geography engendered. The new systematic geography, she
argued, was:

... creating a problem that will increase in acuteness over the
decades ahead for it leads towards subject fragmentation as
fringe specialisms in systematic fields proliferate and are pursued independently to the neglect of the very core of our
discipline — a core that largely justified its existence. Geography in our universities is in fact becoming so sophisticated,
and its numerous branches in diverse fields at times so narrow-

ly specialized, that sooner or later, the question must arise as to how much longer the subject can effectively be held together.[45]

The implications of this analysis are clear:

So my first plea to the academic teachers who will be the leaders of tomorrow must be: let there never be question (other than at an advanced post–graduate and reserach level) of the coexistence of two geographies, physical and social, regarded as one without reference to the other. University departments have a duty to ensure that, at least at the first degree level, the core of our subject is neither forgotten nor neglected, and that the synthesis of the specialist fields and their relevance to the core are clearly appreciated by our undergraduate students. In my mind, it is only on the foundation of a first degree course structure so designed that a geographer is basically qualified either to teach in our schools or to carry his studies further at a postgraduate research level.[46]

The overwhelming worry reflected in this quote was that the myth of the discipline would be exposed. Geography was supposedly a unified academic discipline into which the school teacher initiated young pupils. If there was no obvious link between university and school geography this version of events — the Hirstian vision of school subjects — would stand exposed. Teachers themselves became very worried: 'Geography was in a state of ferment . . . it was moving too quickly. . . Let alone in the schools even many of the universities didn't have new geography';[47] and 'This new approach, however you felt about it, caused a sort of schism . . . both at university and at school level'.[48]

Fears of this schism were expressed in a number of contemporary books. The gap between schools and universities, of which there is much evidence in previous periods, was thought particularly worrying:

Techniques of study are changing more rapidly in modern goegraphy than at any previous time in the subject's history. As a result there is a great need for a dialogue between research workers and those being admitted to the mysteries of the subject. Teachers provide the necessary link; and it is dangerous for the vitality and future health of geography that some teachers find current developments either incomprehensible or unacceptable.[49]

Rex Walford (1973) made a similar diagnosis: 'The need for unity within the subject is more than a practical one of preparing sixth formers for their first lectures on campus; it is, I would assert, a basic requirement for the continued existence of the subject'.[50]

In spite of the opposition of teachers and academics, many of who saw regional geography as the 'real geography', there were strong pressures working in favour of the advocates of new geography. Beyond the problems in schools, the scholars in universities who controlled the new definitions of the subject were concerned to progress to the front rank of university academic disciplines. (Their concerns would of course be reflected in greater sixth form status.) New geography was conceived and promoted to achieve this end. The alliance between university status and school status ensured that ultimately the Geographical Association would embrace 'new geography'.

The perceived problems encountered by school geography were used as an argument for change. The change then moved in those directions most likely to satisfy geography's aspiration for the full acceptance as a first rank academic discipline in universities and sixth forms. The changes emanating from universities were partly mediated through the Geographical Association to the schools. At stages, where the gap between the two widened, the Association was always on hand to warn against too rapid redefinition and to exhort teachers to change and to encourage their re-training. In recent years, fears about 'new geography' seem to have subsided and a period of consolidation has set in. Of the Cambidge base of Chorley and Haggett, it was recently written, by David Walker (1975), himself a protagonist: 'The academic revolution of quantification which has battered traditional scholarship in fields like economic history and linguistics has taken its toll in geography in recent years, but the Cambridge department which Professor Darby took over in 1966 remains on even keel. The tripos system continues to offer a fine balance of specialization and liberal education'.[51]

Perceptions of the subject as being in crisis have considerably mellowed. A professor, who is on the Executive Committee and past holder of a number of positions in the Geographical Association stated: 'I see geography traditionally as a core to understand why places are as they are' but said of the present condition of geography: 'It isn't in flux ... there is no end to the subject ... of course the techniques by which you advance the subject will change ... if the present emphasis on quantitative techniques helps our preciseness who could deny that it is an advance within the subject'.[52]

Ultimately, the reconciliation with new geography was closely linked with geography's long aspiration to be viewed as a scientific discipline. In a previous decade Professor Wooldridge (1956) had written a book on *The Geographer as Scientist*, [53] but in 1970 Fitzgerald, reviewing the implications of new geography for teaching wrote: 'The change which many think is at the heart of geography is that towards the use of the scientific method in approaching problems'.[54] Similarly, M. Yeates (1968) wrote: 'Geography can be regarded as a science concerned with the rational development and testing of theories that explain and predict the spatial distribution and location of various characteristics on the surface of the earthe'.[55]

At the twenty-first International Geographic Congress at New Delhi in 1968, Professor Norton Ginsburg identified *social* science as the 'fraternity' to aspire to. He saw: 'the beginnings of a new age for human geography as a fully-fledged member of the social science fraternity ... the future of geography as a major research discipline will, I submit, be determined on the intellectual battlefields of the universities, where competition and conflict are intense; and where ideas are the hallmark of achievement'.[56] He considered that 'research has moved rapidly, albeit erratically, towards the formulation of general propositions and theories of organization and behaviour and away from preoccupation with patterns *per se*. In this sense geography's internal organization and intellectual apparatus have come to resemble those of the social sciences, whereas formerly they were markedly at variance with them'. Hence by 1970, geography had finished its 'long march' to acceptance as an academic discipline; from now on its future would indeed be determined not in the school classroom but on 'the intellectual battlefields of the universities'.

Conclusion

The establishment of geography — how geography was rendered a discipline — was a protracted, painstaking and fiercely contested process. The story is not of the translation of an academic discipline, devised by ('dominant') groups of scholars in universities, into a pedagogic version to be used as a school subject. Rather the story unfolds in reverse order and can be seen as a drive on the part of low status groups at school level progressively to colonize areas within the university sector — thereby earning the right for scholars in the new field to define knowledge that could be viewed as a discipline. The process of development for school subjects can be seen not as a pattern of disciplines 'translated' *down* or of 'domination' *downwards* but very much as a process of 'aspiration' *upwards*.

To summarize the stages in the emergence of geography: in the earlier stages teaching was anything but 'messianic', for the subject was taught by non-specialists and comprised a 'dreary collection of geographical facts and figures'. The threshold for take-off on the route to academic establishment began with MacKinder's remarkably successful recipe for the subject's promotion drawn up in 1903. In the MacKinder manifesto the geography teacher is to set the exams and is to choose exams that are best for the 'common acceptation' of the subject the teaching of geography is to be exclusively in the hands of trained geographers and the universities are to be encouraged to establish schools of geography 'where geographers can be made'.

The strategy offered solutions for the major problems geography faced in its development. Most notable of these was the idiosyncratic and information-based nature of school geography. Initially, the subject stressed personal, pedagogic and vocational arguments for its inclusion in curricula: 'we seek to train future citizens' and moreover a citizen 'must have a topographical background if he is to keep order in the mass of information which accumulates in the course of this life' (1919). Later, the subject was advocated because 'travel and correspondence have now become general (1927). But the result of these utilitarian and pedagogic emphases was that comments arose as to the 'expansiveness' of the subject and the fact that it came 'more and more to be a 'world citizenship' subject' (1930s).

The problem was that identified by MacKinder in 1903: geographers needed to be 'made' in the universities, then any piecemeal changes in pursuit of school relevance or utility could be controlled and directed. The growth of the subject in the schools provided an overwhelming argument for the subject to be taught in the universities. As Wooldridge noted later, 'it has been conceded that if geography is to be taught in schools it must be learned in universities'. Slowly, therefore, a uniformity in the subject was established to answer those who observed the chameleon nature of the subject's knowledge structure. Alice Garnett noted that it was not until after 1945 that most school departments of geography were directed by specialist-trained geographers but as a result of this training 'most of the initial marked differences and contrasts in subject personality had been blurred or obliterated'. (One might say 'masked and mystified'.)

The definition of geography through the universities rapidly replaced any pedagogic or utilitarian promotional bias with arguments for academic rigour: and as early as 1927 Hadow had contended that 'the main objective in good geographical teaching is to develop, as in the case of history, an attitude of mind and mode of thought characteristic of the subject'. However, for several decades university geography was plagued both by the image of the subject as essentially for school children, and by the idiosyncratic interpretations of the various university departments, especially in respect to fieldwork. Thus, while establishment in universities solved the status problems of the subject within schools, within universities themselves the subject's status still remained low. The launching of 'new geography' with aspirations to scientific or social scientific rigour is therefore partly to be understood as a strategy for finally establishing geography's status at the highest level. In this respect the current position of the subject in universities would seem to confirm the success of new geography's push for parity of esteem with other university disciplines.

The aspiration to become an academic subject and the successful promotion employed by geography teachers and educationists, particularly in the work of the Geographical Association, has been clearly evidenced. We know what happened in the history of geography: less evidence has been presented as to why this should be so. A clue can be found in Garnett's presidential address to the Geography Association in 1968; a clear link was presented between 'the recognition of our subject's status among university disciplines' and 'the costly provision made available for its study'. Plainly the drive towards higher status is accompanied by opportunities to command larger finance and resources.

The close connection between academic status and resources is a fundamental feature of our educational system. The origin of this connection is the examination system created by universities from the late 1850s and culminating in the school certificate system founded in 1917. As a result, the so-called 'academic' subjects provide examinations which are suitable for 'able' students whilst other subjects are not.

Byrne's work has provided data on resource allocation within schools. She discerned that: 'two assumptions which might be questioned have been seen consistently to underlay educational planning and the consequent resource allocation for the more able children. First, that these necessarily need longer in school than non-grammar pupils, and secondly, that they necessarily need more staff, more highly paid staff and more money for equipment and books'.[57] The implications of the preferential treatment of academic subjects for the material self-interest of teachers are clear: better staffing ratios, higher salaries, higher capitation allowances, more graded posts, better careers prospects. The link between academic status and resource allocation provides the major explanatory framework for understanding the aspirational imperative to become an academic subject. Basically, since more resources are given to the academic examination subject taught to able students the conflict over the status of examinable knowledge is, above all, a battle over the material resources and career prospects of each subject teacher or subject community.

The historical profile tentatively discerned for geography exposes certain omissions, in some cases misconceptions, within the main philosophical and sociological accounts. The philosophical perspective has provided support for the view that school subjects derive from forms of fields of knowledge or 'disciplines'. Of course, once a school subject has brought about the establishment of an academic discipline base, it is persuasively self-fulfilling to argue that the school subject receives intellectual direction and inputs from university scholars. This version of events simply celebrates a *fait accompli* in the history of the school subject and associated disciplines. What is left unexplained and unrecorded are the stages of evolution towards the culminating pattern and the forces which push aspiring academic subjects to follow similar routes. By starting with the final historical product philosophical studies forego the opportunity to examine school subjects fully.

In a way, sociological accounts also celebrate the *fait accompli* and assume that university control of school subjects reflects a continuing pattern of pervasive domination. As we have seen the major agencies actively involved in constructing this pattern were the teachers of school subjects themselves — not so much domination by dominant forces, more solicitous surrender by subordinate groups. The stress on domination leads to an emphasis on teachers 'being socialized within institutionalized structures' which legitimate high status patterns of academic subjects. Far from this socialization in dominant institutions being the major factor creating the pattern we have examined, it was much more considerations of teachers' material self-interest in their working lives. Since the misconception is purveyed by sociologists who often exhort us 'to understand the teachers' real world' they should really know better. High status academic knowledge gains its adherents and aspirants less through control of the curricula which socialize than through well-established connection with patterns of resource allocation and the associated work and career prospects these ensure. The historical study of school subjects directs our attention to the development of patterns of resource allocation and I think shows how generative this approach might be in replacing crude notions of domination with patterns of control in which subordinate groups can be seen actively at work.

Notes and References

1 MUSGROVE, F. 'The contribution of sociology to the study of the curriculum,' in KERR, J.F. (Ed), *Changing the Curriculum*, (University of London Press, 1968) p. 101.

2 BERNSTEIN, B. 'On the classification and framing of educational knowledge', in YOUNG, M. (Ed), *Knowledge and Control*, (London, Collier, Macullan. 1971) p. 47.

3 YOUNG, M. 'An approach to the study of curricula as socially organised knowledge' in YOUNG, M. (Ed), (1971) p. 31.

4 *Ibid.*, p. 34.

5 *Ibid.*, p. 22.

6 *Ibid.*, p. 36.

7 BOURDIEU, P. 'Systems of education and systems of thought and intellectual field and creative project', in YOUNG, M. (Ed) (1971).

8 BOURDIEU, P. and PASSERON, J.C. *Reproduction in Education, Society and Culture*, (London, Sage, 1977).

9 YOUNG, M. 'Curriculum change: Limits and possibilities' in YOUNG, M. and WHITTY, G. (Eds), *Society State and Schooling*, (Lewes, Falmer Press, 1977) pp. 248–249.

10 APPLE, M.W. 'Ideology, reproduction and educational reform', *Comparative Education Review*, 22, (1978) p. 380.

11 *op. cit.*, YOUNG, p. 23.

12 HIRST, P. *The Educational Implications of Social and Economic Change* in Schools Council Working Paper No. 12, (London, HMSO, 1967).

13 PHENIX, P.M. *The Realms of Meaning*, (New York, McGraw-Hill, 1964) p. 317.

14 JENKINS, D. and SHIPMAN, M.P. *Curriculum: an Introduction*, (Open Books, 1976) p. 107.

15 ESLAND, G.M. and DALE, R. (Eds), *School and Society*, Course E282 Unit 2, (Open University, Milton Keynes, 1973) pp. 70–71.

16 LAYTON, D. 'Science as general education', *Trends in Education*, (1972).

17 MACKINDER, H.J. 'On the scope and methods of geography', *Proceedings of the Royal Geographical Society*, Vol. IX, (1887).

18 GARNETT, A. 'Teaching geography: Some reflections', *Geography, 54*, (1969) p. 36.

19 BIRD, C. 'Limitations and possibilities of geographical teaching in day schools', *The Geographical Teacher*, Vol. 1, (1901).

20 Manifesto of Geographical Association printed on the inside cover of all copies of *Geography*.

21 MACKINDER, H.J. *Report of the Discussion on Geographical Education*, (1903) pp. 95–101.

22 COUNCIL of the GEOGRAPHICAL ASSOCIATION, 'The position of geography', *The Geographical Teacher*, Vol. 10, (1919).

23 BOARD of EDUCATION, *Report of the Consultative Committee: the Education of the Adolescent*, Hadlow Report, (London, HMSO, 1927).

24 The Norwood Report, *Curriculum and Examinations in Secondary Schools*. (London, HMSO, 1943) pp. 101–102.

25 HONEYBONE, R.C. 'Balance in geography and education', *Geography*, 34, 186 (1954).

26 GARNETT, A. 'Teaching geography: Some reflections', *Geography, 54*, (1969) p. 387.

27 WALKER, D. 'The well-rounded geographers', *The Times Educational Supplement*, 28th November, (1975) p. 6.

28 DAVID, T. 'Against geography' in BALE, D. GRAVES, N. and WALFORD, R. (Eds), *Perspectives in Geographical Education*, (Edinburgh, 1973) pp. 12–13.

29 *Ibid.*

30 *op. cit.*, Walker, p. 6.

31 *op. cit.*, Garnett, p. 368.

32 *op. cit.*, HONEYBONE, (1954).

33 *Society and the Young School Leaver*, Working Paper No. 11, (London, HMSO, 1967) p. 3.

34 Interview (30 June 1976).

35 GOWING, D. 'A fresh look at objectives' in WATFORD, R. (Ed), *New Directions in Geography Teaching*, (London, Longmans, 1973) p. 153.

36 MARCHANT, E.C. 'Some responsibilities of the teacher of geography, *Geography, 3*, (1965) p. 133.

37 WRIGLEY, E.A. 'Changes in the philosophy of geography' in CHORLEY, R. and HAGGETT P. (Eds), *Frontiers in Geographical Teaching*, (London, Methuen, 1965) p. 13.

38 CHORLEY, R. and HAGGETT, P. (1965).

39 GILBERT, E.W. 'The idea of the region', *Geography*, Vol. 45, No. 1, (1961).

40 Personal interview; college of education lecturer, 5 January 1977.

41 WALFORD, R. 'Models, simulations and games' in WALFORD, R. (Ed), (1973) p. 95.

42 CHORLEY, R. and HAGGETT, P. *Models in Geography*, (London, Methuen, 1967).

43 SLAYMAKER, O. 'Review', *Geographical Journal*, Vol. 134, Part 2 September 1966.

44 PRC. 'Review', *Geography*, Vol. 53, Part 4, November, 1968.

45 *op. cit.*, Garnett, pp. 388–389.

46 *Ibid.*, p. 389.

47 *op. cit.*, interview, 30 June 1976.

48 *Ibid.*

49 COOKE, R. and JOHNSON, J.M. *Trends in Geography*, (London, Methuen, 1969) p. 8.

50 *op., cit.*, Walford, p. 97.

51 *op., cit.*, Walker, p. 6.

52 Interview geography professor, 14 December 1978.

53 WOOLDRIDGE, S.W. *The Geographer as Scientist*, (London, Nelson, 1956).
54 FITZGERALD, B.P. 'Scientific method, quantitative techniques and the teaching of geography' in WALFORD, R. (Ed), (1973) p. 85.
55 YEATES, M.H. *An Introduction to Quantative Analysis in Economic Geography*, (New York, McGraw-Hill, 1968) p. 1.
56 GINSBURG, N. 'Tasks of geography', *Geography, 54*, (1969) pp. 403–404.
57 BYRNE, E.M. *Planning and Educational Inequality*, (Slough, NFER, 1974) p. 29.

11   *The Making of Curriculum*

The Making of Curriculum

C. Wright Mills (1977) argued that 'the production of historians may be thought of as a great file indispensable to all social science' and that 'every social science — or better, every well-considered social study — requires historical scope and a full use of historical materials'.[1] If we use these criteria, it is plain that most of our studies of schools, certainly in relation to curriculum, are not 'well considered'; the great file indispensable to all social science has proved eminently dispensable.

In undertaking studies of curriculum production it has been contended that historical research should indeed be viewed as indispensable. Three levels of historical study were discerned in chapter 7: (i) the individual life history; (ii) the group or collective level: by professions, or the communities which make up subjects and disciplines; (iii) the relational level: the various permutations of relations between groups and between individuals and groups.

Whilst much of curriculum study has either been prescriptive or ahistorical, the work of some of the sociologists of knowledge has directed our attention to the curriculum as a socio-historical product. In this sense their work has sought to employ historical data and perspective to elucidate our understanding of curriculum and its relationship to schooling. But the use of historical data is some distance from the use of historical methods. There is a danger of 'raiding' history where studies span centuries of change at all levels of content and context. A more systematic *evolutionary* (although not in any Darwinian or uncontested sense) understanding of how the curriculum is negotiated is therefore needed. One is concerned to ensure that histories make evolutionary connections partly to secure against 'raiding' but more constructively to facilitate the use of such histories in developing theoretical frameworks. A continuity thesis cannot be assumed but has to be established (or disproven) over time. It is most decidedly at the centre of the sociological as well as historical enterprise to examine curriculum transformation and reproduction at work over time. But such complex undertakings cannot be fully elucidated by 'snapshots' of unique events which may be entirely aberrant and without general significance.

By this view to seek to provide from the macro level theories of schooling and curriculum without related empirical studies of how the curriculum has been negotiated at mezo and micro level over time is an unsatisfactory and thoroughly dangerous sequence through which to proceed. On the other hand, developing studies of the complexity of curriculum action and negotiation over time is a meaningful sequence through which to approach theory. Besides acting as a 'seedbed' for theory such work is a vital complement to macro-level theorizing.

Modes of Historical Study

In arguing for curriculum as a central source in the investigation of schooling and in juxtaposing history and curriculum study, there is an evident and basic problem. History is not first and foremost a theoretical mode of study. Above all, the concern is with particular historical situations which are, in their nature, unique. The process of explanation, generalization and theorizing is of necessity secondary to the pursuit of understanding at this level. Ricoeur (1981) puts it this way:

> Explanation in history is not an end in itself: it serves to mediate historical understanding which is tied in turn to the narrativity of the historical text.[2]

Yet, accepting the primacy of the pursuit of understanding unique historicial events and situations does not deny history explanatory potential. In this sense the Ricoeur quote is exact: there is a place for explanation, even if not pride of place. Moreover, the *recurrence* of factors and events in a range of unique locations can help in discerning explanatory frameworks, in testing and contributing to theory.

Curriculum historians need to ensure that their capacity to develop their 'great file indispensable to all social science' makes optimum connections with strategies for explanation and theory. The current debate over *realism* in the philosophy of science is an instructive example.

Roy Bhasker (1978) states that realist explanations develop the distinction between observed regularities and those underlying 'mechanisms' which account for these regularities. Bhaskar discerns three levels of reality: firstly 'mechanisms', causally efficacious processes, secondly 'events', those consequences or effects of mechanisms and thirdly 'experiences', subjectively perceived aspects of events. Bhaskar argues that:

> Once it is granted that mechanisms and structures may be said to be real, we can provide an interpretation of the independence of causal laws from the pattern of events, and *a fotiori* of the rationale of experimental activity. For the real basis of this independence lies in the independence of the generative mechanisms of nature from the events they generate. Such mechanisms endure when not acting...

Some of these mechanisms:

> Act through the flux of conditions that determine whether they are active and co-determine the manifest outcome of their activity. That is to say, it entails that generative mechanisms endure when inactive and act even where, as in open systems, there is no one-to-one relationship between the causal law representing the characteristic mode of operation of the mechanism and the particular sequence of events that occurs.[3]

Deriving from Bhaskar, Olin Wright sees a realist process of explanation proceeding in this manner:

1   regularities are identified (within a conceptual field which makes such observational regularities possible);
2   a mechanism is postulated in the imagination: it is *invented* by the creative activity of the scientist acting on existing explanations and theories;
3   the reality of the entities and processes postulated in the mechanism is then checked through empirical investigation (experiment, quasi-experiment or some other procedure).[4]

Now clearly the sequence or posture to theory is starkly different for the historian. But, at the same time, it should be evident that historical study can be a useful mode for those investigations which may test or contribute to such theories. 'Regularities' or 'mechanisms' may then be identified or scrutinized as operant in particular historical locales: their status or existence may then be clarified, elaborated or modified.

Whilst historical studies may indeed discern 'regularities' these have to be consistently related to changing historical contexts. Regularities cannot be assumed as timeless and invariant. The historian starts, so to speak, from the other end. To give one example: in the next section certain explanatory frameworks are tentatively advanced, certain regularities if you will. But they are historically specific; they refer to a period of some stability in curriculum history when an integrated structure of examinations and associated resource allocations has been paramount. It has not always been so and given the current British Government's intentions will most decidedly not stay so. Educational 'systems' themselves are subject to historical flux. Yet as has been seen in previous instances we do tend to take the present system for granted, to assume that at least some of the salient features are pervasive and continuous.

Developing Studies of Context: An Historical Instance of English Schooling in the Twentieth Century

The studies undertaken of life histories and curriculum histories point to the importance of aspects of the structure of the educational system in understanding the actions at individual, collective, and relational levels. These structures, which might be viewed from the actors' standpoint as the 'rules of the game', arise at a particular point in history, for particular reasons: until changed they act as a structural legacy constraining, but also enabling, contemporary actors. The pervasiveness of these structures and degree of similarity of response at all levels allows some explanatory frameworks or studies of context to be developed as the following instance I think indicates. This is not to argue that structures are timeless or invariant; it is strictly an instance relating to a particular period of curriculum history. There are many indications that this curriculum structure is currently coming under stress and new modes of control and operation can be discerned. So fundamental might the change be that groups currently 'outside' the educational system — such as the Manpower Service Commission may be viewed as entering the terrain.

Above all, the historical study of teachers' life histories and school subjects' histories in recent decades directs our attention to the structuring of material interests — and to the associated structuring of the internal discourse on the school curriculum — in particular, the manner in which resources and career chances are distributed and status attributed. We are here focussing on the political economy of the curriculum, in particular the 'convention' of the school subject.

The main historical period for the emergence of this salient structure was 1904–1917. The 1904 Secondary Regulations (in which Morant played such a central defining role) list and prioritize that subjects suitable for education in the secondary grammar schools. These were largely those that have come to be seen as 'academic' subjects, a view confirmed and consolidated by their enshrinement in the School Certificate examinations launched in 1917.

1.1   From 1917 onwards examination subjects, the 'academic' subjects, inherited the priority treatment in finance and resources directed at the grammar schools. It should be noted that the examination system itself had developed for a comparable clientele. The foundation of these examinations in 1858 'was the universities' response to petitions that they should help in the development of 'schools for the middle classes'. (The genesis of examinations and their subsequent centrality in the structure of the educational systems are a particularly good example of the importance of historical factors for those developing theories about curriculum and schooling.)

1.2   The structure of resources linked to examinations has effectively survived the ensuing changes in the educational system (although currently these are now subject to challenge). Byrne (1974) for instance has stated 'that more resources are given to able students and hence to academic subjects', the two are still synonomous 'since it has been assumed that they necessarily need more staff, more highly paid staff and more money for equipment and books'.

1.3   The material interests of teachers — their pay, promotion and conditions — are intimately interlinked with the fate of their specialist subject. School subjects are organized within schools in departments. The subject teacher's career is pursued within such departments and the department's status depends on the subject's status. The 'academic' subject is placed at the top of the hierarchy of subjects because resource allocation takes place on the basis of assumptions that such subjects are best suited for the 'able' students (and *vice versa* of course) who, it is further assumed, should receive favourable treatment.

1.4   Thus in secondary schools the material and self-interest of subject teachers is interlinked with the status of the subject, judged in terms of its examination status. Academic subjects provide the teacher with a career structure characterized by better promotion prospects and pay than less academic subjects. As previous chapters bear testimony, the conflict over the status of examinable knowledge, as perceived and fought at individual and collective level, is essentially a battle over material resources and career prospects. This battle is reflected in the way that the discourse over school subjects, the debate about their form, content and structure, is constructed and organized. 'Academic' subjects are those which attract 'able' students, hence 'the need for a scholarly discipline' characterizes the way in which the discourse on curriculum is structured and narrowed. Locating our studies at these points ensures that exploration will focus on relationships between aspects of structure and action.

Structure and Mediation: Internal and External Factors During the Process of Subject Establishment

Studies of context with regard to subject teachers and communities provide us with a 'cognitive map of curriculum influence' (or, more basically, the 'rules of the game'). Essentially the 'rules of the game' discerned in the limited number of studies so far conducted are those 'internal' to the educational system. Since external factors are also of eminent importance broader theories of context will need to be elaborated if more general models of change are to be envisaged. In the section which follows therefore the 'internal affairs' of curriculum are linked with 'external relations'.

Internal Affairs

1 *'Invention'*

    1.1   In one model of subject evolution the early stages focus on pedagogic and utilitarian functions but, plainly, there are stages which proceed the formation of subject groups. In this situation, the 'ideas necessary for creation are normally available over a relatively prolonged period of time in several places'.[5]

    1.2   Westbury (1984) has conceptualized this initial stage as 'invention'. These inventions may originate with educators themselves trying out new ideas or practices; or they may sometimes be a result of pupil demands or of pupil resistance to existing forms; or they may arise in response to new 'climates of opinion'. They may also come from 'inventions in the outside world', e.g. squared graph paper, books, micros.[6]

    1.3   Internally, there is one overwhelming reason for the take-up of 'inventions' by subject groups. 'Inventions' normally exist in several places over a long period of time but 'only a few of these potential beginnings lead to further growth':

such growth occurs where and when persons become interested in the new idea, not only as intellectual content but also as a potential means of establishing a new intellectual identity and particularly a new occupationl role.[*7]

2 Subjects as 'coalitions'

2.1   The process model developed by Bucher and Strauss (1976) for the study of professions provides valuable guidelines for those studying school subjects. Within a profession, they argue, are varied identities, values and interests. Hence, professions are to be seen as 'loose amalgamation of segments pursuing different objectives in different manner and more or less delicately held together under a common name at particular periods in history'.[8] The most frequent conflicts arise over the gaining of institutional footholds, over recruitment and over external relations with clients and other institutions. At times, when conflicts such as these become intense, professional associations may be created, or, if already in existence, become more strongly institutionalized.

2.2   The Bucher and Strauss model of profession suggests that perhaps the 'subject community' should not be viewed as a homogeneous group whose members share similar values and definition of role, common interests and identity. Rather, the subject community should be seen as comprising a range of conflicting groups, segments or factions (referred to as subject sub-groups). The importance of these groups might vary considerably over time. As with professions, school subject associations (e.g. the Geographical Association) often develop at particular points in time when there is an intensification of conflict over school curriculum and resources and over recruitment and training.

3 Establishment: Coalitions in action

3.1   Initially a subject is often a very loose coalition of sub-groups and less coherent, even idiosyncratic versions and the focus is on pedagogic and utilitarian concerns.

---

[*] It is instructive to note that after this contention Ben-David and Collins conclude that: 'the conditions under which such interest can be identified and used as a basis for eventually building a predictive theory'.

3.2   A sub-group emerges arguing for the subject to become an 'academic discipline' so as to be able to claim resources and status.

3.3   At the point of conflict between earlier sub-groups and the proselytizing 'academic' sub-group, a subject association is often formed. The association increasingly act to unify sub-groups with a *dominant coalition* promoting academic. The dominant coalition promotes the subject as a 'scholarly discipline', or a 'real science', defined by university scholars.

3.4   For the successful establishment of an 'academic' subject the culminating phase is the creation of the 'university discipline' base. The subject boundaries are now increasingly defined by university scholars and it is to the structure of their material interests and resulting aspirations that we must look to explain curriculum change.

External Relations

As we have noted some of the 'inventions' which initiate internal curriculum change begin externally. But 'external relations' are of more importance than as initiators of change at this level. There is considerable evidence that for many subjects, especially the more 'applicable' subjects, the influence of industrial and commercial interests can be substantial. This, it should be noted, is not to argue a direct 'correspondence' thesis nor for the existence of a 'selective tradition' where all content opposed to capitalism is ultimately 'purged' from aspiring curriculum categories.

Much of the latter work has focussed on textbooks. Anyon (1979), for example, has persuasively shown how US social studies texts do omit much of labour history.[9] Clearly textbooks are an important 'external' factor but they are dependent on internal take-up and can be supplemented internally. Ultimately, we are back with which models of internal curriculum can be sustained: in this act of sustenance external relations are vital.

In sustaining internal models of curriculum, the role of agencies external to the school is of central import. Herbert Blumer (1986) elaborated the concept of 'public' to characterize the groups who collectively use of view a particular service and, therefore, contribute to the 'public debate' about it.[10] But as C. Wright Mills (1977) pointed out:

> The problem of 'the public' in western societies arises out
> of the transformation of the traditional and conventional

consensus of medieval society; it reaches its present-day climax in the idea of a mass society. What were called 'publics' in the eighteenth and nineteenth centuries are being transformed into a society of 'masses'. Moreover the structural relevance of publics is declining, as men at large become 'mass men' each trapped in quite powerless *milieu*.[11]

Because of the power of particular 'publics' the ideologies of dominant 'publics' relate to particular views of education and particular 'rhetorics of legitimation' or 'discourses'. Esland (1972) has begun to conceptualize a range of questions which surround this issue:

> The question one would be asking about these publics is, what characterizes their thinking about education? How are changing conceptual thresholds for defining valid school experience communicated and made plausible to the teacher and to other publics? How is the dialogue between consumers of education and its professional exponents indicative of changing concepts of order and control? The institutional correlates of these processes will be manifested in the career flow of teacher and pupil and the definitions which are attached to particular mental states and experiences.

The rhetorics and ideologies of 'publics' are of course located in the socio-cultural processes which support and label particular kinds of enterprise as educationally worthwhile.[12]

The work of John Meyer is valuable in allowing us to conceptualize external relations.[13] His work, concerned with the US, has been modified by Reid (1984) with the UK system in mind. In this approach 'external forces and structures emerge not merely as sources of ideas, promptings, inducements and constraints, but as definers and carriers of the categories of content, role and activity to which the practice of schools must approximate in order to attract support and legitimation'. In short, these external constituencies are vital elements in the discursive formation, the way in which the debate on school curriculum is constructed and organized. External relations then are seen less in terms of formal or conventional groups such as parents, employers, trade unions and universities, but in terms of more broadly conceived *'publics'* or *'constituencies'* which include all these people but go more widely to include scholars, politicians, administrators and others.

These interested publics which pay for and support education hand over its work to the professionals in only a limited and unexpected sense. For while it may appear that the professionals have power to determine what is taught (at school, district or national level, depending on the country in question) their scope is limited by the fact that only the forms and activities which have significance for external publics can, in the long run, survive.[14]

In winning the support of the crucial 'publics' or 'constituencies' suitable categories or rhetorics need to be defined. Reid has painstakingly constructed the evolution of one such category, the 'sixth form', and the associated evolution of the supporting constituency. Reid claims that we have to take the logic of these categories seriously and accept that 'within the terms of such logic, success rhetoric *are* realities'. Though teachers and administrators:

> ... have to be careful that dysfunctions between practice and belief do not escalate to the point where credibility collapses, nonetheless it remains true that what is most important for the success of school subjects is not the delivery of 'goods' which can be publicly evaluated, but the development and maintenance of legimating rhetorics which provide automatic support for correctly labelled activity.

Hence Reid concludes:

> The choice of appropriate labels and the association of them in the public mind with plausible rhetorics of justification can be seen as the core mission of those who work to advance or defend the subject of the curriculum.[15]

Curriculum Change as Political Process: An Example of The Process of Academic Establishment

The internal affairs and external relations of curriculum change point to a socio-historical or, more specifically, a political process at work. Placing the internal and external together leads to evolutionary or historical models of political action which mediate aspects of the structure of the educational system. Hence, in one such model of change, school subjects might be seen as progressing through a number of stages in pursuit of academic establishment (once established of course new ground rules may operate).

    1 *Invention* may come about from the activities or ideas of

educators; sometimes as a response to 'climates of opinion' or pupil demands or resistance or from inventions in the 'outside world':

> The ideas necessary for creation . . . are usually available over a relatively prolonged period of time in several places. Only a few of these inventions will lead to further action.[16]

2   *Promotion*   by educator groups internal to the educational system. Inventions will be taken up 'where and when persons become interested in the new idea, not only as intellectual content but also as a means of establishing a new intellectual identity and particularly a new occupational role'. Hence, subjects with low status, poor career patterns and even with actual survival problems may readily embrace and promote new inventions such as environmental studies. Conversely high-status subjects may ignore quite major opportunities as they are already satisfactorily resourced and provide existing desirable careers. The response of science groups to 'technology' or (possibly) contemporary mathematics groups to 'computer studies' are cases in point. Promotion of invention arises from a perception of the possibility of basic improvements in occupational role and status.

3   *Legislation*   The promotion of new inventions, if successful, leads to the establishment of new categories or subjects. Whilst promotion is initially primarily internally generated, it has to develop external relations with sustaining 'constituencies'. This will be a major stage in ensuring that new categories or subjects are fully accepted, established and institutionalized. And further, that having been established, they can be sustained and supported over time. Legislation is associated with the development and maintenance of those discourses or legitimating rhetorics which provide automatic support for correctly labelled activity.

4   *Mythologization*   Once automatic support has been achieved for a subject or category, a fairly wide range of activities can be undertaken. The limits are any activities which threaten the legitimating rhetoric and hence constituency support. The subject at this point is mythological. It represents essentially a licence that has been granted, (or perhaps a 'patent' or 'monopoly rights'), with the full force of the law and establishment behind it. At this point when the subject has been successfully 'invented', the process of invention and of establishment is completed.

Curriculum histories point to the evolutionary nature of subjects as coalitions 'more or less delicately held together under a common name at particular periods'. The nature of these coalitions responds to both the structuring of material interests and discourse and to the 'changing climates' for action. Because of the manner in which resources (and associated career prospects) are distributed, and status attributed, 'academic' subjects groups most often develop as 'dominant coalitions'. The conflict over the status of examinable knowledge therefore becomes the crucial conflict arena where the subject coalitions (and their representative associations) contest the right to material resources and career prospects. The dominance of 'academicism' can be shown over the last century or more. But historical studies pose questions about in whose interests this dominance prevails: professional groups, culturally dominant groups or industrial or financial captial. Academicism may be the past cultural consequence of previous domination rather than a guarantee of future domination.

In fact, the studies in this book would lead us to reconceptualize curriculum change and conflict. For instance, in the United Kingdom the current Government's initiatives look like an attack on a system (and associated bureaucracy) that was conceived in response to middle class pressure and moulded by a Government bureaucracy steeped in public school values. Once, it most definitely served dominant interst groups. But since then, the system and bureaucracy have developed progressive autonomy and their one vested interest (or seen alternatively from the radical right grown flatulent, stale and obsolecent). The latest governmental strategies challenge this model arguing for more direct connections with economic and financial interests. At present, it appears curriculum conflict resembles less a clash between dominant and subservient groups than a clash between *once* dominant and *currently* dominant bureaucracies.

Notes and References

1   MILLS, C. WRIGHT *The Sociological Imagination*, (Pelican, 1977) pp. 161–162.
2   RICOEUR, P. *Hermeneutics and the Human Sciences*, (Cambridge, 1981) p. 17.
3   BHASKAR, R. *A Realist Theory of Science*, (Harvester Press, 1978).
4   E. OLIN WRIGHT unpublished papers.
5   BEN-DAVID T. and COLLINS, R. 'Social factors in the origins of a new science: The case of psychology', *American Sociological Review*, Vol. 31, No. 4, (August 1966).
6   WESTBURY, I. '"Invention" of curricula', notes to open a theme for discussion, Paper at AERA, (New Orleans, April 1984).
7   *op. cit.*, Ben-David and Collins.
8   BUCHER, R. and STRAUSS, A. 'Professions in process' in HAMMERSLEY,

M. and WOODS, P. (Eds), *The Process of Schooling*, (Routledge and Kegan Paul, 1976) p. 19.

9 ANYON, J. 'Ideology and United States history textbooks', *Harvard Educational Review*, Vol. 41, (1979) p. 361–386.

10 BLUMER, H. *Symbolic Interactionism — Perspective and Method*, (Berkeley and Los Angeles University of California Press, 1986) pp. 195–208.

11 *op. cit.*, Mills, p. 62.

12 *op. cit.*, Esland (1972) p. 109.

13 MEYER, J.W. 'The structure of educational organisation' in MEYER, J.W. and MARSHALL, W. *et al.*, (Eds), *Environments and Organisations*, (San Francisco, Jossey Bass) and MEYER, J.W. 'Levels of the educational system and schooling effects' in BIDWELL, C.E. and WINDHAM, D.M. (Eds), *The Analysis of Educational Productivity*, 2 vols., (Cambridge, Massachusetts, Ballinger).

14 REID, W.A. 'Curriculum topics as institutional categories: Implications for theory and research in the history and sociology of school subjects' in GOODSON, I.F. and BALL, S.J. (Eds), *Defining the Curriculum: Histories and Ethnographies*, (Lewes, Falmer Press, 1984) p. 68. (I am indebted to Bill Reid for drawing my attention to Meyer and for his collaboration over a number of years.)

15 *Ibid.*, p. 75.

16 *op. cit.*, Ben-David and Collins.

12   Cases, Conclusions and Complexities

This book has argued that studying the curriculum as an historical source beside its intrinsic value is of use in a more broadly conceived investigation of schooling. Alongside the investigation of curriculum as a source stands an associated argument that a wider range of methodological approaches will need to be employed and integrated. Life history and curriculum history work are focal in this reconceptualization of our studies. The foregoing essays have exemplified some of these methodological approaches as they impinge on curriculum as a source for the study of schooling.

The emergence of curriculum as a concept has been briefly traced and linked to the development of a class and classroom system in schooling and to the origins of state schooling for a mass clientele. Curriculum emerged in part as a mechanism seeking to designate the content and activity of classroom teaching and learning. The capacity to *designate* was rapidly linked to the capacity to *differentiate* as instanced in the 1868 Taunton Report. In time, a new epistemological triad defining pedagogy, curriculum and examination developed. The genesis of an examination system in the 1850s was, in one of the instances, cited related to particular class groupings being initiated 'in response to petitions from the middle classes'. From this point on, *differentiation* and *examination* became closely interlinked. Over time, this examination system closely allied to the developing subject-based curriculum listed in the State's 1904 secondary regulations was enshrined in the 1917 School Certificate system for Secondary Schools. In this way, a particular patterning and prioritizing of school subjects, the so-called 'academic' subjects, established supremacy. The modern epistemology of pedagogy, curriculum and examination, which developed from the mid nineteenth century, was progressively refined so that by the second decade of the twentieth century a general system, built around the school subjects listed in the Secondary Regulations and the School Certificate, was effectively established. With minor changes, the paramouncy of the content and form of the 'academic' school subjects designated therein retained their supreme position in state secondary schools through to the post-war situations that are studied.

The case studies provided in chapters 6 to 11 offer an opportunity to examine and estimate the continuing power of this political 'settlement' particularly over the curriculum of state schooling in England *circa* 1965–1980, as the tripartite system was changed to a more comprehensive system of schooling. We are, therefore, able to examine the manner in which political decisions over organizational change linked to specific political objectives actually work their way through into the detail of schooling as designated by curriculum. Studying schools at a point where *all* pupils were to be offered 'equality of opportunity' in the same school offers a chance to study how the curriculum settlement which had given supremacy to the academic grammar school curriculum responded to this 'reorganization' of schooling and to the stated change in political ethos and rationale. As we have argued, curriculum as an historical source offers a litmus test of political intervention and purpose.

The antecedent curriculum structures inherited by comprehensive schools followed the hierarchy of style articulated in the Norwood report. The 'academic' curriculum for the grammar school, a small and relatively insignificant technical stream and a practical curriculum for the secondary modern schools. The academic curriculum led to professional and management careers, the practical curriculum to manual careers. The academic curriculum was then distinct from the practical curriculum, not just in *content* terms but in its pervasive *form*, comprising written bodies of knowledge divorced from practical matters to be learnt 'for their own sake'.

In assessing which modes of curriculum gained ascendancy in the newly organized comprehensive schools, the case studies in chapters 6 to 11 offer fairly conclusive testimony. They pinpoint a process of 'symbolic drift' in comprehensive secondary state schooling towards one dominant model of form and content — the 'academic' subject supposedly based on the 'scholarly discipline'.

The studies show how, at the level of personal lives, subject groups and subject associations, the pursuit of finance, resources and careers (and indeed survival) led widely different individuals and groups to follow similar course. The discourse identified shares an acceptance of the primacy of 'academic' subjects. We can see how such *discursive formation* functions through the way in which the debate over curriculum and schooling is constructed, conducted and organized. We can illustrate also how this is underpinned by the *structuring of material interests*: what one teacher called 'the kindly eye of the state', once again sponsoring the academic mode of curriculum (and associated pattern of schooling) throughout the period under scrutiny.

The studies illustrate how the struggle to present subject matter as 'academic' crucially affects the 'form' as well as the content. Echoing the fate of the 'science of common things', we saw how experiments in rural education as 'the hub of the curriculum wheel', in communities where such rural education was central to the life experience and work of the people, were marginalized. In turn we saw how in a conclusively practical subject like rural studies teachers were asked to renege on the subject's history and heritage. The subject groups were forced to embrace a form and content of curricula, develop a written theoretical body of knowledge, in order to survive and win resources. Thus to win status and resources the original clientele of the subject effectively had to be abandoned. We can see clearly how the charges of the rural studies teacher 'were once more squeezed into a forgotten heap of frustrating unimportance'. The testimony of such contemporary witnesses is subsequently echoed by one of the leaders of the redefinitions of rural studies.

Studying the social construction of a curriculum area then allows us some insights into the various agendas and purposes of state schooling. Likewise, the study of the progression towards scholarly definition in geography discerns evidence that Layton's tentative model for science has relevance. We are urged to investigate the emergence of a form of schooling which structures and finances a mode of curriculum whose culminating phase is characterized by a leading educationalist as one in which most students 'are initiated into a tradition, their attitudes approaching passivity and resignation, a prelude to disenchantment'.

Yet our case histories show how such a situation may have arisen: in a way, Waring's phrase 'monumental accretion' captures the process fairly well. In the century following Taunton, different sectors of schools developed with their own distinctive curriculum. The deliberate nature of this differentiation is made clear by Taunton, as is its definite social class (and gender) basis. Over the following century, particular social classes attended specific types of schools and were versed in specific styles of curriculum. Over time, then, a degree of curriculum continuity established for distinct social classes a working notion of 'cultural capital'. The essence of this curriculum and class continuity is evidenced in the Norwood Report.

In the post-war period state schooling (private schools, of course, notwithstanding) was forced to open to all pupils in one kind of school, the comprehensive school. Yet a deep structure of curriculum, differentiation linked to a social base, continued to operate. The enormous importance of curriculum as a mechanism to *designate* and *differentiate* within schooling has been noted. Yet in the comprehensive era of state schooling, the force of this mechanism existed beyond the attempts to 'reorganize' the schools. As we have seen the mode of curriculum which achieved dominance in the comprehensive school in terms of status, finance and resources was in fact that mode most closely related historically to the grammar schools and the middle classes. The implications of this for political slogans like 'equality of opportunity' in schooling can be easily evidenced in the case of rural studies and in the evolutionary profile of geography — once again the unwanted children are 'made the servants of the juggernaut of documented evidence, the inflated examination'. The modality developed partly in response to 'the petitions of the middle classes' in 1858 thereby established supremacy within state comprehensive schools a century or so after. The disjuncture between the political rhetoric and the internal detail of schooling can, I think, begin to be recovered through such case histories of curriculum. In this way, these studies present a view, albeit altogether too partial a view, of the validity of curriculum as a source for studying the agendas and purposes of state schooling.

But there is a danger in presenting a culminating pattern to a situation which is always in contestation. We are describing a situation which has been fought and for the moment 'achieved'. But challenges continue. Whilst the structure, the epistemology are clearly seen to reward the academic tradition, at least in the evidence of the witnesses in our case studies, plainly alternative visions continued, Johnson's alternative dream; the Science of Common Things, rural education, continuing aspects of adult education all work with alternative views of epistemology. In modern comprehensives these alternative views also remain within certain mainstream subjects like English and in more 'marginal' subjects like music, art and physical education. As we have said, even though the structure of material interests and discourses most often result in a 'dominant coalition' within subjects supporting the academic mode, nonetheless sub-groups within subjects also continue to define and develop alternative epistemologies. Curriculum then, like all the social arenas, is potentially a site of ongoing and dialectical action. Redefinition (and resistance) can be sponsored from 'below'.

Moreover, new facilities for action are developed in the external as well as the internal domain. We have seen how differentiation was initially promoted through distinct types of schools, types of curriculum and types of examination. With the birth of the common school we saw how increasingly curriculum and examination were left as the mechanisms of differentiation.

The current state regime in England, however, faces major problems which are leading to a wide range of new initiatives. The ground rules defined in these case studies may therefore be subject to fundamental change in the next period of state schooling. Certainly, the government's concern over a dysfunctional economy has led to some radical initiatives in technical education. Even more significantly, these are funded and operationalized by agencies outside the school system. Within the schools a common examination system is about to be launched. This might again change the mode of differentiation through distinct examinations; however, the form and content of the curriculum to be examined need to be closely scrutinized. Once again, we are exhorted to use the curriculum as a source for insights into the new regimes of state schooling.

The complexities associated with new initiatives in English state schooling are, of course, echoed in the period under review in the cases presented. The insights presented are in their nature tentative, for far more studies need to be undertaken of other teachers' life histories; of other school subjects, for instance classics, economics, sociology or English (where a wide range of alternative versions have been defined and promoted); of the effects of private schooling; of internal school processes; of the relationship between histories of pedagogy and histories of curriculum. We need work on other historical periods and, crucially, in other countries. Plainly, this is just a beginning but the school curriculum is a social artefact, conceived of and made for deliberate human purposes. I believe there are few better sources for future studies of schooling.

Of course, studies of preactive curricula are of little use on their own. For, at the end of the day, the critical question is who gets what and what do they do with it. For its part, this book has sought to argue that the struggle over preactive curriculum is a crucial and neglected part of this question. Preactive curricula have in-built biases and prejudices, in-built continuities with particular social groups and their associated cultural capitals.

These built-in biases help set the agenda for all future negotiations in the school and classroom. Though the analogy is far from exact I am often reminded in the debate about curriculum of the notion of trying to sell refrigerators to the eskimos. It is as if the students of pedagogy urge us to concentrate on the negotiations over the sale of the refrigerators; the ethnographers of school and institutional context urge us to look at the social context of the particular eskimo locale; and the students of school process meanwhile would have us look at which pupils get refrigerators and which get coolers (and, we might add, which pupils get frozen out altogether). Nobody asks the question of why refrigerators, of how such an inappropriate product came to be at the centre of the action. Likewise, the agenda-setting conducted through the making of curriculum has been too often left out in our studies of schooling. It is time for a full-scale exploration of the potential of such work in elucidating the complex conundrum of schooling.

Bibliography

ADAMSON, J.W., *English Education 1789–1802*, (Cambridge 'At the University Press', 1930).

ADAMSON, J.W., *Pioneers of Modern Education 1600–1700*, (1951).

ALLEN, A.B., *Rural Education*, (London, Allman and Sons, 1950).

ANDERSON, N., *The Hobo*, (University of Chicago Press, 1923).

ANDREWS, A., 'In pursuit of the past: Some problems in the collection, analysis and use of historical documentary evidence', paper delivered at Whitelands College Workshop on *Qualitative Methodology and the Study of Education*, July 1983.

ANYON, J., 'Ideology and United States history textbooks', *Harvard Educational Review*, Vol. 41, (1979).

APPLE, M.W., 'Ideology, reproduction and educational reform', *Comparative Education Review, 22*, (1978).

ARMSTRONG, M., 'Reconstructing knowledge: An example' in WATTS, J. (Ed), *The Countesthorpe Experience*, (London, George Allen and Unwin, 1977).

ARMSTRONG, M. and KING, L., 'Schools within schools' in WATTS, J. (Ed), *The Countesthorpe Experience*, (London, George Allen and Unwin, 1977).

BARNARD, H.C., 'J.W. Adamson' in *British Journal of Educational Studies*, Vol. X, No. 1, November 1961.

BARROW, R., *Giving Teaching Back to Teachers: A Critical Introduction to Curriculum Theory*, (Brighton, Wheatsheaf and Althouse, 1984).

BECKER, H.S., 'The Career of the Chicago public school teacher', *American Journal of Sociology*, Vol. 57, (1952).

BECKER, H.S., *et al.*, *Boys in White*, (University of Chicago Press, 1961).

BECKER, H.S., *Sociological Work: Method and Substance*, (Chicago, Aldine, 1970).

BECKER, H.S. and GEER, B., 'Latent culture: A note on the theory of latent social roles' in COSIN, B.R. *et al.*, *School and Society: A Sociological Reader*, (London, Routledge and Kegan Paul, 1971).

BEN-DAVID, T. and COLLINS, R., 'Social factors in the origins of a new science: The case of pyschology', *American Sociological Review*, Vol. 31, No. 4. (August 1966).

BERGER, P., *Invitation to Sociology*, (Doubleday, 1963) and BERGER, P., and LUCKMANN, T., *The Social Construction of Reality*, (London, Allen Lane, 1967).

BERNSTEIN, B., 'On the classification and framing of educational knowledge' in YOUNG, M. (Ed), *Knowledge and Control*, (London, Collier, Macmillan, 1971).

BERTAUX, D. (Ed), *Biography and Society: The Life History Approach in the Social Sciences*, (London, Sage, 1981).

BHASKAR, R., *A Realist Theory of Science*, (Harvester Press, 1978).

BIRD, C., 'Limitations and possibilities of geographical teaching in day schools', *The Geographical Teacher*, Vol. 1, (1901).

BLUMER, H., *Symbolic Interactionism: Perspective and Method*, (Englewood Cliffs, Prentice Hall, 1969).

BLUMER, H., *Symbolic Interactionism: Perspective and Method*, (Berkeley and Los Angeles University of California Press, 1986).

BOARD of EDUCATION Memorandum on the *Principle and Methods of Rural Education*, (1911).

BOARD of EDUCATION, *Report for 1910–1911*, (London, HMSO, 1911).

BOARD of EDUCATION, *Report for 1904–1939*, (London, HMSO, 1939).

BOARD of EDUCATION, *Report for the Consultative Committee: the Education of the Adolescent*, Hadlow Report, (London, HMSO, 1927).

BOARD of EDUCATION *Rural Education Circular 1365*, (London, HMSO, 1925).

BOGDAN, R. and TAYLOR, S., *Introduction to Qualitative Research Methods*, (Wiley, 1970).

BOGDAN, R., *Being Different: The Autobiography of Jane Fry*, (Wiley, 1974).

BOURDIEU, P., 'Systems of education and systems of thought, and Intellectual field and creative project' in YOUNG, M. (Ed), *op. cit.*, (1971).

BOURDIEU, P. and PASSERON, J.C., *Reproduction in Education, Society and Culture*, (London, Sage, 1977).

BROCKLEHURST, J.B., *Music in Schools*, (London, Routledge and Kegan Paul, 1962).

BUCHER, R. and STRAUSS, A., 'Professions in process' in HAMMERSLEY, M. and WOODS, P. (Eds), *The Process of Schooling*, (London, Routledge and Kegan Paul, 1976).

BYRNE, E.M., *Planning and Educational Inequality*, (Slough, NFER, 1974.

CARSON, S. and COLTON, R., *The Teaching of Rural Studies*, (London, Edward Arnold, 1962).

CARSON, S., *The Use and Content and Effective Objectives in Rural Studies Courses*, (M.Ed. Thesis, University of Manchester, 1967).

CARSON, S. (Ed), *Environmental Studies: The Construction of an 'A' Level Syllabus*, (Slough, NFER, 1971).

CHAMBLISS, W., *Boxman: A Professional Thief's Journey*, (Harper and Row, 1972).

CHARLTON, K., 'The contribution of History to the study of curriculum' in KERR, J.F. (Ed), *Changing the Curriculum*, (London, University of London Press, 1968).

CHORLEY, R. and HAGGETT, P., *Frontiers in Geographical Teaching*, (London, Methuen, 1965).

CHORLEY, R. and HAGGETT, P., *Models in Geography*, (London, Methuen, 1967).

Civics and European Education, Resolution adopted by Minister Deputies at the Council of Europe, 6 October 1964.

CLARKE, F., *Education and Social Change: An English Interpretation*, (London, The Sheldon Press, 1940).

COOKE, R. and JOHNSON, J.M., *Trends in Geography*, (London, Methuen, 1969).

CORNWELL, C. and SUTHERLAND, E. *The Professional Thief*, (University of Chicago Press, 1937).

COUNCIL of the GEOGRAPHICAL ASSOCIATION, 'The position of geography', *The Geographical Teacher*, Vol. 10, (1919).

CUBAN, L., *How Teachers Taught: Constancy and Change in American Classrooms 1890–1980*, (New York, Longman, 1984).

DES *Organisation of Secondary Education*, Circular 10/65, (London, HMSO, 1965).

DAVID, T., 'Against geography' in BALE, D., GRAVES, N. and WALFORD, R., (Eds), *Perspectives in Geographical Education*, (Edinburgh, 1973).

DAVIS, R.H.C., 'The content of History', *History*, Vol. 66, No. 218, October 1981.

DENZIN, N., *Sociological Methods: A Sourcebook*, (Butterworths, London, 1970).

DENZIN, N.K., *The Research Act*, (Chicago, Aldine), 1970.

DOLLARD, J., *Criteria for the Life History*, (Yale University Press, 1949).

DURKHEIM, E., *The Evolution of Educational Thought*, (London, Routledge and Kegan Paul, 1977).

ESLAND, G.M., Teaching and learning as the organisation of knowledge in YOUNG, M.F.D., (Ed) *Knowledge and Control: New Directions for the Sociology of Education*, (London, Collier Macmillan, 1971).

ESLAND, G.M, and DALE (Eds), *School and Society*, Course E282, Unit 2, (Open University, Milton Keynes, 1972).

LEA, *European Studies in E. and W. Sussex*, (LEA Survey, 1977).

FARADAY, A. and PLUMMER, K., 'Doing life histories', *Sociological Review*, Vol. 27, No. 4, (1979).

FARIS, R., *Chicago Sociology*, (University of Chicago Press, 1967).

FEINBERG, W., *Understanding Education: Towards a Reconstruction of Educational Enquiry*, (Cambridge University Press, 1983).

FITZGERALD, B.P., 'Scientific method, quantitative techniques and the teaching of geography' in WALFORD (Ed), *op. cit.*

FRANKLIN, B.M., 'Curriculum history: Its nature and boundaries', *Curriculum Inquiry 7.1.* (1977).

GARDNER and LAMBERT, *Attitudes and Motivation in Modern Language Learning*.

GARNETT, A., 'Teaching geography: Some reflections', *Geography*, 54, (1969).

GIBBERD. K., *No Place Like School*, (London, Michael Joseph, 1962).

GIDDENS, A., *The Constitution of Society*, (Berkeley and Los Angeles University of California Press, 1986).

GILBERT, E.W., 'The idea of the region', *Geography*, Vol. 45, No. 1, (1961).

GINSBURG, N., 'Tasks of geography', *Geography*, 54, (1969).

GLASS, D.V., 'Education and social change in modern Britain' in HOOPER, R. (Ed), *The Curriculum Context, Design and Development*, (Edinburgh, Oliver and Boyd, 1971).

GLENDENING, V., 'Slaughterhouse epilogue', *Sunday Times*, 20 February 1983.

GOODSON, I.F., 'Evaluation and evolution' in NORRIS, N. (Ed), *Theory in Practice*, SAFARI Project, Centre for Applied Research in Education, University of East Anglia, (1977).

GOODSON, I.F. and McGIVNEY, V., *Europe in the School*, Research Project, (University of Sussex, 1982, Mimeo).

GOODSON, I.F., *Curriculum Conflict 1895–1975* unpublished, D. Phil, Sussex 1980.

GOODSON, I.F., *School Subjects and Curriculum Change*, (London and Sydney, Croom Helm, 1983).

GOODSON, I.F. (Ed), *Social Histories of the Secondary Curriculum: Subjects for Study*, (Lewes, Falmer, 1985).

GOODSON, I.F. (Ed), *International Perspectives in Curriculum History*, (Croom Helm, London and Sydney, 1987).

GOWING, D., 'A fresh look at objectives' in WATFORD, R. (Ed), *New Directions in Geography Teaching*, (London, Longmans, 1973).

GREENE, M., 'Curriculum and consciousness', *The Record*, F.3. No. 2, (1971).

HAMILTON, D., 'Adam Smith and the moral economy of the classroom system', *Journal of Curriculum Studies, Vol. 12, No. 4*, October–December 1980.

HAMILTON, D., *On Simultaneous Instruction and the Early Evolution of Class Teaching*. Mimeo of paper given at the History Workshop Conference, (Brighton, November 1980).

HAMILTON, D. and GIBBONS, M., *Notes on the Origins of the Educational Terms Class and Curriculum*. Paper presented at the Annual Convention of the American Educational Research Association, (Boston, 1980).

HARGREAVES, D., HESTER, S. and MELLOR, F., *Deviance in Classrooms*, (Routledge and Kegan Paul, 1975).

HARGREAVES, D., 'Whatever happened to symbolic interactionism' in BARTON, L. and MEIGHAN, R. *Sociological Interpretations of Schooling and Classrooms: A Reappraisal*, (Nafferton Books, 1978).

HARRISON, J.F.C., *The Common People*, (London, Flamingo, 1984).

Hertfordshire Teachers Rural Studies Association Journal, October 1963.

HIRST, P., *The Educational Implications of Social and Economic Change* in Schools Council Working Paper No. 12, (London, HMSO, 1967).

HOBSBAWM, E. and RANGER, T. (Eds), *The Invention of Tradition*, (Cambridge University Press, 1985).

HODSON, D., 'Science curriculum change in Victorian England: A case study of the science of common things' in GOODSON, I.F. (Ed), *International Perspectives in Curriculum History*, (London, Croom Helm, 1987).

HONEYBONE, R.C., 'Balance in geography and education', *Geography*, Vol. 34, No. 184, (1954).

HUDSPETH, W.H., *The History of the Teaching of Biological Subjects including Nature Study in English schools since 1900*, (M.Ed. Thesis, University of Durham, 1962).

JACKSON, P.W., *Life in Classrooms*, (New York, Holt Rinehart and Winston Inc., 1968).

JENKINS, D. and SHIPMAN, M.P., *Curriculum: an Introduction*, (London, Open Books, 1976).

JOTTERAND, R., *Introducing Europe to the Senior Pupils*, (Council for Cultural Cooperation of the Council of Europe, 1966).

Journal of the Kent Association of Teachers of Gardening and Rural Science, April 1953, September 1958.

JUDD, C.M., *The Training of Teachers in England, Scotland and Germany*, (Washington, USA, Bureau of Education, 1914).

Kent Journal, No. 4, 1954.

KERR, J., 'The problem of curriculum reform' in HOOPER, R. (Ed), *The Curriculum Context, Design and Development*, (Edinburgh, Oliver and Boyd, 1971).

KLIEBARD, H., 'Persistant curriculum issues in historical perspective' in PINAR, W. (Ed), *Curriculum Theorizing*, (Berkeley, McCutchan, 1975).

KLOCKARS, C., *The Professional Fence*, (London, Tavistock, 1975).

LACEY, C., *The Socialization of Teachers*, (London, Methuen, 1977).

LAURIE, S.S., *Studies in the History of Educational Opinion from the Renaissance*, quoted in B. Simon, 'The history of Education; in TIBBLE, J.W. (Ed), *The Study of Education*, (London, Routledge and Kegan Paul, 1966).

LAYTON, D., Science as general education, *Trends in Education*, (1972).

LAYTON, D., *Science for the People*, (London, George Allen and Unwin, 1973).

MACDONALD, B. and WALKER, R., *Changing the Curriculum*, (London, Open Books, 1976).

MACKINDER, H.J., 'On the scope and methods of geography', *Proceedings of the Royal Geographical Society*, Vol. IX, (1887).

MACKINDER, H.J., *Report of the Discussion on Geographical Education*, (1903).

Manifesto of Geographical Association printed on the inside cover of all copies of *Geography*.

MANNHEIM, K., *Ideology and Utopia: An Introduction to the Sociology of Knowledge*, (London, Routledge and Kegan Paul, 1972).

MARCHANT, E.C., 'Some responsibilities of the teacher of geography', *Geography, 3*, (1965).

MARSDEN, D., *Politicians, Equality and Comprehensives*, T. 411, (London, Fabian Society, 1971).

MARSDEN, W.E., 'Historical approaches to curricular studies' in MARSDEN, W.E. (Ed), *Postwar Curriculum Development: An historical appraisal*, History of Education Society Conference Papers, December 1978, (1979), V. 82.

McLEISH, J., *Students' Attitudes and College Environment*. Quoted in LACEY, C. *The Socialisation of Teachers*, (London, Metheun, 1970).

MEYER, J.W., 'The structure of educational organisation' in MEYER, J.W. and MARSHALL, W. *et al.*, (Eds), *Environments and Organisations*, (San Francisco, Jossey Bass) and MEYER, J.W. 'Levels of the educational system and schooling effects', in BIDWELL, C.E. and WINDHAM, D.M. (Eds), *The Analysis of Educational Productivity*, 2 vols., (Cambridge, Massachusetts, Ballinger).

MORRIS, M., *An Excursion into Creative Sociology*, (Blackwell, 1977).

MORTIMER, J., *Clinging to the Wreckage*, (London, Penguin, 1983).

MUSGROVE, F., 'The contribution of sociology to the study of the curriculum' in KERR, J.F. (Ed), *Changing the Curriculum*, (University of London Press, 1968).

National Rural Studies Association Journal, (1961).

National Rural Studies Association Journal, (1961–1970).

National Rural Studies Association Journal, (1966).

NEWSOM, T., *Half our Future*, Report of the Central Advisory Council for Education, (London, HMSO, 1963).

NISBET, R.A., 'Social change and history', (1969) quoted in WESKER, J.R. 'Curriculum change and crisis', *British Journal of Educational Studies*, 3, October 1971.

PRO Ed Documents 4403, 13 January 1941, Mr. Cleary memo, items 2, 3. (University of Leeds Library).

Papers of the Society for the Study of Curriculum History, (Pennsylvania State University, Spring 1981).

PARLETT, M. and HAMILTON, D., '*Evaluation as Illumination: a new approach to the study of innovatory programs*', Occasional paper 9, Edinburgh Centre for Research in Educational Sciences, (1972).

PARTRIDGE, J., *Life in a Secondary Modern School*, (Harmondsworth, Pelican, 1968).

PAYNE, G., 'Making a lesson happen' in HAMMERSLEY, M. and WOODS, P. (Eds), *Schooling and Society: A Reader*, (Open University, 1976).

PHENIX, P.M., *The Realms of Meaning*, (New York, McGraw-Hill, 1964).

PLUMMER, K., *Documents of Life: An Introduction to the Problems and Literature of a Humanistic Method*, (London, George Allen and Unwin, 1983).

PRC, 'Review', *Geography*, Vol. 53, Part 4, November, (1968).

PRITCHARD, M., 'The rural science teacher in the school society'. *Journal of the Hertfordshire Association of Gardening and Rural Subjects*, No. 2, September 1957.

QUANT, P.L., 'Rural studies and Newsom courses', *Hertfordshire Rural Studies Journal*, (1967).

REID, W.A., *The University and the Sixth Form Curriculum*, (London, Macmillan, 1972).

REID, W.A., 'Curriculum topics as institutional categories: Implications for theory and research in the history and sociology of school subjects' in GOODSON, I.F. and BALL, S.J. (Eds), *Defining the Curriculum: Histories and Ethnographies*, (Falmer Press, 1984).

REID, W.A., 'Curriculum change and the evolution of educational constituencies: The English sixth form in the nineteenth century' in IVOR GOODSON (Ed), *Social Histories of the Secondary Curriculum: Subjects for Study*, (Lewes, Falmer Press, 1985).

Report on *Rural Subjects and Gardening in Secondary Schools in Hertfordshire*, (Mimeo, 1957).

Report of the Central Advisory Council for Education, *England School and Life*, (London, HMSO, 1947).

REYNOLDS, D. and SULLIVAN, M., 'The comprehensive experience' in BARTON, L. and WALKER, S. (Eds) *Schools, Teachers and Teaching*, (Lewes, Falmer Press, 1981).

RICOEUR, P., *Hermeneutics and the Human Sciences*, (Cambridge, 1981).

ROTHBLATT, S., *Tradition and Change In English Liberal Education: an Essay in History and Culture*, (London, Faber and Faber, 1976).

RUBINSTEIN, D. and SIMON, B., *The Evolution of the Comprehensive School 1926–1972*, (London, Routledge and Kegan Paul, 1975).

RUDOLPH, F., *Curriculum: A History of the American Undergraduate Course of Study since 1636*, (San Francisco, Jossey Bass, 1977).

Rural Science News, Vol. 10. No. 1, January 1957.

Rural Studies Draft Report, *The Certificate of Secondary Education Experimental Examination*, (Mimeo).

Schools Council Working Paper 24: *Rural Studies in Secondary Schools*, (London, Evans/Methuen Education, 1969).

SEABORNE, M., 'The History of Education' in TIBBLE, J.W. (Ed) *An Introduction to the Study of Education*, (London, Routledge and Kegan Paul, 1971).

SELLECK, R.J.W., *The New Education: The English Background 1870–1914*, (Melbourne, Pitman, 1968).

SHAW, C.R., *The Tack Roller*, (Universtiy of Chicago Press, 1930).

SHIPMAN, M., 'Curriculum for inequality' in HOOPER, R. *The Curriculum: Context, Design and Development*, (Edinburgh, Oliver and Boyd, 1971).

SIKES, P.J., MEASOR, L. and WOODS, P., *Teacher Careers: Crises and Continuities*, (Lewes, Falmer, 1985).

SIMON, B., 'The History of Education in the 1980s', *British Journal of Educational Studies*, Vol, XXX, No. 1, February 1982.

SIMON, B., *Does Education Matter?*, (London, Lawrence and Wisehart, 1985).

SMELSER, N. *Essays in Sociological Explanation*, (New Jersey, Prentice Hall, 1968).

SMITH, L. and GEOFFREY, W., *The Complexities of an Urban Classroom*, (Holt, Rinehart and Winston, New York, 1968).

SMITH, L. and KEITH, P., *Anatomy of an Educational Innovation*, (Wiley, New York, 1971).

SMITH, L., 'Archival case records: Issues and illustrations'. Paper presented for SSRC sponsored Case Records Conference, (York, 1980).

Society and the Young School Leaver, Working Paper No. 11, (London, HMSO, 1967).

SLAYMAKER, O., 'Review', *Geographical Journal*, Vol. 134, Part 2, September, (1960).

STENHOUSE, L., *Case Study as a Basis for Research in a Theoretical Contemporary History of Education*. (Mimeo).

Survey by Herfordshire Association of Teachers of Gardening and Rural Subjects, (1957).

SUTHERLAND, E. and CORNWELL, C. *The Professional Thief*, (University of Chicago Press, 1937).

The Hadow Report. *The Education of the Adolescent*. Report of the Consultative Committee, (London, HMSO, 1927).

The Norwood Report, *Curriculum and Examinations in Secondary Schools*. Report of the Committee of the Secondary School Examinations Council, appointed by the President of the Board of Education in 1941, (London, HMSO, 1943).

The Raising of the School Leaving Age, Second Pilot Course for Experienced Teachers, (University of London, Goldsmiths College, 1965).

THOMAS, W.I. and ZNANIECKI, F., *The Polish Peasant in Europe and America*, (New York, 1927).

THOMPSON, E.P., *Education and Experience*. Fifth Mansbridge Memorial Lecture, (Leeds University Press, 1968).

THOMPSON, P., *The Voices of the Past: Oral History*, (Opus, 1978).

THRASHER, F.M., *The Gang: A Study of 1313 Gangs in Chicago*, (University of Chicago Press, 1928).

Trends in Education, (London, DES, October 1967), (article on 'Rural Studies in Schools').

UNIVERSITY OF CAMBRIDGE LOCAL EXAMINATIONS SYNDICATE, One Hundredth Annual Report to University, 29 May 1958.

VULLIAMY, G., 'What counts as school music' in WHITTY, G. and YOUNG, M. (Eds) *Explorations in the Politics of School Knowledge*, (Driffield, Nafferton, 1976).

WALFORD, R., 'Models, simulations and games' in WALFORD, R. (Ed), *op. cit.*, (1973).

WALKER, D., 'The well-rounded geographers', *The Times Educational Supplement*, 28 November, (1975).

WALKER, R., 'The conduct of educational case study' in *Innovation, Evolution, Research and the Problem of Control: Some Interim Papers*, SAFARI Project, Centre for Applied Research in Education, University of East Anglia, (1974).

WARE, F., *Educational Reform*, (London, Methuen, 1900).

WARING, M., *Social Pressures and Curriculum Innovation: A Study of the Nuffield Foundation Science Teaching Project*, (London, Methuen, 1979).

WARING, M., *Aspects of the Dynamics of Curriculum Reform in Secondary School Science*, Phd., University of London (1975).

WARWICK, D., *Team Teaching*, (University of London Press, 1972).

WARWICK, D. and WILLIAMS, J., 'History and the sociology of education', *British Journal of Sociology of Education*, Vol. 1, No. 3, 1980.

WATSON, F., *The Beginnings of the Teaching of Modern Subjects in England*, (London, Pitman, 1909).

WEBSTER, J.R., 'Curriculum Change and "Crisis"', *British Journal of Educational Studies*, Vol. xxiv, No. 3, October 1976.

WESTBURY, I., 'Invention' of Curricula, notes to open a theme for Discussion Paper at AERA, (New Orleans, April 1984).

WILLIAMS, M., *Teaching European Studies*, (London Heinemann, 1977).

WILLIAMS, R., *The Long Revolution*, (London, Penguin, 1961).

WILLIAMS, R., *The Long Revolution*, (London, Penguin, 1975).

WILLIAMS, R., *Politics and Letters*, (London, New Left Books, 1974).

WIRTH, L., *The Ghetto*, (University of Chicago Press, 1928).

WOODS, P. and HAMMERSLEY, M. (Eds), *School Experience*, (Croom Helm, 1977).

WOODS, P., *The Divided School*, (London, Routledge and Kegan Paul, 1979).

WOODS, P., *Pupil Strategies*, (Croom Helm, 1980).

WOODS, P., *Teacher Strategies*, (Croom Helm, 1980).

WOOLDRIDGE, S.W., *The Geographer as Scientist*, (London, Nelson, 1956).

WRIGHT MILLS, C., *The Sociological Imagination*, (Oxford University Press, 1959).

WRIGHT MILLS, C., *The Sociological Imagination*, (London, Penguin, 1970).

WRIGLEY, E.A., 'Changes in the philosophy of geography' in CHORLEY, R.

and HAGGETT, P. (Eds), *Frontiers in Geographical Teaching*, (London, Methuen, 1967).

YEATES, M.H., *An Introduction to Quantative Analysis in Economic Geography*, (New York, McGraw-Hill, 1968).

YOUNG, M.F.D., (Ed), *Knowledge and Control: New Directions for the Sociology of Education*, (London, Collier-MacMillan, 1971).

YOUNG, M., 'An approach to the study of curricula as socially organised knowledge' in YOUNG, M. (Ed), (1971), *op. cit.*

YOUNG, M., 'Curriculum change: Limits and possibilities', in YOUNG, M. and WHITTY, G. (Eds), *Society State and Schooling*, (Lewes Falmer Press, 1977).

YOUNG, M., and WHITTY, G., *Society, State and Schooling*, (Lewes, Falmer Press, 1977).

ZORBAUGH, H.V., *The Gold Coast and the Slum: a Sociological Study of Chicago's North Side*, (University of Chicago Press, 1929).

Index

'A' Level   30, 121, 129, 150, 153, 156, 166, 172
  in Environmental Studies   97, 110, 136, 138
  in Rural Studies   128, 130–4, 136–8
'academic disciplines'   31, 32, 36
'academic' subjects   30, 32, 36, 138
'academicism' 195
'Acts and Facts'   41, 43, 44, 48, 49, 51, 56
Acts of Parliament
  Education (1870)   34, 167
    (1902)   167
    (1944)   30, 46, 99, 124
  Secondary Regulations (1904)   9, 29, 122, 167, 188, 198
Adamson, Professor J.W.: *English Education 1789–1902*   48
'adult education'   35, 36
Allen, A.B.   124
American Historical Society   47
Andrews, A.   44–5
Anyon, J.   191
Apple, M.W.   162
Armstrong, M.   37

Baas Hill Secondary Modern School 135
Barnard, H.C.   48
Barrow, R.   25
Becker, H.S.   72–3, 75–7, 79, 80, 84
  Career of the Chicago Public School Teacher   84

Beloe Report   110, 125
Ben-David, T.   190
Bernstein, B.   28, 160
Bertaux, D.   66, 114
  Biography and Society   61, 74
Bhaskar, Roy   186
Blumer, Herbert   52–3, 76, 191
Blythe, Ronald   50, 74
Board of Education   122–4
Bogdan, R.   84
Bourdieu, P.   161, 162
British Association for the Advancement of Science   20
British Sociological Association 119, 146
Broad   109
Brocklehurst, J.B.   19
Bryce Commission   167
Bucher, R.   90
Byrne, E.M.   139, 179, 188

Caeser, Mr. A.A.L.   170
Calvin, John   26
Calvinism   37
Cambridge, University of, Local Examinations Syndicate   28, 170
Carson, Sean   105, 126–7, 129–30, 131, 132, 136, 137–8
Central Advisory Council for Education   124
Certificate of Secondary Education *see* CSE
Charlton, K.   52
Chicago, University of   60
Chorley, R.   173, 176

3